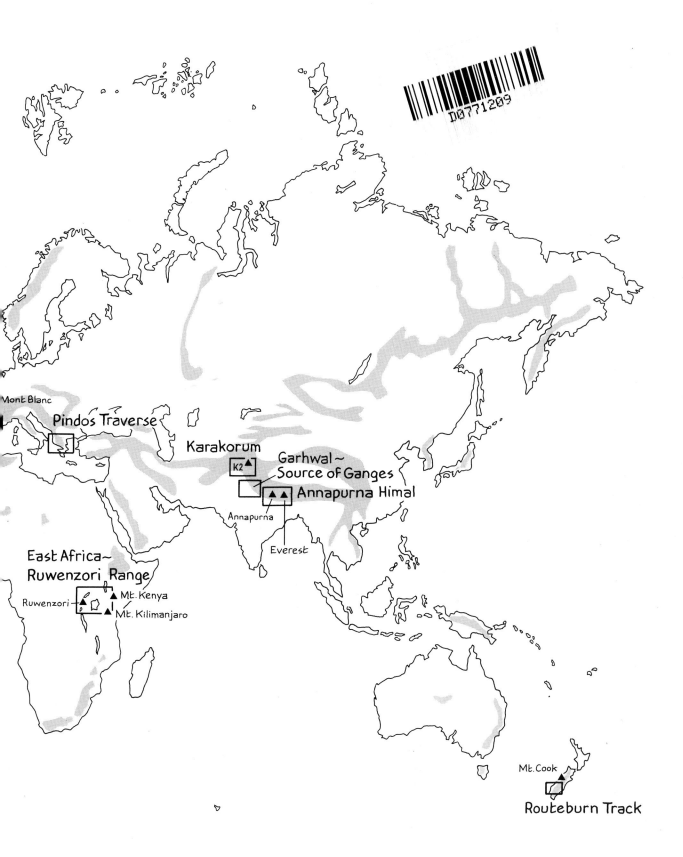

Mont Blanc

Pindos Traverse

Karakorum

K2

Garhwal ~
Source of Ganges

Annapurna Himal

Annapurna

Everest

East Africa ~
Ruwenzori Range

Ruwenzori

Mt. Kenya

Mt. Kilimanjaro

Mt. Cook

Routeburn Track

D0771209

TREKKING
Great Walks of the World

John Cleare

UNWIN

HYMAN

LONDON SYDNEY WELLINGTON

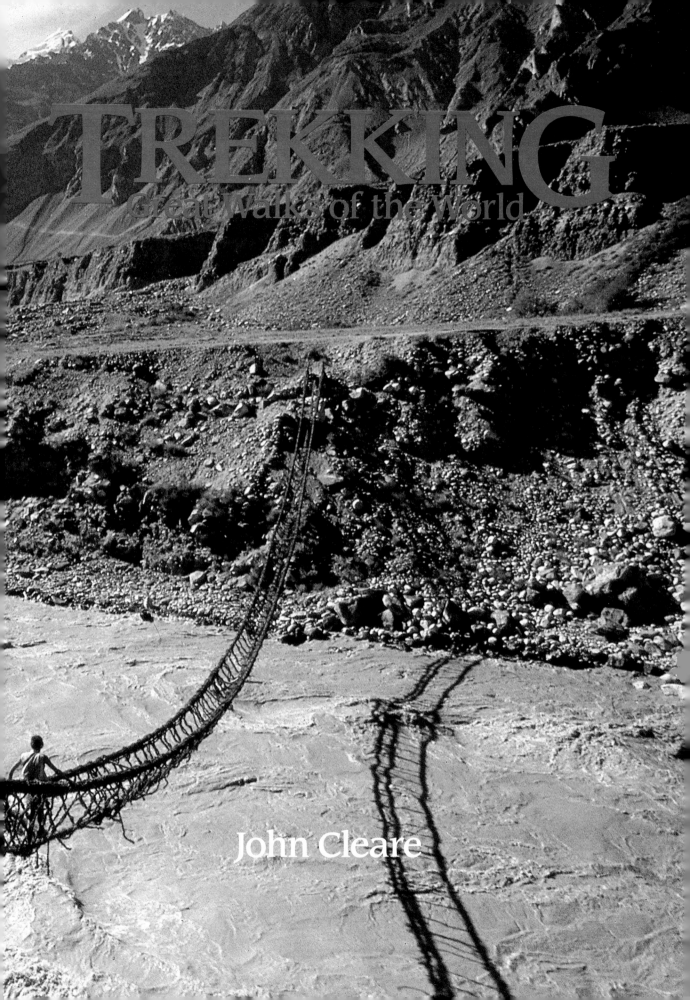

TREKKING
Great Walks of the World

John Cleare

First published in Great Britain by
the Trade Division of Unwin Hyman Limited, 1988.
Copyright © in each chapter remains with the author 1988
Copyright © in the compilation: John Cleare 1988
Copyright © in the photographs remains with the photographer 1988
Copyright © line drawings: Michelle Ross 1988
Copyright © maps: Don Sargeant 1988

Unwin Hyman Limited
15/17 Broadwick Street
London W1V 1FP

Allen & Unwin Australia Pty Ltd
8 Napier Street, North Sydney, NSW 2060, Australia

Allen & Unwin New Zealand Pty Ltd with Port Nicholson Press
60 Cambridge Terrace, Wellington, New Zealand

British Library Cataloguing in Publication Data

Trekking : great treks of the world
   1. Trekking
   I. Cleare, John
   796.5'1

   ISBN 0–04–440135–3

Photographs are by the author of each chapter unless credited otherwise.

Designed by Legend, Bristol
Typeset by Latimer Trend & Company Ltd, Plymouth
Printed in Italy by New Interlitho S.P.A.

CONTENTS

INTRODUCTION

Nearly 250 years ago, in a letter to his son, Lord Chesterfield wrote: *'The World is a country which nobody ever yet knew by description; one must travel through it one's self to be acquainted with it . . .'*

Today, the entire land surface of the world has – in theory – been explored, its remotest corners have been mapped by satellite, its strangest sights made familiar by television. Unlike Lord Chesterfield's son, the modern armchair traveller is extremely well informed and the plethora of knowledge and description available to him in both words and pictures is nothing short of miraculous. Yet the noble Lord's advice is no less apposite today. Only by actually going and doing and seeing first-hand can the traveller hope to add true perspective to the picture, however well it has been described, or to experience the very feelings, tastes and smells which, though inexpressable in words, will flesh out the factual skeleton of his journey and later become the piquant flavour of memories. Second-hand adventure is no real substitute.

This then is a dual-purpose book. It should be of equal interest both to those who *do* as well as those who only *read*. Many travel books are aimed solely at the armchair reader, the authors endeavouring to share, as best they can, something of their experiences with those who, for one reason or another, cannot themselves undertake the same journey. All too often such books, though thoroughly entertaining, assume that the reader has no wish to make the journey described and thus practical information and useful facts are frustratingly omitted. Other books are mere guides. Full of facts, they are useful, if typically uninspiring, and hardly a compelling read on a long winter's night. Doubtless publishers assume that the traveller, having already decided on his goal, now needs information rather than inspiration.

I recall once, years ago, suggesting a potential feature to the editor of a well-known glossy magazine.

'All right!' he cried. 'Enthuse me!' And tilting back in his swivel chair he proceeded to spin round and round while I – suitably distracted – did my best to wax lyrical about my projected story; I must have been successful for my idea

was finally commissioned. In a similar way this book will, I hope, *enthuse* its readers besides merely entertaining them. It will also inform them, for there is a route description written between the lines of each chapter and a wealth of useful information collected at its end, enough to interest not only the intending traveller but the questioning armchair reader as well.

Happily we live in a decade when travel is easier, cheaper, and readily available to more people than ever before. But every time I board a Jumbo to endure cramped hours and plastic food, I ponder how pleasant it must have been to travel sedately to India by ocean liner as recently as 30 years ago. Or how delightful it must have been to walk up to Gangotri before roads writhed into the valleys of Garhwal. Kathmandu, in the 20 years that I have known the city, has gradually been strangled by the internal combustion engine. Though the world has surely shrunk we have paid a severe penalty for it. Nevertheless it is ironic that thanks to modern politics more of the world is actually inaccessible today than it was to stalwart travellers a century ago.

While much has changed in 30 years, much more will change in the next 30. Travel may become easier still but people-pressure will surely increase. Unless we care, the already shrinking wilderness will continue to shrink, and its very future depends on both private and public sanctions on those who would destroy it, sanctions not only from those of us who know the wild places but also from those who read about them. I well recall my first glimpse of Uganda's Murchison Falls National Park. Beneath black clouds, grey pillars of thunder storms marched across a vast, rolling plain of rippling green, alive with elephants. As far as the eye could see there were elephants, hundreds and hundreds of them. Here was the second largest elephant concentration in Africa, I was told. Just four years later I spent a couple of days driving round Uganda's other great reserve, the Rwenzori National Park, famous for holding the world's largest elephant population. Not one did we see; in fact there were precious few animals of any kind. 'Alas, Bwana' explained a dispirited and down-at-heel warden, 'the army comes here

for target practice and the tanks win when they fight with elephants.'

A true horror story, indeed. But the thin end of the same wedge is the litter of plastic bottles on the beaches of Vancouver Island and sloshing in the tide even on Antarctic shores. It is the piles of rusting cans at Everest Base Camp and the discarded oxygen bottles on the South Col. It is the polluted streams beside the Baltoro Glacier and the unburied faeces, the fluttering pink and blue toilet paper that ring the more popular Khumbu camp sites. The private traveller had no sanction on Idi Amin's army, but the individual trekker has complete control over his or her impact on the wilderness. It is an indictment of the many visitors to the foot of Mount Everest, often now mere tourists out of tune with the environment – and equally of their leaders and organisers who should know better – that a certain concerned trekking company has been organising low-key 'clean-up' treks to remove the rubbish others have abandoned. There can be no excuse for ignoring the unwritten rule 'Leave nothing but footprints, take nothing but photographs.'

Indeed, the responsible trekker respects not only his environment but also the people who live there, the people whose uninvited guest he has become. Respect means fair treatment in many different ways. Entering one remote village recently I was greeted with a barrage of dung where a few years before we were welcomed with smiles. Obviously other Western visitors had upset the villagers meanwhile. Sometimes, in more travelled regions, I have been besieged by children pulling my clothes and chanting 'Bon-bon! Caramele!' or just plain 'Baksheesh!' – indicating that generous but unthinking Europeans have recently passed by. Candy is not a kind gift where dental care is non-existent, nor are small coins in regions where an adult's annual income might be $200. Picture postcards, exercise books and ball-point pens, the latter ideally presented via the village school-master, are sensible gifts and graciously received.

The wise trekker should strive to understand and comply with local customs, habits and religious sensibilities, however pointless they may seem. In the Himalaya, for instance, one should always pass *chortens* and *mane* walls, or turn prayer wheels, in a clockwise direction. Likewise it is considered an insult when dealing with local people to use the left hand alone. In the Karakorum it is not done to photograph local women or defensive and strategic works – indeed expedition leaders sign an undertaking that their parties will not do so. Respect for such customs engenders respect for the traveller, and

the best local guide book will usually explain such things.

I have always considered maps to be of vital importance in any travel book. A good photograph is worth a thousand words, they say, but I'd suggest that a good map is worth two thousand! Practical maps of genuine use in the field in Third World or politically unstable countries are characteristically unobtainable, although some can be purchased from specialist shops such as Edward Stanford Ltd, London. If all else fails, the maps in this book are sufficiently accurate and detailed in most cases to use in the field – at a pinch. Our cartographer, Don Sargeant, is himself a well-travelled expeditionary mountaineer and much skill and experience has gone into his work. Naturally each map is aligned with north towards the top of the page. On the relevant maps glaciers are marked with a grey tone, while major summits or points are marked thus ▲, 7,000 metre (23,000 ft) .peaks thus △, and the 8,000 metre (26,250 ft) giants thus △.

Needless to say, proficiency with map – however basic – and compass is an essential skill for wilderness travellers in whatever environment, not only as a means of navigation but also when working out just what mountain they are looking at. An ability to navigate by compass is often taken for granted here in Britain, where the upland weather is so often misty, but it's a skill rarely required on the average trek through more exotic climes. Yet in perilous situations – during an unexpected blizzard on the Thorong La for instance, or when lost in thick mist in trackless Ruwenzori rainforest – compass skills can literally mean survival and in non-hazardous situations they are likely to save wasted time and energy.

Adequate preparation is often ignored by many first-time trekkers. The experienced traveller will prepare as thoroughly as possible, although always retaining the flexibility to enjoy a satisfying journey despite unavoidable changes of plan, due perhaps to weather, politics, transport cancellations and so on. Obviously adequate insurance is a sensible precaution and in remote or mountainous areas it should cover the cost of rescue, especially if a helicopter might have to be used – as in the Alps or the Himalaya. I know of a trekker whose appendix was removed on the Baltoro Glacier – by a scratch team of international expedition doctors to be sure – but he would have been in a sorry state had it not been possible eventually to evacuate him by 'chopper'. Luckily such dire emergencies are rare but when they do occur they are extremely expensive.

INTRODUCTION

Medical preparations are no less important, and the appropriate immunizations and inoculations should include that for hepatitis, not infrequently contracted by independent trekkers in Third World countries. And obviously a first aid course before you go is extremely useful. Simple hygiene, such as washing hands and peeling fruit, while usually common sense, is all too easily neglected, with unpleasant results at best. Trekkers should familiarise themselves with a wilderness medical handbook before departure, it will prove an invaluable investment. Three such excellent and readable books are listed in the bibliography at the end of the Annapurna chapter. While aimed at expeditionary mountaineers, they cover all travel in the wild and on a trek I always keep one in my rucksack. They also enlarge upon the dangers of altitude sickness which are mentioned in several chapters of this book.

One of my favourite quotations is from the 17th century Chinese poet Hsu Hsia-k'o: *'The body roams the mountains; and the spirit is set free'*. How true! Most of us can identifiy with his sentiment, well translated into present day terms by the late James Ramsey Ullman — the American writer —when he claimed that mountains *'. . . may well be a way of escape — from the cities and men, from the turmoil and doubt . . . But in the truest and most profound sense it is an* *escape not from but to reality.'* It is no surprise that of our thirteen chapters, eleven cover treks in the high country. But both writers might just as well have used the word *wilderness* instead of *mountains*, for mountains are only the most obvious, most timeless and least destroyable manifestations of the global wilderness — excepting of course the great oceans that occupy seven-tenths of our planet's surface. Other manifestations, no less adventurous and as spiritually refreshing, though perhaps less strenuous and certainly more threatened, are the great forests and the remote coasts that are the subjects of our two remaining chapters, and the wide deserts along whose fringes rise two of the mountain ranges we visit. I have personally enjoyed exciting and deeply satisfying journeys in all three of these very different environments, but I could wish for more, and as this book slowly came together, so my feet became more and more itchy. There are still so many places to go and so many journeys worth making. Voyages of discovery are always adventures and if this book has pointed you at your first trek, at pastures new, or has merely entertained you, then it will have succeeded. It was Goethe who wrote:

> *Whatever you can do, or dream you can do, begin it.*
> *Boldness has genius, power, and magic in it.*

John Cleare
Fonthill Gifford
Wiltshire
May 1988

The Bhagirathi River — the infant Ganges — thunders through the gorges near Gangani in August during the close of the monsoon. It was just here that the road was wiped out and our party had to abandon our bus.

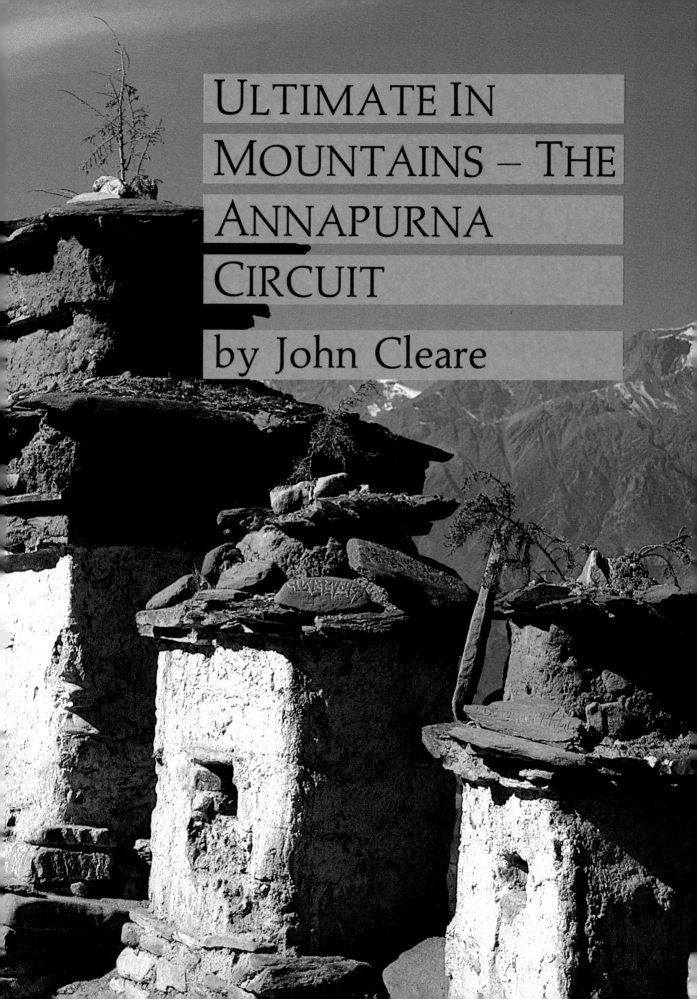

ULTIMATE IN MOUNTAINS – THE ANNAPURNA CIRCUIT

by John Cleare

*'. . . Northward soared
the stainless ramp of huge Himala's wall
Ranged in white ranks against the blue. . . .
It seemed to stand in heaven and speak with Gods'*
Edwin Arnold, *The Light of Asia*

To watch the dawn sweep over the Annapurna Himal, its 40 mile (60 kms) crystal rampart rising sheer some 22,000 feet (6,700 m) above the lush green fields and mirrored lakes of the Pokhara Valley is indeed one of the great privileges of the traveller in Central Nepal. The rumpled ridges of intervening foothills, textured with forest and wreathed with morning mists, serve only to isolate still further these mountains from the world at their feet, humdrum though it is not, stressing – if indeed stress were needed – that these are the Himalaya – the Ultimate Mountains.

This impressive segment of the Great Himalayan Chain, which holds no less than eleven '7,000 metre' (23,000 ft) summits, stands almost isolated by profound valleys from neighbouring mountain groups to east and west and from the Tibetan Marginal Chain (or Zaskar Crest) to the north. The region was virtually unknown to foreigners until 1950, when Maurice Herzog's French team entered the Kali Gandaki gorges to the west in an eventually successful expedition to Annapurna I (26,545 ft/8,091 m), while Bill Tilman's British party penetrated the easterly defiles of the Marsyandi Khola to explore the valley of Manang at its head and attempt Annapurna IV (24,688 ft/ 7,525 m).

The French traversed both the Thorong La and the Tilicho La and reached Manang Village in the quest for their peak and a short while later Tilman's men crossed over from Manang to Muktinath, but for many years thereafter the area remained a genuine 'lost valley', all but cut off from the outside world and virtually closed to foreigners.

There were political problems – and Tibetan rebels – along Nepal's northern marches in the '60s and early '70s, and it was not until these matters were resolved that the Government finally opened the Manang Valley in 1977, making possible for the first time the 150-mile (240 kms) circumnavigation of the entire Annapurna massif, a journey which is now one of the most celebrated treks in the world.

The popular starting point is Dumre, a village in the broad Marsyandi vale at an altitude of only 1,200 ft (360 m) beside the Kathmandu–Pokhara highway. Unfortunately a road is now being pushed up the Marsyandi Valley and although the technical problems would appear to be insurmountable, it is scheduled eventually to reach Manang Village at 11,300 ft (3,450 m). By early 1988 it had reached the village of Phalesangu at about 2,000 ft (600 m), some two days' walk above Dumre. I prefer to take the new spur road to the small hill town of Gorkha. Some two days, hiking through unspoilt country before reaching the river at Tarkughat Bazaar, means enduring the road works for only a few dusty miles.

Personally I am a strong opponent of indiscriminate road building in the mountains of Nepal, an act which many Western countries are vying with each other to finance and engineer. Not only are roads destroying the 'goose that lays the golden eggs' – the unspoilt mountain environment that attracts the visitors who are Nepal's largest source of revenue – but they are destroying a fragile rural economic system in one of the world's poorest nations.

Normally all goods are carried on the backs of thousands of relatively high-earning professional porters (and also in some places on those of yaks and mules) and their spending on food and lodging en route diffuses widely into the countryside. With the coming of a road expenditure is concentrated at either end and earnings accumulate in the pockets of a minimal number of already affluent city entrepreneurs – truck owners, fuel merchants and drivers.

November is my favourite month in Nepal and in the perfect autumn weather those first three days before joining the regular trail were a pleasant rest cure from the chores of organizing the trip and the frustrating hassles of travel in the Indian subcontinent.

It was fascinating to explore the historic little town of Gorkha, happily unspoilt by motor vehicles as the road ends just outside town, a reflection perhaps of what Kathmandu and Pokhara had been only 40 years before. Gorkha is the ancient seat of the present royal dynasty and from there King Prithvi Narayan Shah sallied forth in 1768 to conquer Kathmandu and unify Nepal.

We climbed from the town for 1,000 steep feet (300 m) to the fortress-like hilltop temples of Gorkhanath and Kalika where a superb view unfolded to the north. Seeming to hang in the sky beyond hazy green valleys and crumpled blue ridges were the four glinting white fangs of the Gurkha Himal – Manaslu, Peak 29, Himalchuli and Bhauda. Gyaljen – our *sardar* (headman) – had been to the summit of Manaslu and I had once led an attempt on Himalchuli so we were able to point out the routes on these formidable peaks to our ten panting, yet spellbound companions. All of them

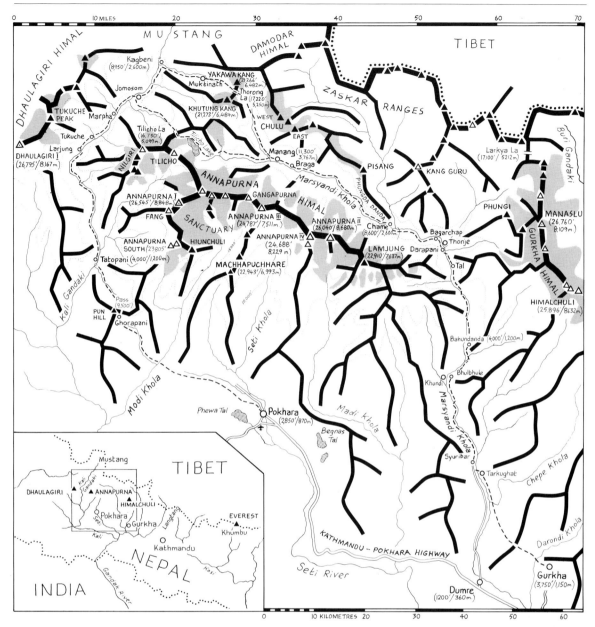

mountaineers, it was their first real view of the Himalaya. Then we descended at a leisurely pace along a delightful ridge-top path, arriving a couple of hours later at our first camp, where a small goat-boy was playing his flute and tea was ready and waiting. It was the perfect start to a Himalayan journey.

Next day we were away soon after dawn – standard trekking practice – descending through dewy forests where monkeys chattered in the trees and Andrew, the toughest young member of our party, skidded on the slippery path and twisted his ankle. It is during these first few days of any trek that such minor problems occur as folk get used to regular exercise again, to sustained walking and simple food. This is usually when such things as blisters and tummy

troubles manifest themselves – the latter a legacy of long flights and eastern cities – and with any luck soon run their course.

It was harvest time in the valley below and there was constant activity in the rice paddies beside the trail. In one place we watched an old fellow carving millstones with a simple chisel beside his primitive watermill. I bought ripe bananas and small, sweet oranges for our party from smiling villagers in a pretty village while excited children clamoured to practice their English and never once begged for 'mithai' (candy) or pens – a sure sign that we were well off the tourist track. Incidentally the former must be discouraged for dental reasons and donations of the latter should ideally be made direct to the village schoolmaster. Eventually we reached the

13

broad and lush vale of the Marsyandi where we camped on the shingly banks of the Chepe Khola, one of its major tributaries.

The following morning, gentle dawn mists hung over the river and huge spiders clung to dew-spangled webs stretched above the path. And then, as the sun rose higher, the white battlements of first Lamjung (22,910 ft/6,983 m) and later Himalchuli (25,896 ft/7,893 m) soared above the dissolving wreaths. Before long we reached the Marsyandi itself, marred by the nasty scar of the road works and noisy, battered jeeps heading for Syuribar. At so low an altitude we were soon hot and sweaty and stopped occasionally to swim in the welcoming pools of the river or its tributaries while kingfishers

darted overhead if we kept still and silent.

But we soon passed the road head and the valley regained its tranquillity, gradually narrowing as the steepening hillsides crowded in on the river. By the time we reached Bhulbhule (2,700 ft/820 m), four nights out from Gorkha, the river was a wide, foaming torrent with waterfalls pouring over nearby cliffs to join it. The day had been humid and I felt we'd earned some refreshment so Gyaljen and I introduced our companions to the delights of the village *chhang* house. *Chhang* is the tasty – and heady – local beer. Its consistency varies from 'bouillon' to 'borscht' and it can be brewed from rice, barley or, in this case, from millet. An overdose seems to cause little ill effect. It is an acquired

taste, but I'm partial to the stuff and Andrew, who said it was good for his sore ankle, rapidly became a devotee. Kathy and Sheila were less sure.

Three hours beyond here, perched on a saddle above the valley floor, the little bazaar — and police check-post — of Bahundanda (4,000 ft/1,200 m) is the last major village of the well-populated lower valley, and soon afterwards the trail plunges into the first gorges. Scrubby forest, vertical vegetation and occasional terraces of barley and millet cling to craggy hillsides that rise steeply several thousand feet above the already tumultuous river while the spray of a fine waterfall occasionally draws a rainbow curtain across the defile. The narrow trail —

Left — *The ancient settlement of Braga, built into an arc of crags at some 11,400 ft (3,470 m). The white* gompa — *or temple — is in the centre. Due westward rises the icy wall of Tilicho Peak (23,406 ft/7,134 m).*

Below — *A* mane *wall beneath fluttering prayer flags outside Manang Village. Across the valley rear the savage northern flanks of Annapurna II (26,040 ft/7,937 m) — left — and Annapurna IV (24,688 ft/7,525 m) — right.*

sometimes cut into the living rock and the sole highway into the Manang Valley — crosses and recrosses the river on rickety wire suspension bridges beneath beetling cliffs. An impressive place indeed.

Here we were actually passing through the Great Himalaya — between the buttresses of the Annapurna and Gurkha Himals — and so deep is the valley that the sun rarely reaches Tal Meadows where we made our sixth camp at 5,500 ft (1,650 m). Waterfalls plunge from the surrounding cliffs on to the strangely flat floor of the gorge where a few herdsman's cottages and a teahouse cluster beside the temporarily tranquil river. Apparently the gorge was once blocked here by a huge terminal moraine and the lake thus impounded eventually silted up to form this peculiar meadow. There is a very similar meadow at the same altitude in the Buri Gandaki gorges on the far side of the Gurkha Himal. But it's a gloomy place and I've felt strangely apprehensive whenever I've camped here though nothing untoward has happened. Perhaps it was once the scene of a cataclysmic tragedy?

Two hours beyond Tal, past the villages of Darapani and Thonje, the valley turns sharply westward and widens again. Here, at 6,000 ft (1,800 m), there is a new luminosity in the atmosphere, there are rhododendrons and pine woods and cool winds blow off the eternal snows. I sensed that everyone felt happier. Now we were entering the rain-shadow region beyond the Himalaya — the region of the Buddhist culture of the north. We shared the trail with proud, Tibetan-looking folk, the men in long crimson coats and tall felt boots, the pretty

women wearing the colourful striped aprons of the Bhotiya (ethnic Tibetan) peoples, flaunting silver jewellery studded with turquoise and coral, coloured threads woven into their sleek black hair. We passed for the first time wayside *chortens* — stylized shrines — and *mane* walls carved with the mystic runes *'Om mane padme hum'* and sometimes set with prayer wheels. The next village, Bagarchap, was neat and tidy, with sherpa-style houses and fluttering prayer flags. I was relieved to see distant views once again, and was able to point out savage Phungi (20,990 ft/6,398 m) — an outlier of Manaslu — and the lovely fluted ice of Annapurna II (26,040 ft/7,937 m) to my companions.

Chame (8,630 ft/2,630 m), a few miles onward, is the principle town of the valley. We registered at the police post and John — who is 'something in the City' — managed to his great delight and our amusement, to change a traveller's cheque at the bank, a decrepit wooden shack outside which the manager and his clerk were playing cards beneath an awning of drying washing, guarded by a large, frowning fellow with a cartridge belt hung round his ample paunch and a rusty shotgun cradled in his arms.

A little further on the valley narrows again to a rock-walled gorge and here we actually camped in an orchard. Frost dusted the stunted apple trees throughout the day, probably indicating a sheltered site with plenty of summer sunshine up here beyond the rains. Kaji, our cook, brought us a bowl of wonderful-tasting apples with our supper. I warned everyone to use their double sleeping bags that night and was justified when the temperature dropped to minus 15°C (5°F).

In the chill dawn we climbed steeply through aromatic pine forest beneath a spectacular wall of icicle-hung rock slabs which stretches for almost two miles (three kms), rising all of 5,000 ft (1,500 m) to the crest of the Phungda Danda. Several of my younger companions got quite excited about climbing it — one day perhaps, but meanwhile there are real mountains to climb. When we emerged from the forest we found ourselves in the Manang Valley.

It seems surprising that the people who live up here — Bhotiyas of Tibetan origin and culture — are traditionally traders. Ancient royal dispensations allowed them special customs concessions and many have become international merchants familiar with the great cities of the Orient. Tilman recounts how a Manangi he attempted to photograph in 1950 retorted by whipping out a camera himself! I once saw a sophisticated battery-operated hi-fi in a house in Chame and the leather-faced man you pass on the trail, wearing a Tibetan 'toga' and high felt boots, may be on his way to Sydney or Bangkok. But yak caravans still ply the valley and horses are ridden, a means of transport rare elsewhere in Nepal.

The Manang Valley itself extends for some twelve miles (20 kms) and a succession of hanging glaciers pour down from the Annapurnas to its arid floor at an altitude of nearly 11,000 ft (3,400 m) — occasionally the main trail is blocked by the debris of great ice avalanches. Here the infant Marsyandi flows between dusty irrigated fields of barley and potato and through scattered pine woods. Braga is the finest of the several picturesque villages

where clusters of medieval stone houses typically flaunt elaborately decorated windows and fluttering prayer flags. Their flat roofs piled with firewood and winter hay, these houses nestle into eroded conglomerate crags – the remains of a cataclysmic ancient landslide – as much for defence as for protection against the weather. The *gompa* (a Buddhist temple or monastery) at Braga is over 500 years old and for a few rupees I persuaded the 'verger' to allow me to photograph its thousand gilded Buddhas.

On this particular visit to Manang we climbed Chulu East (c.20,000 + ft/6,000 + m), one of the three so-called 'Trekking Peaks' – Pisang, Chulu East and Chulu West – that rise from the first crest immediately above the valley. They provide an interesting diversion of a week or so for experienced and properly equipped climbers, for they are not especially difficult and the necessary permits are easily obtained in Kathmandu. On another occasion we spent a necessary acclimatisation day picnicking beside a lone white *chorten* high on the hillside above Braga watching the avalanches pouring off Gangapurna and marvelling at the eagles spiralling against the sky.

The valley forks at Manang Village and the regular route to the Thorong La follows the northern branch. One can also ascend the western fork to the frozen Tilicho Lake and cross the Tilicho La above it into the valley of the Kali Gandaki. But though some 500 ft (150 m) lower, this is a rather more serious proposition. It also approaches a sensitive area and currently requires a military permit. And a strong party of New Zealand trekkers was marooned up here for over

a week by heavy snowfall in October 1985. Three sherpas were killed and the trekkers were lucky to survive.

The valley ahead is desolate, now well above the tree line and climbing gradually some 3,000 ft (900 m) in ten miles (16 kms). The dusty trail winds along rocky slopes where sparse yellow grass lies flat against the wind. At dawn and dusk I've seen herds of the rare 'blue sheep' (*Pseudois nayaur*) and Tibetan gazelle on the hillsides and a giant lammergeier once swept so low over my head that I could hear the wind in its feathers.

Two days above Braga the valley reaches an abrupt end at 14,700 ft (4,500 m). In '79 we camped here beneath steep screes leading upwards between Dolomite-like cliffs. The night was bitterly cold and I sat up late with the sherpas at their yak-dung fire, sipping fierce *rakshi* (a rice spirit) and recalling the adventures we had shared together in the past. Our porters' little fires flickered from caves amid the surrounding crags. Today there is a tea-house where we camped – indeed it's the third since Manang Village – but the Thorong La above has become no less strenuous.

We breakfasted at 3.30 am and started upwards soon after four. The moon had set and the dark night was full of stars. It was bitterly cold. The trail up the screes was easy enough to follow by torchlight but the porters needed shepherding and encouragement. Before long we came to a rocky traverse where the whole

A mule train heads north on the long trail to Mustang.

hillside was sheathed in a film of water ice and I had to cut steps while the sherpas helped the porters across. One of the kitchen boys slipped and his basket full of pots, pans and kettles went clattering off into the darkness. It made an incredible din but it was a point of honour that all was safely recovered.

Eventually the angle eased, dawn rose out of Tibet and I started to warm up. We crossed large snow patches, wound through ancient moraines and at eight – soon after the sun had hit us – we reached a wide, desolate scree saddle where a large cairn, hung with tattered prayer flags, marks the summit of the Thorong La at 17,200 ft (5,240 m). We had crossed, as I'd planned, before the wind arrived.

Lying between two 21,000 ft (6,400 m) peaks – Yakawa Kang to the north and Khutung Kang (or 'Thorongtse') to the south – the pass breaches the narrow chain that links the Annapurna massif to the Zaskar ranges. As an important local trade route it is regularly traversed with ponies and yaks. The first European to cross was probably Gaston Rebuffat in 1950, but it is snow covered for much of the year and navigation in bad weather can be difficult. There is no shelter above 14,700 ft (4,500 m) on the east side or above a new tea house at about 12,700 ft (3,900 m) on the west, although I have used a rather exposed campsite, with a water trickle, in a scree hollow at 16,200 ft (4,900 m) on the Manang flank. Unprepared or unacclimatized trekkers have perished up here so the Thorong La should be treated with due respect.

It had been fairly painless for most of us although our doctor, who was over 60, was very tired. He and I found a sheltered hollow among the moraines where we ate our brunch of jam *chapattis* and wondered at the almost snowless desert mountains that rise to 20,000 ft (6,000 m) along the north-eastern horizon. The Thorong La is not a particularly good viewing point although a much better panorama, which includes Dhaulagiri, opens up during the seemingly endless, knee-jarring, 5,000 ft (1,500 m) descent to Muktinath.

We camped near the police check post at the village edge where the pyjama-clad constables seem engaged in a perpetual card game. This is

The summit of Thorong La at 17,220 ft (5,250 m) is a desolate place. This cairn, hung with tattered prayer flags and piled with ancient mane stones, *stands on the crest of the pass. The view is westwards towards the Dhaula Himal and forbidden Dolpo.*

the frontier with the mysterious and still forbidden Mustang region to the north. The landscape here is semi-desert, the only green a few stunted willows and patches of terraced cultivation beside the irrigation ditches. The village itself is ugly, but in a tranquil poplar grove nearby stands a complex of temples where a sacred flame fed by natural gas flickers from the same rock fissure as flows a spring of water. A lama once told me that the 'burning water' is a sign of God's omnipotence, which seems fair enough. It is an important place of pilgrimage, sacred to Buddhist and Hindu alike.

The local people are Thakalis — ethnic Tibetans and entrepreneurs — and a sales team immediately descended on our camp with all manner of souvenirs. Local specialities include turquoise-set trinkets and ammonite fossils and, with considerable circumspection, I acquired one or two bargains.

From a hill just above Muktinath — where ammonites can be found if you know where to look — there is an incredible view southwards. The twisting Kali Gandaki glints in the sun far below, its canyon nearly 23,000 ft (7,000 m) beneath the summits of Annapurna and Dhaulagiri, themselves only 21 miles (43 kms) apart. This is the deepest valley on earth. Dhaulagiri I (26,795 ft/8,167 m) dominates the view from Muktinath itself and at dusk we all scrambled a little way up the hillside above our camp to watch the sun slide behind its majestic pyramid and fire the snow plumes that burn gold round its crest.

Another long descent led us down to the river itself at Kagbeni (8,950 ft/2,700 m), a willow-fringed oasis in a steep, ochre-coloured moonscape, a medieval village beneath a frowning *dzong* — or fortified *gompa* — and the gateway to Mustang on the ancient trade route between India and Tibet. Yak and mule caravans, carrying wool and salt south and rice, sugar and shoes to the north, clattered through the narrow arches in the thick defensive walls. Shy urchins peeked and giggled from shadowed doorways as we entered the deep central courtyard at the heart of the village. It seemed a strange and alien place, another world, another time.

Below Kagbeni, the Kali Gandaki is wide and skeined and in late autumn was carrying little water. The river was here, draining the Tibetan plateau, before the Himalaya rose across its course. I was very aware of the awesome geography of these parts but this desolate canyon seemed utterly hostile to life in any form and the prospect of tea awaiting us at Jomosom ensured that we all hurried down its six thirsty miles (ten kms).

Jomosom is an important town, boasting an airstrip, an army base and hydro-electricity. Hung with power cables and seemingly deserted in the noon sun, it reminded me of a decrepit Mexican frontier town in a bad 'B' movie. I located our kitchen with some difficulty and drank many cups of tea with great pleasure. The combination of altitude, sun and exercise is especially dehydrating and drink is far more important in the short term than food.

The route onwards was wide, dusty and fairly busy with porters, soldiers, merchants with their jangling mule trains and, occasionally, white-jodhpured, black-coated government officials scurrying about their business. Once we even came upon four porters gingerly carrying a huge colour TV slung between two poles.

We found no convenient camp site at Marpha, a couple of hours down the canyon, so we spent a pleasant night in a large house where our own cook prepared supper, and we later shared the fireside with our hosts — a large family of several generations — and sang songs for each other. Father and the youngsters spoke fair English but the older ladies could only smile at our strange words.

Marpha is a neat village of substantial whitewashed stone houses, many displaying ornate woodwork and elaborately carved windows, flanking a clean and cobbled main street. It even boasts running water and a stone-built drainage system, an exceptional phenomenon in Nepal. Further on, Tukuche and Larjung are similarly attractive villages, where we were able to buy fresh fruit again, although I half expected Clint Eastwood to stride from a tea-house and leap onto one of the richly harnessed horses haltered outside. The affluence of the local Thakali folk results, of course, from the busy trade route up the valley.

The valley contains little level ground apart from the wide shingle expanse of the river, perhaps a mile across. Scattered pine forests and crags rise steeply towards the snows high on either side. As we crossed the many skeined river below Larjung, dramatically overhung by Dhaulagiri and its tumbling icefall, we were struck by one of the fierce dust storms which sweep up this venturi-like valley. I tied a wet bandana round my face and hid my cameras but it looked worse than it felt and the stinging blast died after a few minutes.

Now the landscape changes yet again. The valley becomes green, forests of pine and rhododendron close in on the river and patches of cultivation appear, token that the monsoon rains penetrate this far up the great canyon. We passed again into narrow gorges where the trail was cut precariously into vertical cliffs while the Kali Gandaki roared angrily below, in two places hurling its full might through narrow boulder chokes between rock walls a mere 60 ft (20 m) apart. The path was busy with gaily caparisoned mule trains and often we had to flatten ourselves into the rock to let the jangling beasts go by. Quite how our porters managed, I don't know.

And then suddenly we emerged into a lush, smiling glen where the icy buttresses of 'Fang' – now Varaha Shikhar – (25,089 ft/7,647 m), close neighbour of Annapurna I, rose above terraced fields and orange trees hung with ripe fruit. At the bazaar village of Tatopani (4,000 ft/1,200 m) – the name means 'hot water' – we threw off our dirty clothes and relaxed in the riverside hot springs, gorging ourselves on fresh fruit. Richard even shaved. It was a blissful moment after three weeks on the trail.

But it was by no means the end of the trek, for we now had to climb out of the Kali Gandaki Valley and make our way eastwards for four days across the grain of the country to Pokhara.

A long ascent of over 5,000 ft (1,500 m) up stone steps and through terraces of newly sown millet and barley led us to camp in a clearing in the rhododendron groves on the long southern spur of Annapurna South. We watched the sunset from the grassy summit of Pun Hill (9,950 ft/3,030 m), above the pass of Ghorapani – a hill that must be one of the world's classic mountain viewpoints – an experience which was perhaps a fitting climax to our journey.

The panorama extends westward from Himalchuli, past Machhapuchhare, Annapurna South, Annapurna I and Fang, to the Dhaula Himal – to Tukuche Peak and Dhaulagiri I and far beyond to Gurja Himal. I also identified, I thought, Dhaulagiris II to VI. We puzzled out which peak was which with map and compass until the alpenglow finally died on Dhaulagiri and we could no longer see to read.

As the moon rose we scrambled down to the camp to enjoy hot rum toddies drunk round a blazing log fire, but we left John – more masochistic perhaps or just searching for karma?

Elaborately decorated windows are a feature of the Manang villages.

Left – Mule train near Chitre descending into the deep Kali Gandaki Valley from the pass of Ghoropani. In the distance are Dhaulagiri I (26,795 ft/ 8,167 m), and Tukuche Peak.

Below – View southward from Point 5,255 m (17,240 ft) above Muktinath, down the gorges of the Kali Gandaki between Dhaulagiri (right) and Annapurna.

– to bivouac on the summit. He had the best view of the dawn but before he rejoined us we had seen a red panda (*Ailus fulgens*) among the rhododendrons.

Three days of pleasant and relaxed hiking led us finally to Pokhara. It is an up and down trail to be sure, but a good one and busy with local folk going about their business, mule trains en route to Jomosom and beyond and often Gurkha soldiers from both the British and Indian Armies returning to or from their villages on furlough, always ready for a chat in passing. This is Gurung territory and military service is a popular – and lucrative – profession for the young men. The villages themselves are neat and prosperous, there are flowers in the gardens and blossom on the trees, the fields are well tended and with

Machhapuchhare – the virgin southern outlier of the Annapurna range and perhaps the most beautiful mountain in the world – ever-present on the northern horizon, this final stage of the journey well displays the typical smiling face of Nepal and its people.

We came at last to the road head on the outskirts of Pokhara, and Gyaljen commandeered a rickety bus to take us through this clamorous small town, heavy with unaccustomed smells and diesel fumes. At an altitude of less than 3,000 ft (1,000 m), the air here seemed thick and cloying and we were glad to reach camp at last beside the lake of Phewa Tal, where we swum in the cool, green waters as the dusk crept over the fluted ice of Annapurna.

Most of these notes, except those obviously specific to the Circuit of Annapurna, are applicable generally to the other high treks in Nepal including those discussed later.

Difficulties/dangers
Well used trails and good bridges all the way. Some stiff but never actually difficult walking and the only steep and strenuous climbs are the final 2,500 ft (700 m) ascent to the Thorong La and the unrelenting 5,000 ft (1,500 m) ascent from Tatopani to Goropani.
Highest point: 17,220 ft (5,250 m) – Thorong La. May involve crossing snow near summit. Sometimes impassable due to stormy weather or heavy snow. See paragraphs in main text about the dangers of this high pass.
Time above 10,000 ft (3,000 m): 5 days minimum + any extra acclimatization period. See notes below under 'Medical considerations'.

Distances/times
The basic circuit, as described, is approximately 150 miles (240 kms) on the map. But it is better measured in days walking at a reasonable pace for some 7 hours each day, in fair weather:
Gurkha to Manang Village: 9 days.
Then ideally allow 2 days in the vicinity for rest and acclimatisation before proceeding.
Manang Village over the Thorong La to Muktinath: 3 days, but enforced wait of several days is possible in bad weather.
Muktinath to Pokhara: 8 days. Total 22 days.

Season/weather
Pre-monsoon season – late April, May.
Post-monsoon season – October, November, early December.
November is the best time for the journey as the weather is typically most settled, the views are clearest and although it is starting to get cold above 10,000 ft (3,000 m), modern clothing and equipment should minimize the problems of low temperatures. But this is mountain country and it can rain – or snow high up – at any time.
Actually, because much of the Annapurna Circuit lies *beyond* the chain of the Great Himalaya, this is one of the few treks feasible during the monsoon from June into September if you are prepared to brave ten days of unpleasant conditions – rain, mud and leeches – at the beginning and end of the journey. If you persevere, this is when the mountain flowers are at their best, although the Thorong La may well prove impassable. Rhododendrons flower from April into the monsoon.

Typical mid-November temperatures
At the lowest altitudes —
mid-day sun: 100°+F/38°+C
shade: 80°F/27°C
night minimum: 60°F/16°C
At the highest altitudes —
mid-day sun: 48°F/9°C
shade: 40°F/5°C
night minimum: 12°F/–11°C

Equipment
Normal gear for trekking from 2,000 to 17,000 ft – (600 to 5,000 m) i.e. shorts and T-shirt low down, warm mountain clothing higher up with fibre-pile and/or down jacket and a wind/waterproof cagoule strongly recommended. Wet feet are unlikely and training shoes are adequate at lower altitudes but light trekking boots (with ankle support) are preferable and safer on the stony ground and long descents at the higher elevations. An umbrella, obtainable locally, may be useful for both sun and showers. A double sleeping bag with three subsequent 'warmth combinations' is recommended. It is stupid to be cold.
Most items of mountain clothing and equipment can be purchased in Kathmandu – though larger sizes may be scarce – and are sometimes available in Pokhara.

Access/permits
A Trekking Permit is essential and can be obtained from the Immigration Office in either Kathmandu or Pokhara. A nominal charge is levied and two passport pictures are necessary. Government regulations covering trekking change from time to time and should be noted.
There are Police Check Posts at irregular intervals where Trekking Permits must be presented.
At the time of writing (early 1988) the valley of the Dudh Khola N.E. of Thonje and all territory north of Muktinath and north and west of Kagbeni (i.e. Mustang and approaches to Dolpo) are closed.

Logistics
Pokhara is reached from Kathmandu by a daily air service, by express bus (approx six hours) or by slower local bus. All buses stop at Dumre. Gurkha lies at the end of a branch road and can be reached by regular bus from Kathmandu.
It is now possible to complete the entire circuit staying at or eating in 'tea-houses' or other wayside accommodation. There is no shortage of good campsites and porters should be available in such centres as Pokhara, Gurkha or Dumre. However, Government regulations stipulate that porters must be properly equipped with shoes, socks and warm clothing to cross the Thorong La.
Several firms in Kathmandu or Pokhara – the best highly efficient and reliable, many less so and some plainly incompetent (you get what you pay for) – will outfit and/or organize the whole journey for you. Such trips can be booked through adventure travel companies in most Western countries, many of whom provide an excellent service.

Medical considerations
Altitude sickness can be lethal. Many trekkers pay scant attention to the business of acclimatization, ignoring at their peril the old rule *Climb high – Sleep low*, and after Manang Village it's uphill all the way to 17,000 ft (5,000 m). Ideally two rest days should be taken before pushing beyond Manang: a side trip or two into the hills above Braga, reaching above 13,000 ft (4,000 m) and returning to the valley to sleep, is rewarding, not only to marvel at the icy wall of the Annapurnas opposite, but also to acclimatize.
Stomach problems can be minimized by eating local food with discretion and drinking only water which is either well boiled or of unimpeachable origin.
A Medical Post for Trekkers, usually presided over by a Western doctor during the most popular trekking seasons, is situated some three miles before Braga near the trail, a short distance west of Ongre airstrip. There is a similar post for Everest trekkers at Pheriche – one day in descent from Base Camp. The nearest hospital is at Pokhara.

Language
English is taught in schools and will be understood to a greater or lesser extent by many local people. In the

villages children will be keen to practice their skill on travellers. A smattering of Nepali (Gurkali) or Hindi can make the journey more enjoyable but is not a necessity.

Other considerations
Although this trek is often attempted clockwise, it is best taken in an *anti-clockwise* direction, east to west. The chief reason is that acclimatisation is easier in this direction. The eastern approach to the Thorong La is far more gradual than from the west and the final day's climb is 3,000 ft (900 m) *less*.

Reading
Maps: Several locally produced dyeline sketch maps are available in Kathmandu bookshops or from trekking agencies. The best of these are more or less accurate near the main trails and are adequate for finding the way, if not for pinpointing the mountains seen en route.

Guide books:
Trekking in Nepal
Steve Bezruchka (Cordee, UK/The Mountaineers, Seattle)
Trekking in the Himalayas
Stan Armington (Lonely Planet)
Trekkers Guide to the Himalaya and Karakorum
Hugh Swift (Hodder & Stoughton, and in USA)
Insight Guide to Nepal
(Apa Productions, Hong Kong)
The Trekking Peaks of Nepal – A Guide
Bill O'Connor (Crowood Press)

Medical books:
Medical Handbook for Mountaineers
Peter Steele MD (Constable)
Mountain Sickness – Prevention, Recognition and Treatment
Peter Hackett MD (American Alpine Club/Cordee, UK)
Medicine for Mountaineering
James Wilkerson MD (The Mountaineers, Seattle/Cordee, UK)

Literature:
Nepal Himalaya – H W Tilman
Republished 1983 as part of *The Seven Mountain-Travel Books* (Diadem UK/The Mountaineers, Seattle)
Annapurna – Maurice Herzog (Jonathan Cape, 1952 and various subsequent editions)
Nepal – Toni Hagen (Kummerly & Frey)
The Sherpas of Nepal – von Furer-Haimendorf (John Murray, 1972)
The Story of Mount Everest National Park Various authors (Cobb/Horwood New Zealand, 1985) Obtainable from the King Mahendra Trust for Nature Conservation in Nepal.

Other Classic treks in the Nepal Himalaya

If one can claim that 'Trekking' was invented in the Himalaya, then its modern form was surely developed in Nepal when Col. Jimmy Roberts decided that while climbing big mountains might be masochism, the approach march to them made a wonderful holiday.

The first modern 'commercial' trek was organised in 1965 by Col. Roberts and was a there-and-back walk from Kathmandu to Everest's southern Base Camp, but before long he and other devotees had worked out many other excellent itineraries in a country where the long distance hill-walking is as good as anywhere in the world. Much of the credit for the subsequent development of today's efficient and enjoyable 'commercial' trek must go to the Colonel and his firm 'Mountain Travel Nepal', still innovative, still breaking new ground and still based in Kathmandu – though now also handling treks and expeditions in many other mountain regions.

Khumbu
Today – for obvious reasons – the 'Everest Trek' is the most popular itinerary in Nepal, but alas very different from what it was before the advent of regular flights to Lukla STOL airstrip (9,400 ft/2,850 m) – a surfeit of visitors and the application of sometimes irresponsible commercialism have seen to that. However, Khumbu with its friendly Sherpa inhabitants *is* special, and well worth a visit. Thankfully, Khumbu is now a National Park.

Most visitors will fly in, thereby avoiding the contrast provided by the delightful approach trek through the foothills which provides a perfect opportunity to get fit and start crucial acclimatization – without which progression far above Lukla can be not only slow and painful but also downright dangerous. I would advise taking the original Everest Trail, joined at *Jiri* – which can now be reached by regular bus from Kathmandu – which lies some nine days below the chief Khumbu village of *Namche Bazar* (11,290 ft/ 3,440 m).

Then, rather than following the regular and well trodden direct route onwards to Everest Base Camp, I prefer to make a circuit via the Ngozumpa Glacier and *Gokyo* (15,600 ft/4,740 m) where the view from the hill above encompasses Cho Oyu, Everest, Lhotse and Makalu, before continuing over the *South Cho La*, a 17,800 ft (5,400 m) snow pass, to join the regular route at *Lobuje*. Although technically straightforward, the pass looks quite intimidating at first sight, the descent is over broken rocky ground and the little patch of glacier on its crest holds a few crevasses and must be crossed with circumspection. But it can be the highlight of the trek and the views from the top are stunning. *Gorakshep*, below the celebrated viewpoint of Kala Pattar, and *Base Camp* (17,600 ft/5,400 m) are one day further on.

Return is made down the regular route past *Thangboche Monastery* and *Namche* to *Lukla* airstrip from where there are regular flights – weather and people pressure permitting – to Kathmandu.

Langtang
This high, glacier-headed valley, running parallel to the main Himalayan crest beneath great ice peaks, is another excellent trekking destination and also a National Park. Like Manang its inhabitants are Bhotiya people, and though the valley's western end is popular with trekkers, the eastern end, between 12 and 15,000 ft (3,500–4,500 m) and beyond habitation, is still wild and fairly remote.

The Langtang Glen is a tributary of the important Trisuli Valley, a major through route into Tibet, and approach is easiest via the new road up the Trisuli Valley which, in early 1988, had reached as far as Dunche village, though it is scheduled eventually to reach Syaburubensi at the confluence of the two valleys. However, I prefer to enter *Langtang* by one of the three high passes over its southern rim – returning by another. In the east, *Tilman's Pass* is for mountaineers only but the central *Ganja La* (16,800 ft/5,100 m) and the western *Laurebina La* (15,100 ft/ 4,600 m) can be crossed by fit trekkers except in winter or bad weather. They lead over from the attractive Sherpa-inhabited *Helmu* Glens and by either of them *Langtang Village* is some nine days walk from Kathmandu, the latter pass leading beside the pretty *Gosainkund Lakes*.

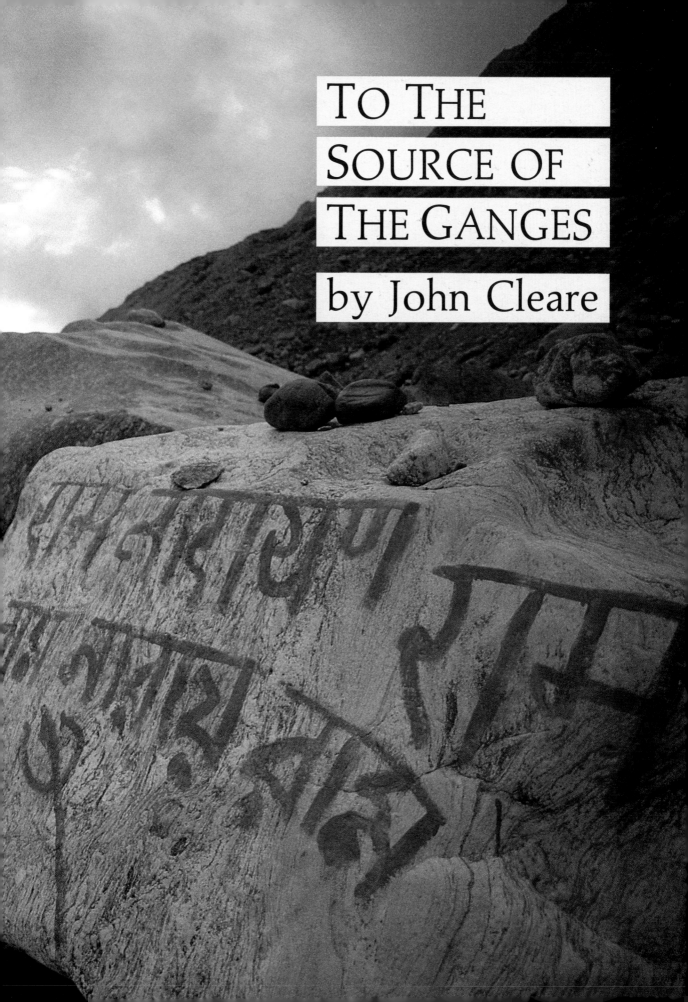

TO THE
SOURCE OF
THE GANGES

by John Cleare

TO THE SOURCE OF THE GANGES

'They had crossed the Siwaliks and the half-tropical Doon . . . and headed north along the narrow hill roads. Day after day they struck deeper into the huddled mountains, and day after day Kim watched the lama return to a man's strength.'
Rudyard Kipling, *Kim*

I awoke fitfully, my legs ached and the ground was very hard. The air was damp and smelt strangely musty. I heard a splash. Where was I? I sat up and remembered. Laurie was standing waist deep in the gently steaming water.

"Wow man – it's hot!" he called. I rolled out of my sleeping bag, limped over the flagstones to the pool's edge and dropped in. It was hot! And sulphury! And just what the doctor ordered after three cramped days in a bus with hundred percent humidity and a bivouac on a stone floor. Wanda poked her head round the cloister corner.

"*Chiya* (tea) up, boys," she announced, "or shall I serve breakfast in the bath?"

Tato Pani is a hot spring – indeed the name means 'Hot Water' throughout the Himalaya – a wide, stone-rimmed pool surrounded by whitewashed cloisters. It stands on a steep, forested hillside above the tumultuous Bhagirathi River at an altitude of just over 6,000 ft (1,800 m) in the Himalaya of Garhwal. Clearly the spring has, at some time, been spruced up to welcome the pilgrims who journey up this tortuous valley from the Indian plains to the holy shrine of Gangotri – and beyond to the source of the Bhagirathi at Gaumukh, held to be the birthplace of the Ganga, the holy Ganges. Perhaps we too were pilgrims of a sort.

The bustling town of Rishikesh, only 1,000 ft (300 m) above the sea yet 800 miles (1,290 kms) from it, sprawls under the green wall of the foothills beside the portal through which the Ganga bursts forth onto the Indian plains. From here our bus had growled its way over the Siwaliks through a curtain of monsoon rain. At dawn the temperature had been in the 80s and as the day drew on, grew far hotter still. Clouds hung in the valleys and wreathed the hills as we wound our way through steep, lush forest in an eerie, green half-light. Beyond this first bastion of the mountains the rain stopped and we halted for glasses of hot, sweet tea in the small town of Chamba, nectar which we agreed was an excellent cure for travel-sickness. Twice as we descended, our Sikh driver slowed to a careful crawl to negotiate landslides but it was under a blue sky that we reached the smiling valley of the Bhagirathi and bounced on into Uttarkashi.

At almost 4,000 ft (1,200 m), Uttarkashi is a scruffy little mountain town, sitting astride the river, surrounded by steep pine forests. I had the feeling that if only the clouds still clinging to the hills would roll back we might even see the snows – it was that sort of place. A swallow-tailed moth larger than my hand fluttered at the window of the Government rest-house where we spent another hot and sticky night. Next morning we purchased our final supplies in the bazaar, including a half-litre of gasoline, contracted to meet two porters at Gangotri, and climbed onto an overloaded local bus which finally lurched away up the valley in a cloud of blue smoke as the rain again started to fall.

The valley narrowed and the last untidy villages were left behind. The dirt road climbed steadily, the rain poured down relentlessly, the windows misted up and I dozed. After a while I became aware that we were grinding along even more slowly than usual. The babble of voices had ceased – there was tension in the air. The driver was bent over the wheel peering intently through a dangling curtain of fairy lights and plastic charms into the rain ahead. We lurched several times and jerked to a skidding halt. Everyone started chattering at once and with several locals Laurie and I scrambled out into the rain.

No wonder we had stopped. The road, no wider than the bus, was cut into the precipitous valley wall while the Bhagirathi roared below through a rocky gorge. A few yards ahead the rutted gravel disappeared into a mound of mud and boulders.

"What's the form, Mr Singh?" I asked our driver. "What do we do about this?"

He looked harassed.

"It is not possible to go forward, isn't it!" he gushed, and glancing apprehensively at the crumbling verge on the lip of the abyss, he confirmed "and it is not possible to turn round or go into reverse! We must await the army. Maybe they will dig out the road tomorrow. Maybe you can stay in the bus."

Laurie groaned.

"But a little way ahead there is a village," he added, helpfully.

Beyond the landslide the rain eased and it felt good to stretch our legs. We strode along, rucksacks heavy on our backs, thankful to be masters of our own destiny. It was a sensational road. We passed two more landslides and came to a layby where small, green-clad soldiers were bustling around a couple of big green trucks. I recognised them to be Gurkhas.

"*Namaste!*" we called. A smart lieutenant came over, a tall Sikh in a crisp green turban, and we shook hands.

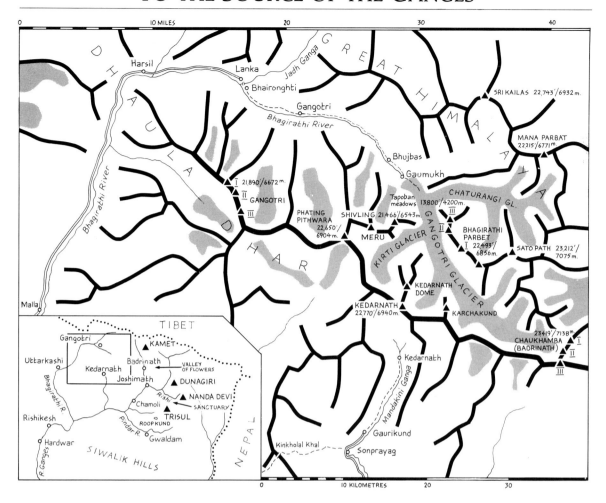

Map scale markings: 0, 10 MILES, 20, 30, 40 (top); 0, 10 KILOMETRES, 20, 30 (bottom)

Labels on main map: Harsil, Lanka, Bhaironghti, Jadh Ganga, GREAT HIMALAYA, SRI KAILAS 22,743'/6932 m., Gangotri, Bhagirathi River, MANA PARBAT 22,215'/6771 m., DHAULA DHAR, Bhagirathi River, Bhujbas, Gaumukh, CHATURANGI GL., I 21,890'/6672 m., II GANGOTRI, III, Tapoban meadows 13,800'/4200 m., GANGOTRI GLACIER, PHATING PITHWARA 22,650'/6904 m., SHIVLING 21,466'/6543 m., MERU, III, II, BHAGIRATHI PARBET I 22,493'/6856 m., SATO PATH 23,212'/7075 m., KIRTI GLACIER, Malla, KEDARNATH DOME, KEDARNATH 22,770'/6940 m., KARCHAKUND, 23,419'/7138 m. CHAUKHAMBA (BADRINATH) I, II, III, Kedarnath, Mandakini Ganga, Gaurikund, Kinkholal Khal, Sonprayag

Inset map labels: TIBET, Gangotri, KAMET, Uttarkashi, Badrinath, VALLEY OF FLOWERS, Kedarnath, Joshimath, DUNAGIRI, Bhagirathi R., Chamoli, Rishi, NANDA DEVI SANCTUARY, NEPAL, Rishikesh, TRISUL, ROOP KUND, Pindar R., Gwaldam, Hardwar, R Ganges, SIWALIK HILLS

"Gangnani is the next village," he explained. "There's nothing much there but you could bivouac at the hot spring a little further on. It'll take us several days to clear the road, but there'll be a bus down from Lanka in the morning and you can go up on it. Can we run you up to the hot spring?" We thanked him gratefully. "Don't mention it," he replied.

Our journey next day beyond Tato Pani was more reassuring. The bus was decrepit and the road steeper, but at least it appeared rather safer as it climbed across the sunny, south-facing slopes of the valley, through alpine meadows thick with flowers and dotted with walnut trees. In this mountain country the air was cool and fresh. We descended into a wide valley, almost a sanctuary, where goats with long, spiral horns blocked the road as it ran through peaceful pastures beside the skeined river. Then we trundled through Harsil, a pretty village of weathered wooden houses strung with yellow marigolds, where grinning children waved from windows. Harsil had once been the headquarters of ex-private Wilson who, in the 1850s, deserted his Highland regiment on the plains, made his

way into the mountains, married a Harsil lass and set up a private kingdom. Apparently his vast wooden palace still exists. Was it he who inspired Kipling to write his splendid tale, *The Man Who Would Be King*?

Thus far the Bhagirathi had been leading north, but here at Harsil the river cuts through the line of the Dhaula Dhar or Lesser Himalaya, then bends sharply south-east towards its source between this crest and the parallel crest of the Great Himalaya. This sudden change of direction was disorienting but I already had a general idea of the basic geography of Garhwal and everything dropped into place. Now we would be travelling in the depression between two of the three major Himalayan folds.

The road climbed again through tall deodars and wound round granite outcrops until eventually the bus halted in a wide clearing where tin shacks, army tents, bustling people, striding soldiers and military mule trains proclaimed the road head at Lanka. We gathered our gear and made for the nearest tea shop, where we studied our maps and asked for directions as we enjoyed our *chiya*. It seemed that here we were on the 'Inner Line' — that imaginary boundary north of which, for security reasons, foreigners are not permitted to venture. Our route, of course, led south-east. We were a mere 20 miles (30-odd kms) from the Tibetan frontier — which explained the military presence and no doubt, originally, the road. I reflected that the first climbing expeditions into the area, travelling with porters and ponies, had taken ten days over a journey which had not yet taken us two. Progress is often unfortunate.

A steep path descended through the pines into a narrow defile where the river foamed in green fury. Soon we came to a major confluence where an incredible gorge joined the main river from the north, sliced through the granite as if by a cyclopean knife. High above, the lattice girders of an uncompleted bridge reached out towards the far side. This tributary is the Jadh Ganga, draining the fold between the Great Himalaya and the northern Zaskar crest, cutting through the former to join the Bhagirathi. We crossed the narrow wooden footbridge spanning the Jadh and climbed to another scruffy clearing in the pines — Bhaironghti — a few hundred yards from Lanka but separated from it by the gorge and more than an hour's walking. Several dusty jeeps stood among the trees and four men in oily singlets were replacing the wheel on a tired-looking bus. They told us that these vehicles had been hauled over the gorge on ropes, that the road did continue to Gangotri and that the bus would go probably get there before dark. We decided to walk.

Five hot, dusty, but not unpleasant miles led up to Gangotri. Flowers grew on the verges of the new dirt road and the ubiquitous pines climbed towards mist-shrouded heights. Here, in the lee of the Himalaya, it seemed almost arid and although the weather was obviously still unstable and we must expect some rain, I was surprised how swiftly we had left behind the monsoon-soaked country south of the Dhaula Dhar crest.

Gangotri means 'Ganga flows north' for here, at 10,000 ft (3,000 m), the river is running north-west towards the Harsil bend. More noteworthy however are the spectacular falls over which the Bhagirathi plunges, the wide river thundering into a rocky cleft almost narrow enough to leap while rainbows play in the spray among the pines. It is no surprise to learn that the Hindu saint Raja Bhagirathi chose this atmospheric site for his meditations and that, with the Ganga's actual source lying only ten miles (16 kms) deeper into the mountains, Gangotri should consequently be considered a holy place and a goal for pilgrims.

We found here a bustling little community, tea houses, *ashrams* and various lodgings scattered among the trees on both sides of the river, with an imposing temple — built by the Gurkha General Anan Singh Thapa in the early 19th century — providing the spiritual heart of the place.

Garhwal has close links with Nepal. The decline of Moghul suzerainty in India coincided with a time of Gurkha ambitions and in the late

Right — *The spiritual heart of Gangotri, a celebrated place of pilgrimage at the falls on the Bhagirathi River, is this Hindu temple in an imposing setting beneath towering cliffs. It was built in the early 19th century by a conquering Gurkha General.*

Below — *Shivling is perhaps the most impressive peak in the Indian Himalaya — and one of the more famous. It has now been climbed by several routes. Here the north-east face is seen at dawn over the shadowed meadows of Tapoban.*

18th century the fierce Nepalese hillmen expanded their territory into the mountains to the west, effectively annexing Garhwal. The warlike Sikhs had meanwhile subjugated the Punjab Himalaya still further west, giving the British East India Company, already angry at the unrest, cause to fear a serious clash along the northern boundary of their plains territories. One of the results of the subsequent Anglo-Gurkha wars was the 1816 Treaty of Sagauli which fixed the Nepali frontier at the Kali River, where it still remains. It also initiated a lasting friendship based on mutual respect between the protagonists. The British, of course, moved into Garhwal. Today many Nepalis seek work there.

Our porters, willing fellows from West Nepal, reported for duty that evening at the little tourist rest-house beside the falls, and early next morning we set off up the excellent trail that led along the northern bank of the Bhagirathi. The wild river ran along a rocky bed, sometimes under great banks of old avalanche snow stuck with broken tree trunks. On either side, steep hillsides covered with scrub and stunted pines swept up to granite walls that reared into the mist. Swirling cloud blocked the valley ahead but through it we caught tantalising hints of distant snows. The sun actually shone on the ancient pilgrim trail as it wound up the valley and we enjoyed the easy walk, occasionally passing boulders gaily painted with religious graffiti. One especially intrigued me – a colourful rendering of the goddess Ganga, signed *Ashoka Art/UK* by the proud artist who had obviously travelled further than most pilgrims. And sometimes we passed pilgrims themselves, bearded and barefoot holy men who would greet us, hands together, with the intonation *'Ram, Ram'* – 'God, God' (more accurately the seventh incarnation of Vishnu), or more worldly folk wearing shoes, flared pants and bomber-jackets, typically clutching large thermos flasks and shouldering ex-army haversacks. But it was still the monsoon season and hardly the best time for pilgrimage.

We stopped at mid-day for a brew and the porters insisted on sharing their chapattis with us. Nothing is more delicious on a trek than hot chapatti spiced with wood smoke and stuffed with onions and cheese or smothered in peanut butter and honey. Luckily for us perhaps, our

This graffito beside the pilgrim trail depicts the goddess Ganga.

friends preferred theirs with a dollop of boiled rice and sprinkled with chopped chilli. In the afternoon we passed a succession of hanging side valleys blocked by moraines and ringed by small, misty, rock peaks streaked with snow patches, while beside the path the slopes were colourful with a profusion of flowers growing among the white boulders. At one place the trail crossed an almost vertical slope of bare, unstable rubble, ancient morainic debris, where several gaps in the path indicated that even the largest boulders protruding from the wall must eventually obey the call of gravity. We scuttled past as swiftly as we could. Then, round the corner, we came to a cluster of huts and tin roofs in a grassy hollow beside the river.

Bhujbas is incongruous – but any building would be in such a situation. As we gazed down on the place the evening cloud rolled back revealing snowy flanks, icy ridges and jagged summits high above us. But over the valley ahead, its feet lost in boiling mists, towered a fierce, double-headed pyramid, its black precipices capped with glinting ice. It looked inviolate, as stylised as a child's drawing, a perfect mountain.

"That" declared Wanda, "is Bhagirathi Parbat!"

A neat, multi-coloured graffito bid us *well come* and indicated *Lal Baba Road*, a path which led between white stones to the *ashram*, for such is Bhujbas. Travellers and especially pilgrims are welcomed and our porters were made comfortable while we opted to lay our sleeping bags in the large, bare dormitory and cook for ourselves, though we could have purchased a simple meal. It was as well that we didn't camp because in the night it rained very hard.

And so we came to Gaumukh, the holy 'Cow's mouth' – the ultimate source of the mighty Ganges. It is only two miles beyond Bhujbas with an ascent of a little over 300 ft (100 m), but the trail is bouldery and rather more rugged than before and the altitude – some 12,000 ft (3,600 m) – was starting to tell. We found ourselves in a desert of stones, gravel and abandoned moraines scattered with bright pink clumps of alpine willowherb, while the sharp summits of Bhagirathi Parabat seemed to tower over the massive moraine wall that marked the end of the Gangotri Glacier, blocking the valley ahead. The trail faded away and little paths wandered off among the boulders, but we knew what we were looking for so we made for the river, a boisterous torrent of milky, grey-green water, and followed it a few hundred yards to where it emerged from a dark cave in a wall of dirty ice under an enormous mound of rubble.

"So that's the Cow's Mouth!" gasped Wanda.

"Yep, the source of the holy Ganges," said Laurie.

"And the snout of the great Gangotri Glacier," I added, as a chunk of rotting ice broke away and crashed into the water.

Gaumukh is the ultimate goal of the hardiest pilgrims but hardly a taxing hike for well fed, properly shod and self-sufficient trekkers and we pushed on. Hints of paths ascended the awkward rubble slopes onto the broad glacier above Gaumukh, where we picked our way through a confusion of mounds and hollows towards the opposite bank. It was a mile of difficult going – but glaciers are like that! Then a path reappeared, zig-zagging steeply up the crumbling lateral moraine of the south bank, a nasty slog of some 400 ft (125 m) we guessed. On the crest we entered an extraordinary sanctuary. An awesome spire of ice-hung granite soared over a wide green meadow carpeted with flowers, across which meandered a lazy stream. There were yellow flowers and pink flowers and red flowers, blue poppies, gentians and edelweiss. A huddle of orange tents stood at the far side. This was the famous meadow of Tapoban, and the bewildering mountain above it was Shivling (21,466 ft/6,543 m).

"And those tents must be our girls on Meru!" exclaimed Wanda excitedly and we hurried through the long grass towards them. Sure enough, it was the base camp of the Polish women's team attempting Meru, the slightly higher but less formidable neighbour to Shivling. Only the doctor and their Indian Liaison Officer were at home but climbers are hospitable folk and Wanda was Poland's foremost woman mountaineer so the two girls entertained us royally with tea and crispy pancakes while we lay in the sun among the poppies, agreed that monsoon rains were worth enduring to catch the flowers in the high country, and gossiping – as climbers will – of mountains and mutual friends.

The beautiful meadows of Tapoban, lying at some 13,800 ft (4,200 m) below Shivling in the *mulde* or lateral trench of the Gangotri Glacier, are probably the safe limit for inexperienced trekkers, and unfortunately there are no simple passes out of the extensive Gangotri basin so they must return the way they came. Our own time was getting short but we planned to push on further still and pitched our tent before dusk at the far end of the upper meadow while our two trusty porters retired to a cave they knew.

The journey onwards along the western bank

of the Gangotri Glacier occupied an exciting day. Initially we contoured the base of Shivling, dropping down an horrific moraine shoot onto the glacier itself, still a wilderness of contorted rubble but dotted with strange, opaque pools of turquoise water. Then, missing a far shorter, easier, but less likely-looking route – which we discovered on our return – we ascended the tributary Kirti Glacier below the stupendous rock walls of Shivling's south face, searching for a reasonable crossing point. Dominating the head of this glacier are the complex icy slopes of Kedarnath (22,770 ft/6,940 m), the peak taking its name from the famous temple and shrine of Shiva, another important place of Hindu pilgrimage, below its formidable southern face. Its satellite, Kedarnath Dome, immediately across the glacier, had recently been ascended by an Indian ski expedition and we tried to work out their route as we lolled on the grassy moraine

lazily nibbling our lunch. Suddenly, with a roar like an errant express train, a large rockfall swept down one of the Shivling gullies behind us and persuaded us to start the crossing. Although we had actually been quite safe we had been scared and it reminded us of the penalty of being in the wrong place in the mountains at the wrong time.

In the *mulde* below the Gangotri flanks of Kedarnath Dome, at around 15,000 ft (4,600 m), we discovered another lovely meadow, smaller and rather less lush than Tapoban but this time graced by a little tarn. Here we camped for a while to explore the area, arranging for our two Nepalis to descend to their cave and return in two days' time. At dawn we watched the light sweep down the incredible wall of Shivling, mirrored in the ice that filmed our tarn. To the south the mountain displays the bizarre twin heads that account for its name, for in Hindu

mythology the *ling* of Shiva is forked. While we breakfasted we watched a herd of rare *bharal* – blue sheep – grazing the slopes above us and marvelled at Bhagirathi Parbet across the glacier, not one mountain but an unexpected chain of four formidable shark's teeth, each throwing down prodigious buttresses of mellow granite. It was an idyllic spot surrounded by so many tantalizing peaks and there was much for each of us to note for future reference.

But all too soon our smiling Nepalis were back and we turned to retrace our steps, back to Tapoban, back to Gangotri and back to civilization. But everything looks different – if strangely familiar – travelling in the opposite direction, and our pilgrimage lasted all the way back to Lanka when we finally clambered onto the snorting bus in a frosty dawn and settled into a blissfully uneventful journey down to the plains.

Above – The terminus at Lanka – a mere clearing in the forest at some 8,700 ft (2,650 m) graced with a few tea-houses and army tents – is a bustling and colourful place when buses arrive or depart.

Left – Dawn lights the southern flank of Shivling, reflected in the frozen surface of a tiny tarn beside the Gangotri Glacier. The twin summits of this incredible mountain are sacred to Shiva, one of the top three gods in the Hindu pantheon, responsible for personal destiny.

To the Source of the Ganges Fact Sheet

Difficulties/dangers/distances/times

The basic pilgrim route is an easy walk on a fair path which could be completed by a fit trekker from *Gaumukh* and back in two days. The total return distance is 19 miles (30 kms) and the height gain a mere 2,800 feet (850 m).

However, most trekkers will wish to press onwards at least to *Tapoban Meadows*, a further 1,100 feet upwards (340 m) and 2½ miles (4 kms) in distance on the map, but the going here is very rough, paths are non-existent in places and very poor at the best, and the route up the lateral moraine is loose and awkward. A strenuous section.

The route onwards along the *Gangotri Glacier*, graced in places by hints of paths, is typically rugged glacier travel on a very broken, debris-covered dry glacier and not without some little hazard from loose rocks and rockfall.

Highest point: Tapoban Meadows: up to 14,000 ft.

Time above 10,000 ft (3,000 m): to Tapoban only, 3 days +.

Season/weather

The Indian Himalaya can be loosely divided into three climatic regions: that to the south of the Lesser Himalaya – the first major Himalayan crest identified in Garhwal as the Dhaula Dhar – which is governed by the monsoon; then a more arid region in its rain shadow but still subject to monsoonal weather of sorts, here very narrow though very extensive westward in the Punjab Himalaya. Finally there is a region of high-altitude, trans-Himalayan semi-desert which stretches behind the Great Himalaya and includes the Zaskar crest and Ladakh mountains further west. In the Garhwal sector this region lies in Tibet.

The Gangotri Basin – in the second of these regions but approached through the first – is, like the rest of Garhwal, at its best from early September, as the monsoon dies, until late October and into November when the first winter snows may start falling. This autumn period enjoys typically settled weather and clear days but nights get colder and colder.

However in Garhwal trekking and climbing are possible in spring during May and June, and throughout the monsoon (July–August) when the flowers are at their best in areas beyond the Dhaula Dhar. Storms may be frequent in spring with views typically hazy and winter snow often still blanketing the high passes, while during the monsoon itself conditions are very unsettled. Spells of clear weather alternate with periods of heavy rain or snow and approaches through the southern valleys may be difficult or flooded.

Typical mid-October temperatures at Tapoban:
mid day 60°F/16°C
night   22°F/−6°C

Equipment

The Equipment Notes for the Annapurna chapter apply equally here except that this is a shorter trek and its higher altitudes are lower and less exposed. Shorts, shirt, pullover and light windproof are adequate by day to Tapoban and even above in September and October, but proper warm clothing and a good sleeping bag are required at night.

While training shoes are adequate for the walk to Gaumukh, stouter boots with proper ankle support are recommended for the rocky going on the glacier.

There is an infant mountain equipment industry in India and certain items of trekking/mountain equipment can be purchased in Delhi. It is also possible to hire gear. The friendly Indian Mountaineering Foundation, with HQ at Benito Juarez Rd, Anand Niketan, New Delhi–110021, will offer advice.

Access/permits

Trekking permits are not currently required for *walking* in India although a permit system may possibly be introduced in the near future. *Special permits are necessary for climbing* however and must be obtained well in advance through the IMF In Garhwal there are restrictions on foreign visitors near the Chinese/Tibet frontier and elsewhere certain politically sensitive and border regions are restricted or closed. Indian Government Tourist Offices should have up-to-date information.

Logistics

There are good bus services from Delhi to Rishikesh via Hardwar – a town some twelve miles (20 hrs) away, which can also be reached by train direct from Delhi. Regular daily services connect to Uttarkashi whence a local service plys onward to Gangotri if the condition of the road allows. Bus services in Garhwal (Uttar Pradesh State) are quite comprehensive and the Uttar Pradesh Government Tourist Office in Janpath, New Delhi, is very helpful in assisting visitors to organize their schedules.

This State is well provided with a system of official 'rest houses' and 'tourist bungalows' which provide simple and inexpensive accommodation, especially useful in such places as Hardwar, Rishikesh and Uttarkashi. There are two such places in Gangotri which should be pre-booked from Uttarkashi if possible.

Porters can be hired and supplies should be purchased in the bazaar at Uttarkashi and for treks from other valleys in similar bazaar towns, e.g. Joshimath, as supplies at the small road head townships will be very limited. The UP Government Tourist Office operates a trekking service with an outpost in Uttarkashi who will assist with porter hire – rates of pay and conditions are covered by local regulations.

Although there are several commercial trekking outfitters operating in Garwhal (both the IMF and the UP Government Tourist Office will advise) the route described can be completed easily without outside logistic support by fit backpackers, and a tent is only necessary for a stopover at Tapoban.

Medical considerations

These are similar to Nepal – see Medical Notes to Annapurna chapter.

Provided overnight stops are made in Uttarkashi, Gangotri and Bhujbas, and the trek itself is taken easily, there should be no serious altitude problems up to Tapoban – though altitude sickness can be lethal and its possibility should never be dismissed.

The lower reaches of Garhwal are malarial and requisite precautions should be taken, particularly during the monsoon.

Language

English is spoken by all educated people, by most officials and often a smattering by many local folk. However a little Hindi can be useful and will make contact with ordinary villagers and pilgrims more meaningful and enjoyable.

Other considerations

Gangotri and Gaumukh – and indeed other holy places elsewhere in the Garhwal mountains – are places of pilgrimage and have considerable religious significance to devout Hindus. Visitors should behave accordingly.

Reading
Maps:
Circulation of modern Survey of India maps, at 1:50,000 scale and fully contoured, is restricted and they are very difficult to obtain.
'Uttar Pradesh – Garhwal Himalaya' 1:200,000 – an excellent kammkarte – is published in three sheets (the trek

described requires sheets No 1 West and No 2 Central) by Yama to Keikokusha Co. Ltd, Tokyo, Japan. Very basic trekking maps in kammkarte style are available through the State Tourist Office and photocopies of pre-1947 Survey of India maps (1:253,440 scale – 4 miles/inch) can be purchased from the India Office Library at 197 Blackfriars Road, London SE1 8NG: originals are available for reference.

American AMS 1:250,000 sheets are better than nothing, sheet NH 44–1 covers the Gangotri area and is obtainable from Stanfords, London.

Guide books

The Himalayas – Playground of the Gods Capt. M S Kohli (Vikas Publishing/New Delhi)

Trekking in the Indian Himalaya Gary Weare (Lonely Planet)

Trekkers Guide to the Himalaya and Karakorum Hugh Swift (Hodder & Stoughton, London+Sierra Club, San Francisco)

Literature

Abode of Snow – Kenneth Mason (Hart-Davis, London, 1955 and recently reissued by Diadem)

Trespassers on the Roof of the World – Peter Hopkirk (Oxford University Press)

Himalayan Odyssey – Trevor Braham (George Allen & Unwin, London, 1974)

Where Men and Mountains Meet and *The Gilgit Game* both by John Keay (John Murray, London)

Nanda Devi – Eric Shipton (Hodder & Stoughton, London, 1936 etc)

The Valley of Flowers' – Frank Smythe (Hodder & Stoughton, London, 1938 etc)

Other treks in Garhwal and the Indian Himalaya

In India trekking is old and yet young. Old because it is a time honoured method of travelling among the highlands and mountains, a method enjoyed in the days of the British Raj by military officers, officials, surveyors and gentlemen of all sorts but for a purpose – and if for recreational purpose then usually for *shikar* (hunting) or even as a mountaineering expedition approach march.

In recent years trekking has developed as a pastime in its own right, but although enjoyed by many Indians, trekking in India is still in its infancy compared to Nepal, certainly as far as development, facilities, publicity and number of foreign

participants are concerned. But the potential is vast and with the trans-Himalayan regions of Zaskar, Ladakh, and – hopefully one day – the Indian areas of the Karakorum included, the trekking could be even more varied than in Nepal. Apart from Garhwal other currently important trekking areas are reached from Srinagar in Kashmir and Manali in the Kulu region of Himachal Pradesh, both accessible from Delhi.

The two most celebrated treks in India are both in Garhwal. The Nanda Devi Sanctuary, the all but inaccessible valley surrounding this great and beautiful peak – the highest entirely in India – was first entered through the wild Rishi Gorge after considerable difficulty by Eric Shipton and Bill Tilman in 1934, and naturally provides an incredible trekking route. The Valley of Flowers was made famous by Frank Smythe whose 1931 exploration is described in his book of the same name. Both these areas were declared National Parks by the Indian Government in 1983 and due to previous overuse of their fragile environments were temporarily closed for several years to facilitate environmental recovery and to enable sound management policies to be organised.

The Valley of Flowers

However a brief visit to the Valley of Flowers – the Bhyuntar Valley – is permitted from the Badrinath road at *Govind Ghat* (6,000 ft/1,800 m) some six miles (ten kms) north of Joshimath. A pilgrim route climbs to *Hempkund*, a lake in a tributary valley at 14,400 ft (4,400 m) sacred to both Hindus and Sikhs: thus far – two to three days – one can stay in the many wayside tea-houses.

From the valley fork at *Ghanghria*, the Valley itself is three miles further on and a day visit is allowed. With a special permit one night can be spent in the Valley and the *Khulia Pass* (16,400 ft/5,000 m) below Nilgiri Parbat can be traversed northwards into the *Khulia Valley* where the glacier is crossed and a descent made to the roadhead at *Mana*, a short way north of Badrinath. This superb circuit, at its best between mid-June and mid-September, can be made in six or seven days.

Among many other excellent itineraries in Garhwal are the following:

Bhagarithi – Kedarnath link

This is a beautiful but fairly strenuous trek which follows another ancient pilgrim route linking the Bhagirathi Valley – and thus Gangotri – to the important shrine to Shiva at Kedarnath, and can thus be conveniently combined with the trek

described in the main narrative.

The route leaves the Gangotri road at *Mala* some 14 miles (22 kms) north of Uttarkashi and strikes first south, then north-east across the grain of the country, crossing three passes, the highest of which, the *Kinkholal Khal*, reaches 13,000 ft (4,000 m). The trail passes through several picturesque villages and valleys thick with superb forest, crosses lovely alpine meadows and passes along airy ridges with wide views of the snowy peaks to the north before eventually joining the road at *Sonprayag*, just three miles before its end at *Gaurikund* (buses to Rishikesh) and a day's walk below the temple complex of *Kedarnath* itself. The trek, road head to road head, should take about five days and accommodation may be found in pilgrim rest-houses en route.

Roop Kund and the Curzon Road

The road head for this route is at *Gwaldam* (6,000 ft/1,830 m) in the Pindar Valley which is reached by bus from Rishikesh and Nainital. A long but pleasant climb northwards leads via the villages of *Mandoli* and *Wan* and over beautiful flowery meadows to the lake of the *Roop Kund* at 15,700 ft (4,800 m) in some six days, although ideally a little longer should be spent en-route for acclimatization. This mysterious lake, in which skeletons of men and horses have been discovered, is a place of pilgrimage every twelve years when thousands of pilgrims come here to worship the goddess Nanda Devi. A steep descent leads to the *Shila Samudru Glacier* below the great western face of Trisul (23,360 ft/7,120 m) and to the nearby *Homakund* (13,00 ft/4,000 m), a most impressive glacial lake at the head of the Nandakini Valley.

The valley, graced with meadows and forest, leads down to the shepherds' huts, several tarns and two tiny temples of *Badnikund* whence a scenic route via the village of *Ramni* crosses a pass northwards at about 10,500 ft (3,200 m) into the *Birehi Valley*, whence an ancient goat trail through a complex knot of hills climbs to the *Kauri Pass* at 14,000 ft (4,300 m) with wonderful views of Nanda Davi, Dunagiri and Bethartoli among other peaks.

Lord Curzon, a Viceroy of India, once trekked this route, hence its name. A steep descent leads to the bazaar town of *Joshimath* with direct buses to Rishikesh. The total distance is about 120 miles (190 kms), for which one should allow some 15 days, while a start in late August is an ideal time to experience the monsoon flowers at their best.

TO THE HEART OF THE KARAKORUM— K2 AND HIDDEN PEAK

by John Cleare

'As far as we could see there was a turbulent ocean of peaks without so much as a glimpse of earth in repose. It hardly seemed possible that there should be so much of so a disturbed landscape.'
Michael Spender, Karakorum explorer, 1937

Do not confuse the Karakorum with the Himalaya! The latter range sweeps around the shoulders of the Indian sub-continent for over 1,500 miles (2,400 kms) between the twin bastions of Namche Barwa in the east and Nanga Parbat in the west. The Karakorum lies northward, *beyond* the Himalaya, a complex 250 mile (400 kms) tangle of savage, magnificent mountains where the very dust tastes of Central Asia and the mighty monsoon that dictates the Himalayan weather usually dies like a damp squib. The Karakorum is arid, virtually a mountain desert, reprieved only by its high winter snowfall, and is as different from the mountains of Nepal as chalk from cheese. Indeed the very name is Turkish and means 'black rubble' – if not inaccurate then hardly apposite for one of the most glittering ranges on earth. Typically great angular ice peaks or fierce rock fangs, these mountains are impressive rather than beautiful and stand in avenues above long glaciers, the largest in the temperate zones, from which tumultuous rivers pour to join the Indus or the doomed Yarkand. Nineteen summits tower above 25,000 ft (7,600 m) while no less than five of the peaks clustering round K2 – the world's second highest point – exceed 26,000 ft (7,925 m). Suffice to say that until you've seen the Karakorum, *'you ain't seen nuthin' yet'*!

We sat in 'Pindi for a week waiting for the weather to clear. Several times we drove to the airport and several times we returned disappointed. But eventually the aged Fokker Friendship climbed through the dawn and the huge, lonesome hulk of Nanga Parbat reared ahead above the haze of the plains. We passed just west of this final Himalayan summit, dropped into the deep defile of the Indus that curls around its feet and started our let-down to Skardu. I crossed my fingers firmly for I knew that in the face of a poor forecast the plane might circle the Skardu airstrip and return to Rawalpindi without landing. But this time we were lucky, and soon we were bowling along in open jeeps down a wide valley scattered by small orchards, lined with tall poplars and walled by gaunt, dun-coloured mountains, a harsh landscape lit by shafts of sunlight from already darkening clouds. By the time the mid-day dust-storm arrived we were enjoying lunch in the comfort of the Government rest-house. At last we were in Baltistan with the Himalaya behind us and the Karakorum ahead.

Skardu is the capital of Pakistan's Baltistan Agency, lying at 7,500 ft (2,300 m) on the Indus, fairly close to the Indo-Pakistan Kashmir cease-fire line. It has always been a strategic centre. The imposing fort of Mindoq Khar, which crowns a great rock above the river, was built around 1600 AD and is still garrisoned by the famous Gilgit Scouts. The name is said to be derived from Iskanderia – or 'City of Alexander' – after Alexander the Great who is supposed to have founded the little town, and though the Baltis are today staunch Shi'ite Muslims, the area was once linked eastwards to Ladakh and Tibet. Until the 15th century its inhabitants were Buddhists who have left several beautiful Bodhisattva rock carvings nearby.

Logistics in the Karakorum are a serious business and any journey into the heart of the mountains, whether actually to climb or just to trek, must be expeditionary in character. We were a 'commercial' trekking group and numbered 15 including our smart and efficient Pakistani liaison officer, Captain 'Joe', and the famous Hunza mountaineer, Nazir Sabir, who, still suffering from an epic climb on Nanga Parbat, was not able to join us but would help us to organize. There was much to arrange before our gear set off two days later, on trailers behind farm tractors. We followed at dawn next day in the ubiquitous jeeps, through the already busy bazaar, up the rough dirt road, across the wide, rushing Indus, over a low, sandy pass and into a moonscape valley floored with the shingly skeins of the Shigar River and flanked by jagged, snow-tipped battlements.

Often the road disappeared but we drove on over sandy flats or bumped gingerly through bouldery draws. After some 40 miles (65 kms) the valley narrowed, the road finally petered out altogether and we saw the tractors, surrounded by a crowd of chattering Baltis, waiting by the river. Nazir had spread the word that an 'expedition' was recruiting porters and with Jo marshalling the troops, our doctor and I, aided by Nazir, checked out more than 200 hopefuls, selecting 120 stalwart fellows from as many different villages as possible who we signed up, issued with tennis shoes – we had purchased every last pair in Skardu – socks, gloves, sun-glasses, blankets and gaily-patterned plastic rain-coats. Despite the oppressive noon-day sun I had to laugh as the grinning tribesmen, flushed with their luck, strutted around wearing their new goodies before each collected a carefully weighed and numbered load and paced off up the valley clutching his *matu*, the traditional

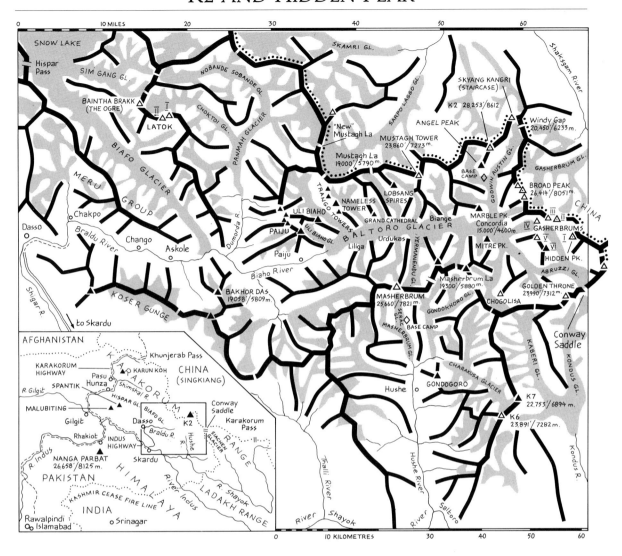

short, T-shaped porter's staff.

We followed, an easy two hour hike up a dusty trail and over a rickety suspension bridge across the foaming Braldu river to the small village of Dasso at about 8,000 ft (2,450 m), an oasis of green terraces clinging to the river bank beneath steep brown slopes. We camped in a grove of willows, bright with new leaves, marvelling at the intricate irrigation ditches which water the tiny patches of barley, the little orchards of apricot and mulberry and the pointed poplars which are such a surprising feature of the landscape around these villages. Beyond Dasso, the valley becomes a desolate defile through which the Braldu roars in its own miniature gorge. Here, on the south-facing slopes above the river, there was no shade and the only vegetation was tufts of sage brush around the boulders that littered the way, and the occasional lonely rose bush hung with pink flowers, charming if incongruous waymarks in this waste

of rock and sand. Chakpo, the next oasis, is only 10 miles (16 kms) on, but the rough path is rarely flat and so early in the trek it made a fair day's journey.

Above Chakpo, the Braldu plunges through a narrow slot in a natural dam of living rock and we photographed each other carefully negotiating the single plank bridge that spanned this awesome channel, watched by an elderly Balti who sat patiently on a nearby rock smiling knowingly at our *salaams*. He knew that the next section was nasty and had no path, the only route lying along the crumbling rubble beside the roaring river. It led to a hollow in which lay a welcoming hot spring where we took turns to bathe away the day's sweat and dust in the steaming little pool.

I'd been warned that the Braldu Gorge was hazardous and a few hundred yards further on we reached the danger zone. For a mile or so, 45 degree slopes of unstable moraine debris and scree drop sheer into the river. No path can last long. Occasionally stones and boulders come tumbling thousands of feet down this fearsome shute and bound into the water, which thunders angrily below in continuous rapids where even the foam is brown with glacial silt. I knew that a British climber had died here the previous year, swept away by a rock fall, his body never recovered. But it is a well used route, traversed by hundreds of local people and expeditions every year, and our porters seemed quite fatalistic about it. However only a fool is blasé about danger so we paused in the lee of a rock bluff while I split the party into three-man groups before we moved as swiftly as possible, a group at a time, from outcrop to sheltering outcrop. Behind each we drew breath before checking the slope ahead and speeding across the sliding rubble to the next haven. A few small stones spun down but no one was hit and we were soon onto safer ground.

Later Reinhold Messner confided to me that he thought the Braldu Gorge was more dangerous than the Eigerwand, but perhaps he'd been less lucky in the gorge than were we.

A day later we climbed 1,500 ft (400 m) out of this claustrophobic defile onto an airy path cut into the cliff face high above the river, rounded a craggy shoulder and dropped into a more tranquil landscape. A wide valley stretched ahead, dotted with little green fields and groves of trees, and dominated by the fine pyramid of Bakhor Das (19,058 ft/5,809 m) at its head. It was a relief to see mountain tops again. For a while another refreshing hot spring claimed our attention, then we passed through several small villages and eventually strode down a shady lane lined with willows, poplars and gnarled walnut trees into Askole.

At 10,000 ft (3,000 m) Askole is the last and largest village in the valley, an oasis of ordered greenery wrested from the arid wilderness by irrigation and centuries of toil. In 1980 medieval

Balti porters engage in an impromptu dance on the eastern bank of the Dumordo River, no doubt excited by the successful crossing by tyrolean traverse. The sharp peak of Bakhor Das rises in the distance.

conditions still prevailed: there were no tractors or telephones, wire fences or concrete, although there were hints that several lavish expeditions had passed this way in recent years. The houses, as in other villages we'd passed, were round-cornered, windowless, flat-roofed structures of mud and stone more like block-houses than homes. Men were ploughing with *dzos* – the cross-bred yak – in fields divided by drystone walls, and once we passed two women working in the young corn. They wore baggy red trousers, black tunics decorated with red appliqué, brass necklaces and broad black whimples, and pointed at us laughing, although they turned away when I stopped. There were no coy smiles as there are in Buddhist or Hindu regions. Women are rarely seen by strangers in Baltistan and indeed we saw few enough local men except inquisitive, be-goitered cretins – inbreeding and iodine deficiency are endemic – and the sick whom our doctor found himself treating at every village campsite.

By now we were paying off redundant porters every day. It may seem extravagant to employ 120 porters to support 15 *sahibs* on a 30 day trek but everything, food, fuel, camping gear and personal kit must be carried from the road head and many of the porters are employed carrying porter rations – it's the old maxim 'the more you employ, the more you employ'. Each evening I sat with Joe and young Jafar, a bright lad from Skardu who spoke English, Urdu and Balti, counting out the rupee notes from my briefcase, signing chitties and collecting thumb prints in return. Each evening there were hassles and each day threats of a strike by one porter clique or another, but that is the way of the Baltis and by fairness, firmness, tact and diplomacy we kept going and remained friends with the porters as our army dwindled until just twelve lads were left when we eventually arrived back at the road head.

Until the recent advent of wire ropes and concrete, rivers in Baltistan were usually crossed either by 'ferries' supported on inflated animal skins, or by *jula* bridges constructed of three 'cables' fashioned from plaited willow and poplar twigs. You step gingerly along the lower swaying cable clutching the other two with your hands, hardly a stable crossing but a triumph of

This cairn at the foot of K2 was erected in 1953 in memory of American climber Art Gilkey and many others who have died on the mountain.

primitive engineering which was never repaired until it broke. Such a bridge still spanned the Braldu at Askole. It was not on our route but we crossed it for photographs and from the far side I managed to recruit as headman one Kassim, a cheery, enthusiastic fellow who had been recommended to me as a replacement for my original headman, an idle poseur I'd been forced to sack, a man who would have left the most disruptive English shop-steward in the shade.

Somehow Kassim had acquired a very long, non-stretch nylon rope – it made him a useful man to know – and now I sent him ahead with his rope, two porters and one of the fittest and strongest *sahibs*. The rest of us followed at a more leisurely pace, clambering over the mountain of rubble which is the snout of the huge Biafo Glacier, completely blocking the valley some four miles (six kms) above Askole. This enormous pathway of ice pours down from the north, from the mysterious Snow Lake, beyond which the equally large Hispar Glacier flows down towards Hunza, creating an icy avenue no less than 62 miles (100 kms) in length! Beyond the Biafo, the main river is known as the Biaho and we followed it for another day to a wide confluence, where the Dumordo River joins the Biaho, beyond which we caught a glimpse of a cluster of impossible-looking icy needles.

"The Paiju peaks," said Jafar, "the gatepost of the Baltoro."

This confluence is a labyrinth of skeined channels. Very early in the season or in winter I knew the Dumordo to be fordable here with care, but the waters were already rising with the summer melt. A couple of miles upstream however there is a narrows where, until a'few years before, a *jula* bridge had hung between rock buttresses either side of the turbulent river. By the time our caravan arrived, Kassim and his little party were standing on the opposite shore. They had continued a further eight miles (13 kms) upriver to its glacial source, crossed the ice and descended the far bank. It was a matter of a few minutes to throw a line across and then rig Kassim's famous rope as a tyrolean traverse 20 ft (six metres) above the water. Using a porter's stick as a seat and a karabiner as a pulley we spent the rest of the day hauling the excited porters, their loads, and the *sahibs* over the river. Luckily several porters returning from a small expedition ahead of us turned up, and were pleased to use our crossing and untie the rope on the far side when we had all crossed. Kassim's rope had saved us three days.

From here we could see Bakhor Das again, from this side an elegant *matterhorn peak* on which we plotted routes. But it was our last link

with Askole, for now cold winds blew down the valley from the east and the rugged snow-capped walls rose higher and higher. For two days we saw hardly a shred of vegetation until, having scrambled over an awkward rocky bluff overhanging the river, where we had to help the porters with their loads, we found ourselves in a glade of stunted willows among patches of juniper and tangles of delicate pink roses. Dark clouds swirled round a veritable forest of gigantic rock fangs ahead and welcome rain began to fall in big heavy drops. This was the famous camping ground of Paiju, last stop before the ice.

After the overnight rain, the dawn was an extraordinary spectacle. Fans of light swept across the heavens before the sun itself burst over a cut-out skyline as spiky as I have ever seen. Below the sun the terminal moraine of the Baltoro Glacier stretched right across the valley, a rubble wall a mile long and several hundred feet high, while a myriad glinting rivers snaked out across the gravel flats at its foot to become the Biaho. Once we had climbed onto its crest we discovered a cratered, convoluted wilderness, a confusion of mountain debris stretching away into the distance. From the vague, cairned trail that crossed the glacier we gaped at the sensational peaks rearing above its northern side: the lovely cone of Paiju, its icy summit encircled by flying buttresses of fluted rock; the phallic column of Uli Biaho; the Nameless Tower – its twisted thumb stabbing skywards amid the iced gables of the Trango Towers; the gothic wings of Grand Cathedral; and, blue shapes in the distance, the lovely Lobsang Spires. For the rock climber a granite dream, for any mountain lover surely a Garden of the Gods?

For five days our caravan wound its way up the great Baltoro Glacier, further and further up this avenue of bewildering peaks, deeper and deeper into the heart of the Karakorum. Sometimes the route lay along the lateral moraine, sometimes in the *mulde* – that secret green trench behind it – but for much of the way we picked our route up the glacier itself, over rubbly hillocks, down deep troughs and around bizarre glacier tables – great boulders balanced on thin stalks of ice – avoiding boulder-lipped crevasses and fording rushing torrents of meltwater.

At the celebrated campsite of Urdukas we enjoyed a well-earned rest day. Urdukas in Balti means 'fallen rocks' and the steep, flower-strewn hillside is studded with great boulders. Here we could look down onto the glacier, now well over a mile wide, amusing ourselves by trying to trace the dozens of differently coloured medial

Left – Gasherbrum I was dubbed 'Hidden Peak' by Martin Conway in 1892 because it is visible only when the traveller reaches the Abruzzi Glacier to the south-west and can see into the remote glacial sanctuary which it dominates. It was first climbed by an American expedition in 1968.

Right – Wild roses, often growing in the most arid situations, are a charming feature of the hard Karakorum. This bush, near the Paiju campsite contrasts the savage grandeur of the Grand Cathedral peaks rearing in the background above the Baltoro Glacier.

Below – Beyond Paiju, the great snout of the Baltoro Glacier blocks the valley wall to wall, birthing the glinting skeins of the Biaho River. In this early morning view, the Trango Towers rise on the left, with the Grand Cathedral massif beyond.

moraines back to their respective tributary glaciers, an intriguing task. For my part I speculated on the forgotten 19,000 ft (5,790 m) Muztagh Pass which was once approached up a side glacier opposite Urdukas, thinking of how, for many centuries, it was a trade route over which yak and pony caravans had crossed into Sinkiang before glacial changes forced its abandonment. I recalled how Younghusband had rediscovered it in 1887, crossing from the north during his epic journey across Central Asia from Peking to Delhi via the Takla Makan desert, and how in 1937 Eric Shipton had located traces of an ancient polo ground at its foot among the Baltoro moraines. What an irresistible lure this 'Roof of the World' still exerts, even if the 'Great Game' is over and done with!

For a while Masherbrum rules the Baltoro, a majestic pile of hanging ice and formidable cliffs below a plume of blowing snow. At 25,660 ft (7,821 m) – a full 12,000 ft (3,650 m) above us – the peculiar rocky finger of its summit held the last light long after dark above our next camp on the glacier itself, a place known as Biange. Sunset is swift in the Karakorum. Never was there the lingering pink alpenglow so common in Nepal or the Alps, instead there is a golden flash as the sun disappears, and then darkness closes in and frost rules the night.

Beyond Urdukas the glacier appears unreal, a crazy architect's perspective dream of stylised mountains. A perfect avenue, it stretches into the distance flanked by rows of steep, ice-runnelled peaks, countless buttresses separated by hanging tributary glaciers. A distinctive shape blocks the head of the glacier, shadowy at first then gaining substance and stature as the sun climbs across the sky. It rises high above its sharp satellites and for two days, as we approached nearer and nearer, it grew to dominate the entire scene. It is no surprise that this distinctive peak is one of few hereabouts to bear an indigenous name, for it must have been familiar to any tribesman bold enough to venture this far up the glacier. Gasherbrum means 'shining wall' – an apt title for this 10,000 ft (3,000 m) trapezoid of pale, ice-dashed limestone that rears to just 26,000 ft (7,925 m). But it actually shares the name with five other peaks that stand hidden behind it, and three are higher still, so it is more properly known as Gasherbrum IV.

Thirteen days after leaving Skardu we reached Concordia. Named after that similar glacier junction in the heart of the Swiss Bernese Alps, it is here that the Baltoro splits, turning sharp right and sharp left at the foot of G IV, a majestic T-junction of icy highways. We pitched camp on a flattish plateau of stony ice at 15,000 ft (4,600 m). Nearby several furious melt-water torrents mingled in an icy grotto before plunging into a fearsome *moulin* (swallow-hole), but in the opposite direction a small tarn of placid green water reflected Marble Peak and Mitre Peak on either side of the glacier, the twin summits of around 20,000 ft (6,000 m) that form the portals of Concordia. Now, for the first time, K2 was visible, its stupendous cone glistening in the sunshine nine miles (15 kms) distant at the far end of the dark defile of the Godwin Austen, the northern glacier branch. This is what we had come to see, indeed many people have no wish to go further, and here I planned to camp for five days.

But by no means was it our journey's end. We split into smaller groups, depending on speed, fitness, laziness or ambition. Taking a couple of light tents and a little food, I led one party up the glacier to K2 Base Camp, a day's journey beneath Broad Peak (26,414 ft/8,051 m), a huge triple-headed mountain that's been dubbed the 'Breithorn of the Baltoro' – and which, like the Breithorn, is technically straightforward by the regular route but formidable in its very scale. Beneath K2 we found Messner's little expedition in residence. I'd worked with Reinhold and he kindly entertained us to a slap-up tea, explaining meanwhile to an avid audience his mountaineering philosophy and tactics. Long after dark I watched the moon rise over Chogolisa, the white and curvaceous 'Bride Peak' southward beyond Concordia. Later I slept, but fitfully, continuously disturbed by the avalanches rumbling off K2.

Weariness had taken its toll and my party wanted to rest. So while Kassim led another group up to K2, I decided to see 'Hidden Peak' – Gasherbrum I. Three porters were keen to accompany me so we set off southward up the so-called Upper Baltoro, lightly laden and moving fast. We traversed another imposing avenue, only this time the mountains were bigger and fewer. While we paused for a brew at midday I watched a Japanese expedition inching their way up Chogolisa through my binoculars. It looked a fine route but I was content where I was. Evening found us at the big corner where the Baltoro becomes the Abruzzi Glacier beneath Golden Throne (23,990 ft/7,312 m), and I enjoyed an excellent meal of chapattis and tea with my happy Balti friends before setting up my bivouac on a high moraine to watch the sun slip behind the twin horns of Mitre Peak and the monstrous chisel of the Muztagh Tower (23,860 ft/7,273 m) turn from blue to black against the golden sky. I remembered Vittorio Sella's famous photograph of the Tower taken from this very spot during the Duke of the Abruzzi's brilliant 1908 expedition. It had always seemed an unlikely picture to me, a flukey angle, but now I could confirm it was real – and yet now *my* dream. I set up my tripod over my sleeping bag, set my alarm for moonrise and slid into sleep, waking every couple of hours to take pictures. It was one of the most memorable nights of my life and dawn came all too soon.

Leaving the Baltis I carried on another three miles (five kms) to the icefall of the Gasherbrum Glacier where I found some Austrian friends of mine setting up their base camp. This would be their home for several weeks. They were very well provisioned and insisted that I shared their delicious breakfast: why are good meals always such important milestones in the wilderness? Behind the camp, above the icefall, Gasherbrums I, II and III, graceful pyramids of rock and ice, their simple angular structure belying their formidable scale, encircled a pristine white cwm. I understand now how well merited is the name 'Hidden Peak' – it could well describe all three. But it was the end of my little odyssey, for over the crest beyond the Abruzzi Glacier lies China, while over the Conway Saddle is Indian territory.

And so began the long journey home.

Unfortunately there is only one practical way out of Concordia for trekkers and that is the way in, but as we retraced our steps most things appeared very different. In particular the rivers had risen. What had been dry *nullahs* two weeks before were now surging torrents of waist deep brown water. Each crossing was an adventure to be tackled warily, sometimes roped but often in human chains, arms locked with our porters, dozens of feet together on the dangerous shifting stones of the river bed. On the lower Baltoro we passed the lavish French national K2 expedition, a host of climbers with hang-gliders and TV equipment – they seemed so intrusive in this empty wilderness and they left an unpleasant taste in our mouths, especially after we had passed the 1,300 porters who followed them. One saving grace was the permanent rope-way, complete with *chaprasis* (watchmen) they had left over the Dumordo River to secure their communications. Better were the great clumps of wild lavender blooming in the wildest places and best of all was the fresh fruit. Small ripe apricots and clusters of juicy mulberrys hung from the trees beside the trail near every village and Kassim assured us that by Balti tradition a traveller may pluck wayside fruit in passing. It was eleven days before we arrived in Skardu and by that time the doctor was very busy.

Rearing above the Baltoro – the vertical granite of the Grand Cathedral and the Lobsang Spires.

Urdukas is a celebrated campsite above the south bank of the Baltoro Glacier. In this dusk view the sun has just slipped behind the clustered Trango Towers across the glacier. On the left rises Paiju Peak (21,654 ft/6,600 m) and in the centre stands the needle of Uli Biaho.

Many of these notes are applicable to other similar high routes in Baltistan and the Karakorum.

Difficulties/dangers
This is an outstanding trek but it is rugged, strenuous and difficult – without doubt the most serious trek in this book. It should be attempted only by fit and experienced walkers.

While there is a regularly used route the entire way, and there are no long steep ascents, the terrain is such that in many places paths do not exist and when they do they are typically rough. Snow may be encountered above Urdukas after bad weather or early in the season and usually lies in patches above Concordia anyway. Though all glaciers up to both K2 and Hidden Peak Base Camps are normally *dry glaciers* they are crevassed and under snow demand great care and possibly even a roped lead party.

The hazards of the Braldu Gorge can be minimized with due circumspection (see main text) but the Gorge should be avoided after heavy rain. The low route described is impassible in high summer and a longer, higher route is more difficult though possibly less dangerous. River crossings may be difficult and hazardous and must be treated seriously.

Highest Point: Concordia at 15,000 ft (4,600 m), though the side trips reach 16,000 ft (4,900 m) at K2 Base Camp and 16,800 ft (5,100 m) at Hidden Peak Base.

Height Gain: On most days the total height gained is only a few hundred feet but the day from Paiju to Liligo gains some 1,200 ft/370 m with 1,000 ft/300 m gained the following day to Urdukas.

Time above 10,000 ft (3,000 m): some 16 days, return journey to Concordia.

Distances/times
The basic route, as described from Dasso Village to Concordia is some 65 miles (100 kms) on the map but is better measured in days . . .
Dasso to Askole: 3 days
Askole to Concordia: 7–8 days (via Dumordo Crossing). This journey could be completed very much quicker by a fit, acclimatized and lightly-laden party but porters work to 'official' stages – ie traditional day stages that have now been legally regularized and must be paid for – of which there are eight between Askole and Concordia.

Season/weather
The Baltoro trekking season is from early May until late October, but severe storms can occur at any time. In normal conditions lower altitude treks are possible elsewhere in the Karakorum as late as December.

Rivers are swollen from late May onwards and by late July certain mountain torrents easily crossed six weeks before may be impassable.

Typical mid-season temperatures
Skardu:	day	98°F/37°C
	night	43°F/6°C
Concordia:	clear day	93°F/34°C
	night	10°F/−12°C

Equipment
Normal trekking gear – see Annapurna chapter – except that a light long-sleeved shirt and a wide-brimmed hat are advisable for protection against the sun. You may consider an umbrella indispensable for the same reason. Boots should be tough and rugged as this trek is likely to destroy any but the best. Nights are very cold.

Access/permits
There are three kinds of trekking areas in Pakistan: *Closed Zones, Restricted Areas* and *Open Areas*. Because this particular trek enters a *Restricted Area* hard against both the Chinese and Indian borders a Trekking Permit is required. This may be obtained with minimal formalities – passport details and three passport photographs – through a local commercial trekking agency. Since 1981 Liaison Officers have not been required, but if a local agency is not employed then an officially approved guide must be. Guide and porters must be insured to official specification.

The permit allows ascents of up to 19,685 ft (6,000 m) in the Baltoro area and in addition covers the side trip to 'Windy Gap' (20,450 ft/6,233 m). Currently there is a police check post at Dasso.

Certain other simple bureaucratic formalities must be observed for this and other routes in Restricted Areas. Copies of the Regulations booklet should be available from Pakistani Embassies or PAI airline offices.

Logistics
Since 1988 the air link from Islamabad (Rawalpindi) to Skardu is flown by Boeing 737 jets, so the service is less affected by weather, much more reliable and still extraordinarily cheap. However Skardu is now connected to Rawalpindi by paved road via the Karakorum Highway and its spur, the Indus Highway. These roads are sometimes cut by landslides, etc, but regular daily bus and minibus services ply between 'Pindi, Gilgit and Skardu, a map distance of some 350 miles (560 kms).

A jeep track now extends beyond Dasso to Foljo Village half way to Chakpo and unfortunately it is planned to continue this road to Askole (!!) – how long it would remain open is open to conjecture.

Porter's wages are expensive but meaningful treks of any length in this remote and scantily populated region are well nigh impossible without their assistance.

Medical considerations
Altitude sickness can be lethal but the ascent to Concordia is a gradual one and with sensible precautions acclimatization should present few problems. Nevertheless it must be borne in mind that should serious altitude sickness (e.g. pulmonary oedema) occur it is impossible to lose height swiftly. It is sensible to take a rest day at Urdukas. (see Height Gain note above and Medical notes to Annapurna).

Sunstroke/heatstroke and dehydration may cause problems and some acclimatization to temperature is sensible, e.g. spend a few days exploring around Skardu.

Sufficient liquid intake is crucial and a water bottle should be carried and used. All water in the Braldu Valley and on the Baltoro Glacier is suspect and must be boiled. Stomach problems can be minimized by eating local food with discretion, by peeling fruit, etc.

Great care should be paid to sanitation, the arid environment is fragile, while camp sites are few, well-used and often already polluted. Leave camp sites as you'd wish to find them and think of those who'll come after you!

Many useful expeditionary 'prescription' drugs are available over the counter in 'Pindi chemist stores. The hospital at Skardu should be used only in emergencies.

Language
English is understood and spoken by officials and all educated Pakistanis. Some local people may have a smattering of English but a few words of Urdu (or closely related Hindi) and/or Pushtu will be useful in remote areas or when dealing with porters.

Other considerations
Dust is omnipresent and gets everywhere. Cameras, binoculars and similar instruments should be well protected.

At time of writing sporadic skirmishing is occurring between Pakistani and Indian forces around the Siachen Glacier. There is currently (1988) a military presence on the

Abruzzi Glacier and an armed outpost on the Conway Saddle not far beyond Hidden Peak Base Camp. Access is doubtless affected.

Reading
Maps:
The beautiful Italian IGM 1:100,000 contour sheet *Baltoro & Concordia* (1969) is difficult to obtain and covers only the glacier and its tributaries.
Polish (Jerzy Wala – Krakow) 1:250,000 kammkarte of entire Karakorum is probably the best general map.
Swiss Foundation for Alpine Research 1:750,000 (1952) sheet *Karakorum* is useful and usually obtainable.
The RGS publishes the superb *Hispar-Biafo Glacial Regions* sheet at 1:253,440, the result of Shipton's 1939 survey, which covers the entire traverse of these glaciers plus the Snow Lake.
American AMS 1:250,000 sheets N143–3 and N143–4 are better than nothing.
Guide books:
Trekkers Guide to the Himalaya and Karakorum – Hugh Swift (Hodder & Stoughton) makes a brief mention of this trek.
Pakistan – a Travel Survival Kit – Roleo (Lonely Planet)
Literature:
In the Throne Room of the Mountain Gods – Galen Rowell (Sierra Club, San Francisco/Allen & Unwin, 1977)
Karakorum – Fosco Maraini (Hutchinson, London, 1961)
Blank on the Map – Eric Shipton, republished 1985 as part of *The Six Mountain Travel Books* (Diadem, UK/The Mountaineers, Seattle)
Abode of Snow – Kenneth Mason (Hart-Davis, London, 1955 and recently reissued by Diadem)
Lure of Karakorams – A Sayeed Khan Qamar (American Book Co., Rawalpindi, 1974)

Other Treks in the Karakorum and Pakistan Himalaya

While there are many straightforward but delightful trekking itineraries of three or four days among the Karakorum valleys, the passes over these fierce mountains tend to be high and rugged and thus meaningful circuits of any length usually follow, like the Concordia Trek, fairly challenging, committing and strenuous routes.

The advent of the Karakorum and Indus Highways has made practical many of these shorter routes and an excellent trekking holiday can be arranged by linking several of them by road, using the occasional hotel, and visiting two or three widely separated and very different regions of the range. A satisfying 'combination trek' of this sort might include:

Hushe Valley and Masherbrum
From *Skardu*, the Indus Valley road is followed eastwards, continuing up the tributary Shyok and Saltoro Rivers to the *Hushe Valley* which is ascended to *Hushe Village*, a long day's journey by jeep. Some may prefer to walk up the Hushe Valley from the *Saltoro River* – a two day trek. *Masherbrum Base Camp* is some nine miles (15 kms) northward from Hushe on the east bank of the *Masherbrum Glacier* at its confluence with the tributary *Serac Glacier*.

Close by, the *Charakusa Glacier* can be ascended towards its imposing cirque, dominated by the savage peaks K6 and K7 (23,891 ft/7,282 m) – some 3 to 4 days above Hushe – while from a side glacier to the south the straightforward small peak of *Gondogoro* (18,500 ft/5,639 m), which rises behind Hushe, can be climbed.

A fine and serious mountaineering journey in the great traditions of Karakorum exploration links these valleys with the *Baltoro* by ascending the *Gandokhoro Glacier*, crossing the *Masherbrum La* (19,300 ft/5,880 m) which, depending on the state of the ice, may involve rapelle pitches, and descending to the Baltoro Glacier near Urdukas.

Hunza area/Karakorum Highway
Other favourite locations for short treks are:

The valleys south-west of Nagar around the *Barpu Glacier*, below the northern flanks of Malubiting (24,449 ft/7,452 m) and Spantik (Yengutz Sar or Golden Peak, 23,054 ft/7,027 m).

West of *Pasu*, where a short circuit can be made round the lower reaches of the *Pasu* and *Batura Glaciers*.

A longer circuit follows the *Shimshal River* east of Pasu, crosses the *Ghujerab Pass* (14,760 ft/ 4,500 m) north of *Shimshal Village*, which leads into really remote country, and returns to the Highway not far from the *Khunjerab Pass* on the Chinese frontier. This twelve day route encircles the Karun Koh massif (24,114 ft/7,350 m).

Biafo and Hispar Glaciers
This is a classic traverse which follows the Baltoro route from *Skardu* to *Askole* but then ascends the great *Biafo Glacier*, lined by incredible rock peaks, to the mysterious *Snow Lake*, the wide ice junction at its head, so named by Sir Martin Conway in 1892. This is about six days above Askole. The straightforward *Hispar Pass* (16,900 ft/5,150 m) is crossed onto the head of the long *Hispar Glacier* – another mighty avenue of peaks – which is followed westward in four days to the jeep road below the glacier snout which connects to the Karakorum Highway at *Karimabad* near Hunza.

This a magnificent, but rugged and serious journey which follows, either on or off the ice, continuous glacier for more than 60 miles (100 kms). To minimize logistic problems two parties should ideally start simultaneously from Askole and Hunza, swapping porter crews when they meet at Snow Lake.

The Nanga Parbat Circuit
Nanga Parbat is undoubtedly one of the world's greatest mountains, not merely in height – 26,658 ft (8,125 m) – but also in aura. Its huge massif, the far western bastion of the Himalayan chain, rises almost isolated some 23,000 ft (7,000 m) above the arid gorges of the Indus and Astor which curl round its feet.

From *Gilgit*, accessible by air or via the Karakorum Highway, the village of *Tarshing* below the huge eastern or Rupal flank, is reached by jeep. Rearing nearly 15,000 ft (4,500 m) this face is probably the highest precipice in the world. An ancient route follows the *Rupal Nullah* for three days before crossing the screes of the straightforward *Mazeno Pass* – at 17,640 ft (5,377 m) – to the *Diamir Nullah* on the western flanks of the mountain. A descent can be made down the *Bunar Valley* to the Karakorum Highway in about six days from Tarshing, or in a further week a system of four lesser passes can be crossed, leading north-east beneath the impressive Diamir and Rakhiot faces of Nanga Parbat to the beautiful 'Fairy Meadow' at 10,800 ft (3,300 m) beside the *Rhakiot Glacier*. From here the Highway is joined at *Rakhiot* some ten miles (16 kms) down valley from the meadow. Climbers can include the straightforward small peak of Shaigiri (19,590 ft/5,971 m) above the south bank of the *Rupal Glacier*, opposite the Mazeno Pass, at the cost of several extra days.

This entire flank of Nanga Parbat is charged with history, for Mummery disappeared on the Diamir flank in 1899 during his explorations with Collie, Bruce and Hastings before successive German failures on the Rakhiot route in the thirties led finally to Herman Buhl's incredible ascent of Nanaga Parbat of 1953. It is worth noting that the monsoon usually hits the mountain in early July.

Four Mohammeds And Their Mules— Across The High Atlas

by Matt Dickinson

'My planet, Earth ... was just a dot in the universe ... From space, not even ... China is recognisable. The intense blue of the oceans, the green of the forests and a reddish trace left by the Atlas mountain chain can be made out. That is all.'
Michael Collins, *Lunar astronaut, 1969*

Everybody has heroes – men and women who live their lives as we would like to live them, who take the risks that we would like to take. And, if I am ever asked, the man who stands at the top of my personal collection of heroes is the great British explorer Wilfred Thesiger. His book, *Arabian Sands*, inspired a love of the desert that, to date, has taken me seven times across the Sahara, living and travelling with the nomadic tribes of the Touareg. But, more importantly, it was Thesiger who turned my travelling eyes to the High Atlas mountains of Morocco.

It all began when I stumbled across an obscure reference to a journey Thesiger had made through the High Atlas in the late 1950s. Though, at that time, the highest peaks were well known, many areas of the range had rarely been visited by Europeans, especially since internal strife on the path to independence from the French had made Morocco a perilous country to travel alone. Nevertheless, Thesiger and a member of an Oxford University expedition he had met by chance, 'left Telouet on 2 August, and with a guide and a single mule they struck east from the kasbah to the isolated lake of Tamda. They took no food, nor did they have to buy any, for wherever they went they were hospitably entertained by the tribesmen. They spent the nights in the mud-built castles of sheiks and rich merchants.' Five weeks later they were back, after what amounted to a complete traverse of the Central High Atlas.

I began some research into the High Atlas range and was surprised at the sheer scale of this, the greatest mountain chain in North Africa. Rising from the Atlantic near Agadir and stretching through Morocco to the Algerian border in the east, the range is some 400 miles (650 kms) in length. At over 13,000 ft (c.4,000 m) the very highest summits match those of the Alps and Jbel Toubkal (13,665 ft/4,167 m) is one of the highest in Africa. Temperate through the summer months, the High Atlas are often snowbound above 10,000 ft (3,000 m) for much of the winter and are capable of whipping up storms that will leave unprepared trekkers and climbers thinking they are anywhere but Africa. Yet no matter how challenging and remote the mountains, for me the main attraction was the thought that the Berber villages of the Atlas might still be as untouched and isolated as they were when Thesiger trekked through them. I resolved to find out.

During the months that I prepared for the trip, fate struck a lucky blow – I was offered a job as a mountain guide with an adventure tour operator. My fortunate destination? The High Atlas! For three months I led small groups on trekking tours of the Toubkal National Park to the south of Marrakech. This is where the highest peaks are to be found and the area has a prolific variety of well-known high and low altitude treks. Even though this is the most popular walking and climbing region of the High Atlas, the villages that lie three or four days' walk from the nearest road head could have been lifted straight from the middle ages – or at least from an age without machines. Wheat is still ground by hand or with millstones powered by ingenious irrigation systems, mules are used to plough the terraced fields cut deep into the mountains and the cattle, fowl and goats live side by side with the Berbers in their huts of mud and stone. The welcome we received in these remote hamlets was always heartwarming after long hours on the trail under the hot African sun. The children would usually spot us first as we snaked through a valley or descended a steep escarpment, our train of baggage mules leading the way. Their childish shouts were often audible from miles away. By the time we got to the village the head man and his family would be ready to receive us with freshly brewed mint tea, hot bread, and sometimes freshly churned butter, a rare treat. Our aching limbs and blistered feet were soothed in the local stream and after a bowl of cous-cous or *tagine* (the local stew), shared communally sitting cross-legged on the dirt floor, we would collapse exhausted into sleeping bags for the night. I made many friends in those villages during the months I trekked the Toubkal region, and also managed to learn something of the Berber language, which I hoped would be useful for my solo journey along Thesiger's route through the more remote Central High Atlas.

The High Atlas themselves offer just about every type of trekking and climbing experience imaginable. As the great Atlas devotee Louis Neltner put it, *'Il n'est plus beau ni moins beau que les Alpes, il est autre'* ('it is neither more nor less beautiful than the Alps, but different'). The overriding sensation while walking these mountains is of being perched on the edge of two climates. The northern slopes stretch away towards the temperate Mediterranean, and at the same time the southern reaches descend gracefully into the Sahara, the rock melting

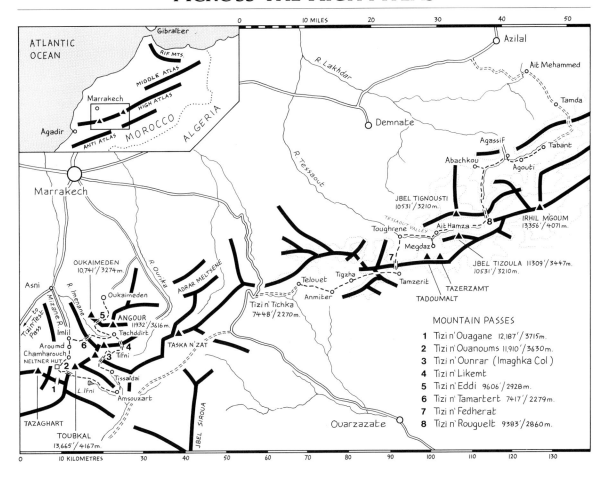

invisibly into sand. From the top of the highest ridges or from the summit of Toubkal and Angour this impression is greatly enhanced, particularly on a clear day in winter. There is something bizarre about standing in deep snow while the yellow sand seas of the Sahara lie clearly on the horizon!

For the most part, the rock surface of the High Atlas is arid and fragmented, which makes technical climbing difficult. However, if you don't mind the dust, trekking is generally along well-defined tracks winding up often tortuous routes to the cols (a col or pass is known locally as a *tizi*). Descents tend to be rapid scrambles down almost vertical scree slopes. Although the aridity of the Atlas sometimes gives the impression that one is walking up the walls of a very steep desert, it is nevertheless host to a surprising variety of insect, animal and plant life. Hares, squirrels and *mouflons* (a type of big-horned wild sheep) are all possible sightings if you have good eyesight, and a prolific range of spiders and scorpions hide under stones ready for the squeamish. One amusing moment during my months as a guide was watching a trick perfected by one member of our group, an

ex-mercenary from South Africa. He delighted in overturning rocks, picking up scorpions with his bare hands (by pinching them just below the sting), and then chasing nervous companions around the camp. He promised more spectacular stunts with a venomous snake but, although we saw them frequently he never managed to catch one – much to everyone's relief.

The circuits we followed on a trek naturally depended on the ability of the group, with the option for everyone of having their baggage carried by pack mules. My favourite schedule used the village of Aroumd (6,040 ft/(1,840 m) as base camp, since guides and mules are easy to find there. For the first three or four days the group would become acclimatized on treks up to 8,000 ft (2,500 m), including overnight stays in the villages of Tachedirt, which has a mountain hut run by the French Alpine Club (CAF), or Tizi Oussem. Training walks finished, we would return to Aroumd and load enough equipment and provisions to be self-sufficient on an eight day trek encircling the entire Toubkal massif. The first day of this follows the well-worn track, past Sidi Charamouch, up the Mizane Valley to the Neltner hut at 10,521 ft (3,720 m). We usually bivouacked near the hut because it tends to get overcrowded with climbers en route for Toubkal. Normally about half the group would be keen to tackle the long, arduous ascent of this giant, the rest deterred perhaps by the necessary dawn start and the notorious scree slopes that steal half a stride from every painful step.

Occasionally, I would vary the itinerary by delaying the ascent until the afternoon and then bivouacking for the night on the summit of Toubkal, and it was on one of these occasions that things went dangerously wrong. One woman in the group was an experienced trekker in her late forties and very fit. However, as we

After the heavy storms there was no shortage of waste wood to use for cooking and brewing the inevitable Berber mint tea.

gained the summit she began to show signs of altitude sickness and was violently ill. Night fell before we could descend to a lower altitude and a vicious, penetrating wind blew light snow across the summit as we brewed soup and tea in an effort to keep her warm. We built a low shelter with rocks by the light of our torches but after 30 minutes her condition had deteriorated dramatically. The warmth seemed to be draining away from her body even though she was wrapped inside the best of our sleeping bags and two emergency survival bags. Within the space of an hour, our Toubkal ascent had changed from an uneventful and pleasurable climb into the most critical situation I have ever encountered in any mountain range. Acute altitude sickness coupled with rapid body heat loss can be a killer. The normal response would be a fast descent but the night was pitch black and the Neltner hut

some four or five hours away across difficult and steep terrain. Even with a totally fit party the risk of getting lost or a fall in the dark was high and the woman was in no state to stand up, let alone walk. We had no choice but to battle it out on the summit until daylight. By midnight the situation had stabilised after non-stop tea and soup-making and all our survival clothing had the desired effect. She finally ceased to lose vital body heat, her coma eased into sleep and we took it in turns to keep watch through the night. At first light we descended safely to the Neltner hut and evacuated the victim back to the base camp at Aroumd, where she recovered immediately. After this episode I never bivouacked on Toubkal again.

Leaving the Mizane Valley by way of the Tizi n'Ounams our route took us to the crystal clear waters of Lake Ifni, where swimming and washing removed most of the ubiquitous Atlas dust. The Berber guides regard this isolated lake with some fear, swearing it is endlessly deep and full of 'djinn' or spirits. I must admit that there is something uncanny about it, something almost supernaturally still about its mirror surface and the total silence that surrounds it, but we always enjoyed our time there.

From Ifni we descended once more to the lush valleys that drain south towards the Sahara. Here, the tracks wind slowly through terraced valleys green with maize and filled with a rich sauna of smells from wild camomile to mint. Old men sit cracking piles of walnuts in the shade

Following the route taken by Wilfred Thesiger in the 1950s, I hired mules in local villages and used guides where routes and maps were unclear.

and young, giggling girls stagger past, bent almost double under the weight of animal fodder or bottles of water. After overnights in the villages of Amsouzart and Tissaldai we climbed the long trail over the Imaghka Col to the remote 'Azib', or grazing land of Tifni, before crossing to the Imenane Valley to spend nights in the villages of Tachedirt and Oukaimeden, where an ascent of the Oukaimeden summit (10,741 ft/3,274 m) provides a superb view, in many ways better than that from Toubkal. An ascent of Angour (11,745 ft/3,580 m) is also possible from Oukaimeden but presents an arduous and difficult route. The same mountain is more easily climbed from the Imenane Valley via Tachedirt. The return to Aroumd and the Mizane Valley over the Tizi n'Tamartert (7,477 ft/2,279 m) is a one or two day trek which neatly concludes the grand tour of the Toubkal National Park.

As winter took the Atlas in an icy grasp, my tour of duty in the Toubkal region ended and I was free to leave for the Central High Atlas and my long-awaited solo trek. After a few days' rest in exotic Marrakech, I travelled by bus and bush taxi to Telouet. It gave me an immense sensation of freedom to be travelling alone again after so long in the close atmosphere of the groups. The kasbah of Telouet was a bustle of activity when I arrived. This mountain stronghold of the formerly powerful Glaoui family is largely ruined now and little remains of its past glory. Nevertheless, it is probably the most impressive *kasbah* (citadel) in the Atlas range and some of the elaborately decorated rooms, though pock-marked by bullet holes and looted by souvenir hunters, can still be seen. I was handed a glass of mint tea and some almonds by the *kasbah* guardian and sat watching as carpets and great cushions were scattered in preparation for

Hidden deep in the Tessaout Gorge, Ichbaccen is a typical Berber village.

a festival with visiting dignitaries from the south.

As night fell I wandered around the village in search of a mule and a guide but, as Thesiger had found 30 years before, it was not easy to find someone who was prepared to leave Telouet for the long journey east to Irhil M'Goun (13,356 ft/4,071 m) and beyond. Eventually, after two frustrating days of false leads, I found an excellent guide, Mohammed, who promised to come with his mule for three days as far as Lake Tamda and Tamzerit. He would then return to Telouet and I would continue east with (hopefully) a new guide and mule. As we negotiated payment, an old man, held in great respect by the village, grasped me hard by the hand and pointed to the distant peaks where jet black storm clouds were gathered. His message was simple to understand even with my basic command of Berber – bad weather was on the way. If I had known just how bad, I might have taken up his offer to stay longer in Telouet.

The rain began at midnight. At first only a few spots, it soon increased to a steady downpour which clattered violently against the mud roof of the hut. Thunderclaps rolled across the valley and lightning flashed white sparks of light through the warped wooden shutters. But as drops of water splashed through the roof and collected in puddles on the floor I still failed to realise how this storm was going to affect my plans.

At dawn I was impatient to load the mule and be on our way but Mohammed insisted that there was something I should see first. As we walked through the deserted village, I became aware of a roaring noise above the steady patter of heavy rain. We arrived at the higher ground near the kasbah and the source of the noise was immediately revealed. A dried-up wadi – nothing but sand and rocks the day before – had become a river some 150 ft (50 m) wide. I had often heard the Berber tribesmen talk of the flooding that comes with prolonged rain but nothing could have prepared me for this unexpected sight – a river created in just six hours! And the rain had not yet stopped.

Mohammed and I obviously had to make a decision quickly because the wadi was filling visibly by the minute and the torrent increasing at an alarming rate. We knew that our route to Anmiter would cross it several times so it was only with great reluctance that Mohammed packed the mule and we set off into the freezing rain. For a couple of hours I remained optimistic but when we reached the first crossing I agreed with Mohammed that we had no hope of getting

the mule across – the water was flowing much too quickly and had become powerful enough to sweep branches and even a couple of floundering goats down from the highlands.

We took the shivering mule back to Telouet and finally got to Anmiter by an alternative, winding route which skirted the wadi and kept to the high valley sides. Here however our luck ran out. There was no way forward unless we crossed a tributary of the principal wadi which was by now several feet deep. Mohammed crossed easily in his bare feet but as I reached the middle I felt the rocks beneath my feet shift with the current, suddenly my legs were swept downstream and I splashed head first into the brown water. I crawled out on all fours after my first Moroccan bath for a long time to find Mohammed laughing hysterically. The Berbers have a great sense of humour!

We continued until just before nightfall when we came to a narrowing of the valley above the village of Tigzha where the wadi was being forced through a canyon in a scene reminiscent of the Himalayan 'white water' rivers. The roar of the water and sinister rumble of stones and rocks clashing together beneath it made any talking impossible. The villagers watched powerless as the river swept away their carefully tended crops and uprooted the trees which provide a major slice of the Berber mountain economy.

Most Berber village houses are built well away from wadis on ground that has proved safe for centuries, but as we entered Tighza a new threat became all too clear as a boulder the size of a car crashed and somersaulted down the steep cliffs behind the village, narrowly missing the most exposed house. There was no doubt that a direct hit would be disastrous, so I pointed out a number of large boulders above the village leaning at crazy angles, just waiting to be eroded away by the rain. True to Berber fashion, they laughed at my fear and invoked the will of God 'Inshallah'.

Mohammed and I were invited to stay in the most impressive house in the village, a four-storey building belonging to the chief. His charming wife cooked a chicken in olive oil, which we ate cross-legged on the floor, Berber-style, while the men of the village talked non-stop about the ceaseless rain. The meal was punctuated by stones and mud plopping from the roof and the chief himself went up several times to clear away the water and prevent it from collapsing under the heavy weight.

My sleeping bag had become a wet, slimy, giant slug and I lay awake most of the night waiting for the roof to fall in or for a huge megalith to come smashing through the wall. Every time a rock clattered down the cliff I muttered 'Inshallah'. The Berbers apparently slept like logs.

It was two days before the *wadi* subsided enough to allow anyone to pass through the canyon and Mohammed returned to his family in Telouet, anxious for his animals and fields. I later found out that Thesiger had been delayed by floods for three days on the eastern side of the Atlas and could understand any frustration he felt. But at last I left Tighza with a new guide – also called Mohammed – for Lake Tamda. We climbed a beautiful valley to a high plateau grassland supporting several nomadic families, then reached the snowline at about 10,500 ft (3,200 m). The mule coped admirably with the snow but Mohammed's dog, which had been so enthusiastic about coming along on the trip, now began to change his mind as we continued up the col. By the time we reached Lake Tamda the snow was too deep for the dog to plough through and he rode piggy-back on the mule for the rest of the day. As we climbed beyond the

frozen waters of the lake we realised that we had mistimed our arrival at Tamzerit and that the last two hours of the trek were inevitably going to be in darkness.

As the light quickly faded we could scarcely see more than a few feet ahead and we both doubted that we would find the village. I suggested to Mohammed that if we got completely lost we could put up my tent and wait until daylight. He thought for a moment, then asked if the dog could also sleep in the tent since it was a bitter night. I reluctantly agreed.

"And", he continued, "what about the mule?" I'll never know if he meant this as a joke but it

On the rocky tracks of the High Atlas the vulnerable hooves of the mules are easily damaged. Most of the troubles can be solved with a new set of shoes but expert 'mule doctors' offer their services at souks throughout the mountains and produce miraculous cures.

restored our good spirits for a while. By nine that evening, we had descended into Tamzerit Valley and torchlight revealed the position of the village. Mohammed had friends who welcomed us with mint tea, warm bread and cous-cous and we slept in the chief's house with goats and voracious bed bugs for company.

A massive bowl of rice supplied a communal breakfast and I then had to negotiate mule hire to the next village. All the talk of journeys inspired the chief to tell me about his pilgrimage to Mecca and, after long and elaborate prayers, he gave me a tour of his beautifully constructed house and, very unusually for these remote traditional villages, made a point of introducing me to his wife and children. He was such a gracious and charming host that I felt completely at home and it was with great reluctance that I packed my bag to leave. When I learned that my next guide was also called Mohammed, I decided that a personal coding system had become essential. So it was that Mohammed II left to return to Tighza with his white mule and I crossed the Tizi n'Fedherat with Mohammed III and his brown mule, bound for Toughrene.

For the first time in a week the clouds cleared to reveal a deep blue winter sky. It was a pleasant and easy walk down the Fedgha Valley, although I lost count of the number of times we had to wade the river where the track had been eroded in the storm. After each crossing I poured the water out of my boots, much to the amusement of Mohammed III who seemed happy to squelch along with what must have been several pints in each plastic shoe. I knew from my map that Toughrene stands on high ground but I was unprepared for the spectacle that greeted us as we approached from the south-west. The view of the village is breathtaking, perched as it is on top of a sheer cliff, its packed stone houses almost seeming to defy gravity. It reminded me of the Etruscan defended villages of Italy, made all the more exciting by the remoteness of the location. We climbed up, to be greeted by a small boy who took my hand and led us to a house. It is an extraordinary feature of travel in the High Atlas that there is never a need to ask for food and shelter. As Thesiger found, the Berbers are a

The village of Ichbaccen is set into a deep valley several days' trek from the nearest road. Situated as it is on one of the main tracks across the High Atlas it survives as an example of how Berber communities have lived for centuries.

naturally hospitable people and still welcome strangers to their houses as soon as they arrive, unknown and unannounced. Even our mule was given a roof over his head and some oats in a manger.

The family I stayed with were in a state of some turmoil, having lost most of their earnings for the year when their fields of potatoes were swept away in the flood. I helped them to salvage whatever they could but where the fields had been was now a tangled mess of branches and trees set into a clay-like red mud inches deep. Just to reinstate the land would take months of work. Yet, despite this disaster, they were in a good mood that evening as we ate delicious *tagine* and wild honey with warm, flat bread. The children of the house gathered in the doorway, whispering and giggling – their white, teeth shining like pearls against grubby faces. Every time I looked in their direction they scattered in hysterical panic. As we finished the meal a cheerful figure entered the room and said he'd heard I was looking for a guide and mule to head east. I took an instant liking to him. Surprisingly enough, Mohammed was his name! The next day Mohammed III returned to Tamzerit and I set off for Megdaz with Mohammed IV.

The Tessaout River was still very high and progress up the valley was slow. We picked our route across banks of boulders and through ruined fields where gangs of villagers were working to restore order to the chaos. At Ait Ali-n-Ito, we branched right and rested for an hour or so in the shade of a walnut tree before loading the mule again and arriving at Megdaz by late afternoon. My feet were beginning to suffer as a result of being almost permanently waterlogged, but the spectacle of this superb Berber stronghold was enough to take my mind off the blisters. No fewer than ten *kasbahs* stand on a steep mountainside, framed against the backdrop of the Tadoumalt and Tazerzamt ranges. In the chief's house we climbed three storeys to a room filled with steam from a shining brass samovar. Five men, dressed in finest *djellabas* (the all-purpose robe worn by Arabs everywhere), were in conference. The effect was like gatecrashing a high-powered board meeting but they welcomed me and the samovar was fired up for mint tea. Mohammed IV was greatly in awe of these dignitaries and I was no less impressed—particularly by one whose appearance was as warlike and formidable as a modern day Ghengis Khan, his face sliced by a deep scar. In the company of these Berber chieftains it was easy to imagine how their iron rule of the Atlas had controlled the northern end of the trans-Saharan routes for centuries.

That night, another warlike tribe – an army of bed bugs – made sleep impossible. Just after dawn we packed the mule and rejoined the Tessaout Valley, this time branching right towards Ait Hamza. A light cloud cover dulled the day and we saw fresh snow fall on the high peaks of the Tignousti range to our north. We lit a fire at lunchtime and charcoaled some sweetcorn given to us by an old man rebuilding the track. It was a bit tough but made a pleasant change from the normal lunch of tinned sardines. On this day, as on most others, we met the occasional Berber traveller on the way to market with firewood, mint, walnuts or vegetables loaded onto a long-suffering mule. Mohammed IV seemed to know just about everyone – probably because his village was on the main trade route to Marrakech. Merchants and holymen, shepherds and fieldworkers – all stopped to pay their respects and swap mountain gossip. Once a whole family passed us, the men leading the mules, the women and children perched on top in their best finery for the journey – a blaze of reds and golds against the arid highland landscape that is typical of the Atlas.

When we arrived at Ichbaccen there was still plenty of daylight and, after consulting the map, I decided we could continue to Amezri a few miles further up the valley. The Berbers swore it was impossible to get there in less than five hours. The map, which had always been spot on, said it would take one. Tempers rose. I couldn't believe the map was wrong and I was convinced that Mohammed IV was employing delaying tactics, but after a great deal more discussion the Berbers won and we stayed in Ichbaccen.

The next day they were proved right. The top right corner of the Skoura 1:100,000 map is a work of complete fiction. The distances, topography and tracks bear no relation to the reality of the terrain. The argument resolved, Mohammed IV and I got back onto the best of terms. Amezri is a beautiful village situated at the head of the Tessaout Valley and flanked by the parallel ridges of the Tignousti and Tizoula (10,531 ft/3,210 m and 11,309 ft/3,447 m respectively). Our route took us up a deep-cut canyon then emerged into a flat moraine plateau before climbing to the village itself. It was a superb morning's trek – slightly marred by the mule, which began to show signs of a limp. The alpine scenery continued to improve as we passed Tasgaiwalt and began to climb up to the Tizi n'Rouguelt (9,383 ft/2,860 m). From this pass we descended just over 3,000 ft in three hours, reaching Rouguelt with minutes to spare before dark. A pack of snarling dogs barked us into the village, announcing our arrival. First priority was to tend the mule. The long day had made the limp much worse and Mohammed prised off the mule's shoe to reveal a bad abscess in the hoof. No one in the village had the tools or expertise to perform the necessary operation, so we decided to wait for the market day at Abachkou, down the Ddaghour Valley, where a mule 'doctor' had a tent.

The weekly *souk* was a magnet for the tribesmen of the region and as much a meeting place as it was a market. We left the mule in the queue for treatment (there was a long line waiting for new shoes) and spent a pleasant day wandering around the makeshift tents. Mohammed met many old friends and drank gallons of mint tea. The Berbers never seem to tire of this sickly sweet drink but I had to refuse after about ten cups.

"What's the matter?" they asked, "are you sick?" Happily I was rescued when a young boy ran over to say the 'doctor' needed help with the mule. When we got there we could see why. The poor beast was wild-eyed and bucking like mad every time its hoof was raised. Eventually it took seven of us to hold it steady while the grisly job was done with a red hot iron, but when we walked the mule around the dusty square, the 'doctor' beamed in triumph – the mule's limp was completely gone.

The weather took a turn for the worse over the next few days as Mohammed IV and I rejoined the Ddaghour Valley and continued east. I often caught my guide scanning the high peaks above the Tizi N'Rougelt, probably because this was the route he would have to take home when we parted. He denied worrying about this but couldn't hide his anxiety every time fresh snow fell. Merchants and mule trains from the *souk* passed us at great speed but we took our time, lingering in the tiny villages and exploring some of the smaller valleys that branch off the Ddaghour. The mule was completely recovered by now, but it almost put an abrupt stop to the trek one day on a high, narrow path we had taken to skirt some washed-out track. We came to a particularly steep section, barely enough for the mule to pass, about 40 ft (12 m) above the river. Instinctively, it refused to move forward and as Mohammed edged past to lead it, bucked and kicked him off the precipice. With lightning reactions Mohammed grabbed the mule's ankle and hauled himself back. I was horrified, but Mohammed later laughed about it for hours and often told it as an after dinner story in the villages, to the amusement of our hosts.

At the head of the valley, we stayed in the village of Agassif. A sheep was slaughtered by the chief in honour of our visit and what seemed to be the entire village joined us by candlelight for the feast that night. A good-natured argument grew when I asked how many people lived there. Some said 30, some said 40, until the chief's son, the only one who could write (he was on holiday from Koranic school), wrote down the name of every man, woman and child and came up with 47. Twenty-two of them were named Mohammed! The gathering obviously enjoyed this impromptu census and they demanded more questions. By the end of the evening I knew how many houses, radios, cattle, fields, mules, sheep and goats comprised the hamlet of Agassif, right down to the last chicken (although estimates on this varied wildly from about 90 to several thousand)!

Full to the brim with mutton and statistics, I left the party and walked to the river. It was a moonlit night and the snowy peaks of M'Goun were bathed in blue light. The sound of the fast-running water echoed around the valley walls and, every now and again, laughter and conversation from the village filtered down to join it.

My almost-solo journey was nearly over. In two days we would cross the last remaining ridge of this great African range and descend to the valley of the Ait Bou Goumez and the bustling market town of Tabant. Mohammed and his long-suffering mule would turn about and head back to Toughrene. I would travel north by truck on the dirt road to Azilal and Marrakech.

Looking back on the experiences of the trek, following in the footsteps of Thesiger, the High Atlas had fulfilled all my expectations and more. The excitement of travelling between villages accessible only by foot is one that will draw me back time and again. The hospitality and generosity that Thesiger found among the Berbers was still intact after 30 years, and the practicality of hiring guides and mules presented no real problem. The mud-built castles of sheiks and rich merchants still stand tall over the villages of the Atlas and the communities that inhabit them are as genuine and tightly knit now as they have ever been. Since the start of the trek I had seen or spoken to no one but the Berbers, and my admiration for their strength, honesty and kindness had grown as a result. My only hope is that future travellers, who will perhaps also set out from Telouet with only a guide and a single mule for companions, whether three, 30 or 300 years from now, will find the Atlas and its people as I have written of them here.

Megdaz is the gem of the High Atlas, perched on a steep mountainside, facing out over a spectacular view of some of the highest peaks in the range. The architecture of the village represents the wealth of the merchants who live there in buildings up to five stories high.

Practical
The High Atlas are still relatively undeveloped, with the exception of the Toubkal region where several tour companies such as Exodus and Explore Worldwide run trekking programmes. The routes themselves are for the most part along well defined and dusty trails. High passes separate the valleys but are not technically difficult assuming a reasonable level of personal fitness.

Distances/times
The Toubkal circuit is a variable route depending on time available. Somewhere between six and nine days would be a reasonable assessment, plus two or three days' acclimatization.

In the Central High Atlas, the tracks run east/west along the spine of the range and itineraries are almost unlimited in terms of time and scope. A limited walk is possible in two weeks. A complete traverse could take months!
Highest point: Jbel Toubkal – 13,665 ft/4, 165 m

Language
English is not spoken at all in any areas of the High Atlas but most villages have one or two people who speak some French. Arabic is little used and the predominant language is the local Berber dialect.

Other considerations
There are no limits to the routes that can be undertaken in the High Atlas. With patience and luck it is possible to hire guides and mules in just about any village. Hospitality is second nature to the Berbers, so no matter how strenuously they object to an offer of payment for food or accommodation, it is always a good idea to make a gesture in the form of a gift or money.

Seasons
The best trekking conditions are in the season between March and September although the summer months of July and August can be very hot. April and May boast the finest variety of flowers and plant growth in the lowlands in contrast to later in the season when the High Atlas can be extremely arid. Water supplies are generally good except for in the high ground above 10,000 ft (3,000 m).

From October to February the Atlas presents a completely different face and the high passes can be snowbound for weeks at a time. The climatic conditions in winter, accentuated by the proximity of the seasonal winds of the Sahara, can vary dramatically from mild to severe . . . much in the style of the Alps. Blizzards and snow storms are always a possibility in winter, as are flash floods and rain storms.

Equipment
In summer, lightweight gear is sufficient but nights can be cold enough to warrant good sleeping bags. Shorts are ideal in the Toubkal area where locals are used to trekking parties, but in more remote regions they are definitely to be avoided as they inevitably cause offence amongst traditional villagers. A tent can be useful in months where rain storms occur.

The scree slopes of the Atlas are notoriously tough on ankles so good robust boots are essential. In winter I would recommend taking equipment capable of high level Alpine trekking. Snow gaiters and crampons can be a good idea if you are tackling any of the major peaks. Maps and other equipment are just about impossible to buy or hire in the Atlas, so go prepared.

Access/permits
The High Atlas is a region refreshingly free from the constraints of bureaucracy and I have never heard of permits required for trekking.

Logistics
The nearest town of any size to the High Atlas is Marrakech. Flights can be found at reasonable rates direct to this magical medieval town from both Paris and London. Food and some medical supplies can be purchased in Marrakech as these are sometimes confiscated on entry by the Customs.

From Marrakech there are shared taxis or buses to any of the points of access into the mountains. As far as accommodation is concerned there are three options. Camping is one, although good ground is sometimes hard to find above 10,000 ft (3,000 m). Villages do not have official rest houses in the style of the

Himalaya but I have never found a Berber village where someone wasn't prepared to offer shelter for a night. The French Alpine Club have several huts for mountaineers, mostly in the Toubkal region. Their standards are generally high but they can become unpleasantly overcrowded at peak times.

Medical considerations
Stomach problems are the main consideration in the High Atlas, particularly if you are eating local food in the villages. An injection of gamma globulin against hepatitis is advisable and medical advice should be sought on other inoculations. In the highlands the stream water is good but if there is any habitation upstream purifying or boiling is essential. No medical supplies are available in the villages and whatever kit you take with you will rapidly become depleted in villages where locals ask for aspirins or bandages. The dry Saharan wind can take its toll, so take lots of moisturizing creams. Altitude sickness is an ever present threat above 10,000 ft (3,000 m), so acclimatize slowly.

Reading
Maps:
The best trekking maps are the *Cartes du Maroc* 1:100,000 produced in Rabat. The detail is sufficient for most climbing and trekking trips although, as noted in the text, these maps are occasionally more fiction than fact. Stanfords Map Centre in London stock these and larger scale maps of Morocco.
Literature:
There are very few books on the Atlas region in the English language. The following are all of use:
Lords of the Atlas – Gavin Maxwell (Century Hutchinson)
Atlas Mountains – Robin Collomb (West Col Productions, 1980)
Morocco That Was – Walter B Harris (Blackwood, 1921)
The following are in French:
Le Haut Atlas Central – André Fougerolles (IDEALE, Casablanca, 1982)
Dans Les Grands Atlas Morocains – Dr Paul Chatinieres (Plon, 1919)
Villes et Montagnes Marocaines (La Porte, Rabat, 1965)

Fact Sheet

Born in Cambridge in 1960, Matt Dickinson lived in Nigeria as a child and after school in the UK got a degree in Archaeology and Anthropology at Durham University, where he was President of the Exploration Society 1981–2. He has travelled widely in countries like Nepal and Tanzania and led expeditions to Madagascar and Niger. The Sahara desert, and particularly the nomadic Touareg peoples, are amongst his main interests.

From 1985 to 1988 he worked as a writer and production manager for BBC Television on programmes as diverse as *The Great Journeys*, *Jim'll Fix It*, *Jasper Carrott* and *Ever Decreasing Circles*. More recently he has been working as an Asssistant Producer on the Central Television series, *The National Geographic Hour*.

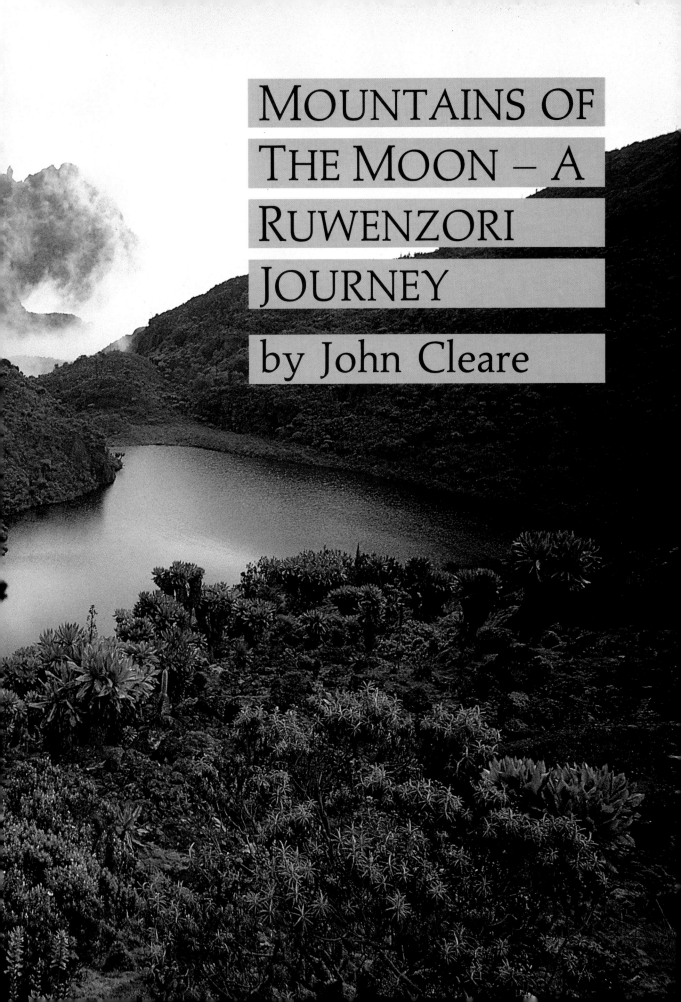

MOUNTAINS OF THE MOON – A RUWENZORI JOURNEY

by John Cleare

'Through a clear and limpid atmosphere there appeared the crest of . . . the Ruwenzori . . . The people of Unyoro say that no one who has attempted its mysteries has ever returned.'
Gaetano Casati, *Ten Years in Equatoria*, 1891

The rain drummed viciously on the tin roof of the old Land Rover. The wipers sloshed impotently across the streaming windscreen. There was nothing to see. Shutting my eyes again, I squeezed in between the bulging rucksacks and two companions with whom I shared the back seat. After jolting over 650 miles (1,100 kms) from Nairobi, pain seemed only relative.

Suddenly the brakes squealed and the vehicle shuddered to a halt. Behind the wheel John Temple swore. Great grey shapes, dimly seen through the curtain of rain, were moving with a stately slowness across the road only yards ahead. Elephants! Twenty or thirty of them! At last they disappeared into the murk and we could set off again. Then suddenly the rain stopped and a large sign beside the road proclaimed: 'The Equator – Drive Safely in the Rwenzori National Park'. We entered the Northern Hemisphere. It was Christmas Eve.

The first sight of the Ruwenzori Mountains came 20 miles (33 kms) later when a red dirt road led us off the main highway towards the village of Ibanda. Ridge upon jagged ridge, seemingly cut from grey-green cardboard, rose beyond a foreground of *shambas* (smallholdings) and creased green foothills against a sky already tinged with that golden flush that heralds the African dusk. At a clearing in a banana grove we halted beside a peculiar octagonal aluminium hut. Smoke drifted through the joints in its conical roof and a wizened old man, an ancient army greatcoat thrown over his frail shoulders, stood grinning in the doorway.

"*Jambo Mzee!*" called out Temple ('Greetings, Old Man') and to us.

"This is the M.C.U. Base Camp Hut – and this is Isaac, the caretaker."

The five of us climbed stiffly down from the Land Rover. So this was the gateway to the mysterious Ruwenzori – the fabled Mountains of the Moon!

In 500 BC Aeschylus wrote of '. . . *Egypt nurtured by the snows . . .*' and 600 years later the geographer Claudius Ptolemy located the source of the Nile at a snow-fed lake in a range he called the Mountains of the Moon, deep in Central Africa. It was not until 1876 however that a European – Henry Morton Stanley, Livingstone's rescuer – actually glimpsed the eternal snows, still 50 miles (83 kms) distant. The

Bakonjo who still today inhabit the eastern flanks of the mountains claimed them as the abode of the god Kitasamba and it was fear of him that precluded their own ventures to the snowline. Nevertheless, by the turn of the century several European explorers had penetrated the thick forests and reached the glaciers – even if they achieved little else. Then in 1906, a full scale expedition arrived led by the ubiquitous Duke of Abruzzi. His companions included four mountain guides from Courmayeur, the renowned mountain photographer, Vittorio Sella, and no less than 150 porters. Together they climbed all the major summits and drew the first maps.

Abruzzi discovered that the Ruwenzori is a series of large massifs each crowned with several individual summits, the six highest massifs holding glaciers, and that no less than ten of the summits rise above 16,000 ft (4,880 m). On the higher peaks he encountered spectacular encrustations of ice-rime forming cornices and mushrooms on rocks and ridges, and at lower altitudes he found cliffs and slabs draped with curtains of moss and lichen. Beneath were deep, narrow valleys choked with giant, exotic plants and usually floored with bog, while a wide belt of tangled foothills covered in dense forest guarded the central heights. Modern aerial surveys have confirmed Abruzzi's maps.

Since then there have been regular visitors to the range but, perhaps understandably, never in great numbers. The now-defunct Mountain Club of Uganda built several mountain huts at strategic locations and before the collapse of Idi Amin's regime in Uganda a couple of climbing parties and several groups of sturdy hikers would reach the mountains each year. They endured tough conditions but the rewards were rich – the freedom of a chain of unique mountains, still holding scope for detailed exploration, and rising from an extraordinary and still entirely unspoilt wilderness. By contrast, the Ruwenzori's less extensive western flank has been visited comparatively rarely, since Zairean independence created major political and logistic hurdles for travellers.

By noon on Christmas Day our little party had set off from the road head hut. Ahead trotted our porters, a dozen ragged Bakonjo tribesmen armed with short spears or stout staves and led by an elderly and shifty-eyed headman, resplendent in floral hat, gaberdine raincoat and black wellies. Each – save the headman – carried a 50 lb (22 kgs) load on a headband, together with the blanket and rations that we had issued – cassava flour, peanuts and smoked fish. A lean yellow dog loped at their heels. The porters had been organized for us by John Matte, the helpful Ugandan who ran the

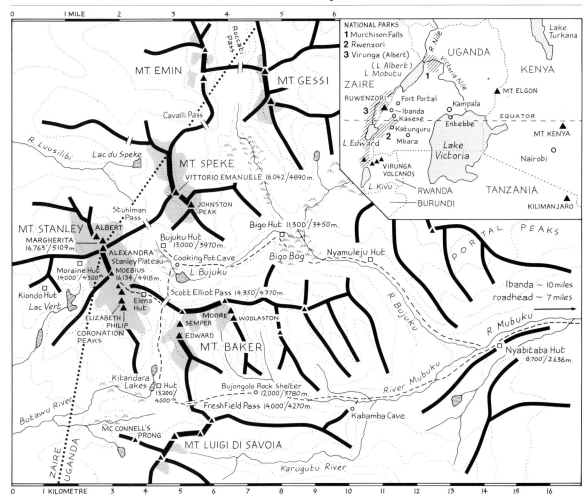

Ibanda store and was once the local M.C.U. agent. He gave us the club's hut keys, a mere formality as it happened, while Temple carried a quantity of money in his rucksack to pay the porters' wages of – in 1975 – about 50p (+ rations) per day. We planned to spend some two weeks in the heart of the mountains, reaching as many summits as possible and attempting several new climbs which we had located on the old aerial photographs Temple had somehow obtained. Meanwhile we would complete the classic Ruwenzori circuit on our approach and return treks.

At first, the trail followed a narrow canyon through ten foot (three metre) yellow grass and up a U-shaped valley below craggy, cloud-capped hillsides. At only 5,000 ft (1,500 m), in shorts and shirt and heavy rucksack, the going was hot and sticky. Soon bush rose on either side and sometimes trees loaded with pink blossom overhung our path. Occasionally an unseen creature crashed away through the undergrowth. Then we came to the glacier-fed Mubuku River that cuts a swath through vine-hung forest on its tumultuous journey to

Lake George and the distant Nile, the trail undulating above its bank often a ribbon of slippery mud marked only by the toes of our bare-foot porters, who were, by now, well ahead. In furious frustration I skidded and slipped, wishing for proper mountain boots instead of the flimsy tennis-shoes we had been advised to wear. On one steep descent I fell, sliding out of control on my bum right through an army of safari ants on the warpath. Entire regiments were scooped into the legs of my shorts and late that night I was still picking ants from my private parts!

A wade through a deep, cool stream raised morale and then we were winding upwards through open forest of bamboo and podocarpus, stepping over earthworms big as snakes while monkeys monitored our progress from the treetops. In waist-deep bracken we crested a steep ridge and there was Nyabitaba Hut, set against a rocky knoll. As we reached it hail stones large as pennies exploded around us, beating a crazy fusilade against the tin walls. We prepared our Christmas dinner in this bare shed with snatches of song and thick smoke wafting from the large caves close by. At least the

porters were enjoying Christmas!

The Bujuku River, rising in the very heart of the range, joins the Mubuku below the hut and it was more convenient for our climbing objectives to ascend the tributary river, later crossing high passes to descend the Mubuku Valley and thus complete the circuit. It was to prove a wise choice. A lattice of fallen trees enabled us to cross the Mubuku and enter the narrow Bujuku Glen, where the river roared in its bouldery bed below forested walls and mossy crags. We climbed steadily beside the torrent and at mid-day passed the Namuleju Hut, another tin shack where slower parties might spend the night. Cloud still choked the valley ahead and we began to wonder if the mountains really existed.

Slowly the gradient eased, the valley broadened and the vegetation changed. Many of the trees we now recognized as giant heather —

Left — *The bizarre crown of a giant tree groundsel* (Senecio adnivalis) *rises near Lake Bujuku against the northern face of the Mount Baker massif.*
Below — *The lichen-covered south-west ridge of Mount Johnston, the first section of the Mount Speke traverse with fine views of the peaks at the southern end of the Stanley Ice Plateau, rising southward across the Bujuku Valley.*

weirdly different from the Scottish variety — and we passed stands of tree-groundsel, giant lobelia and St John's wort, familiar plants at home when merely inches high but here reaching 20 ft (six metres) or more. Moss hung from everything and we noticed pink orchids and other flowers, white, yellow and mauve. Even in the dull light below the leaden clouds, it was strange and beautiful.

We identified the flat green basin ahead as the notorious Bigo Bog. An ocean of verdant sphagnum, studded with grassy tussocks and islets of purple-rosetted lobelia, it fills the valley bottom for over half a mile — obviously a formidable obstacle. Cautiously at first, then more boldly, we leapt from tussock to tussock, following the muddy spoor of the porters. But soon we were wading thigh deep in the fearsome black ooze — never quite glutinous enough to prevent escape. I felt like a small boy again, actually enjoying the mud with no one to gainsay me!

Bigo Hut stands by the Bujuku at 11,300 ft (3,450 m), in a glade of giant heather beyond the Bog. Before starting a brew, we waded waist-deep into the icy river to scrub the mud from body and clothes. Our Bakonjo friends meanwhile left their nearby cave with their spears and the yellow dog and a while later,

fresh hyrax liver supplemented our supper of bacon butties. One young lad proudly sported a new fur cap. The marmot-sized hyrax, closest extant relation to the elephant, is commonly hunted by the Bakonjo for its meat and fur when they tire of banana growing in their *shambas*.

Perhaps the liver was intended to sweeten the blackmail, for next morning the headman declared that wages must be doubled or his team would desert. But John Temple was no greenhorn.

"Right then," he said "you have broken your contract and lost your honour. We *mzungu* are strong, we will carry our own loads. *Ondoka! Kwaheri!* – Go away! Goodbye!"

He sacked the entire team. I was nonplussed – we were left sitting by Bigo Hut surrounded by nearly 500 lb (220 kgs) of assorted food and equipment. But half an hour later – as Temple had anticipated – the five younger porters crept out of the bushes and asked to stay with us for the originally agreed wages. These lads proved cheerful, loyal and devoted, but we still had to reorganize our entire logistics.

Now the walls of the valley closed in again, tier upon tier of rocky walls and forested ledges rising into the cloud. Familiar as I was with lofty Alpine and Himalayan pines, the forested skylines suggested stupendous scale until I realised that the trees were heather and rarely even 50 ft (15 m) high, when everything dropped into perspective – but it was imposing terrain nevertheless. Everything seemed green – the ground, the rock, even the sky. A long climb through a zone of steep moraines swathed in lush vegetation led us to a grove of the now ubiquitous tree groundsel lining the shores of moody and silent Lake Bujuku.

"Where are these mountains then?" growled Jim, Californian and impatient. "Aren't we supposed to be right in the centre . . . ?"

"Just look!" said Temple. "No – up there." He pointed excitedly.

Indeed, snow-plastered buttresses and pinnacles hung in great rents which opened and closed in the curtains of cloud high above us. Yes, we were there at last, right in the middle. And these dark waters were the highest source of the Albert Nile. Now we must pray for good weather!

Soon the tattered cloud was streaming away and we reached our destination, half an hour above the lake, in fitful sunshine. Set among boulders in a groundsel glade at 13,000 ft (3,970 m), the twin Bujuku Huts make a real home from home, one actually weatherproof and still boasting a wooden sleeping-shelf. While our loyal porters settled into the nearby 'Cooking Pot Cave' we hung out our socks to dry, started

Porter rations include peanuts, cassava flour and dried lake fish – a local delicacy.

the tea brewing and marvelled at the mountains that now encircled us. The summit crest of Mount Baker, pinnacled and challenging, reared beyond the lake, snow patches clinging to its great northern precipices. A line of hanging seracs and ice tongues hid the Stanley summits opposite the hut while arcing slabs buttressed the glaciers of the Speke massif above us. Now that the curtain was drawn, the prospects were tantalizing.

The Bujuku Huts are the strategic centre of the range and given reasonable weather and basic glacier experience, several straightforward summits can be gained from it. Vittorio Emanuele, the highest point of Mount Speke, rises to 16,042 ft (4,890 m), is probably the easiest, and should be reached in about five hours. From its rime-plastered summit there are superb views across to the eleven summits that jut above the wide Stanley Plateau. The Plateau itself, a unique ice cap over one and a quarter miles (two kms) long, lying at some 15,500 ft (4,700 m) and only 25 miles (42 kms) north of the Equator, is gained most easily via the tiny Elena Huts above the foot of the Elena Glacier. A few crevasses can be avoided by simple snow slopes and Moebius − a frosted tooth at 16,134 ft (4,918 m) − is only a 15 minute scramble from the crest of the Plateau. From this summit there is a magnificent panorama of the Zairean flanks of Stanley and, with luck, to the Virunga Volcanoes 140 miles (225 kms) southward.

Margherita (16,763 ft/5,109 m), Alexandra and Albert, the highest summits of the Ruwenzori, rising like frozen waves from the northern end of the Plateau, and the spiky Coronation Peaks at the southern end are more serious undertakings and should be attempted only by experienced and properly equipped mountaineers. While we enjoyed some excellent climbs we learnt the hard way that a typical Ruwenzori 'dry season' day starts with a clear, frosty dawn, progressing through a cloudy noon to a snowy afternoon, which finally clears again at dusk. Another major problem we discovered was keeping our sleeping bags dry, while our clothes daily became soggier.

"Trench-foot or frostbite?" I asked Temple. "Take your pick!"

Beyond the hut, the grassy Stuhlmann Pass leads down into Zaire. This western flank of the range is extremely beautiful, but the political frontier is a hypothetical line bearing no relationship to the mountain geography and is easy to cross inadvertently. We had climbed a superb new ice gully on the North Face of Albert − technically just in Zaire − and were bivouacking one day at the ruins of the old Belgian Moraine Hut at 14,000 ft (4,300 m), below the western face of Margherita, when we were 'jumped' by armed Zairean Rangers. Suffice to say that we eventually escaped, scared stiff but unscathed, during the regular evening snowstorm, but only because we were fit and acclimatized and our captors were not. If a short trip is contemplated to this enticing western flank, one should keep high, around glacier snout level, and observe due caution.

From Bujuku, the trekking route now crosses the 14,350 ft (4,370 m) Scott Elliott Pass − so named for a botanical explorer of the 1890s − to reach Kitandara on the headwaters of the westward-flowing Butawu River. We gained the Pass easily but steeply, a broad saddle where giant groundsel grows between the boulders. We paused at the head of the green gorge beyond, its floor falling steeply to the twin Kitandara Lakes, tiny jewels set in the forest a mile down. On our right, cliffs and terraces rose to the ice-hung South Stanley peaks. On our left reared the most stupendous rock wall in the Ruwenzori, glinting damply in the morning sunshine and streaked with black stains. Two thousand blank feet (600 m) above, we could see the jutting edge of an ice terrace hanging from Mount Baker's crest. Only two thread-thin ice gullies slashed the wall.

"Oh wow! An African El Cap!" gasped Jim, as awed as the rest of us.

"Yer' wouldn't catch me on it," said Temple forcefully, "I prefer to enjoy my climbing, it looks bloody 'orrific!"

"Mean, damp and dangerous," I agreed. "I'll bet that ice wipes off the lichen periodically. I'll stick to Yosemite with you, Jim!"

Down the gorge we went, shoulder-high through helichrysum thickets heavy with tiny, white everlasting flowers and ever mindful of ice − or rock − falls from those walls overhead.

The Kitandara Hut stands in an idyllic setting on the wooded shores of the second tarn and is larger, less ruinous and more comfortable than the other huts. Here we planned a rest day. We arrived in a sudden, blinding snowstorm which left the lush foliage of lobelia and groundsel that overhung the dark waters looking like a line drawing. When the sun returned and the snow-powdered tooth of McConnell's Prong, high on the sharp shoulder of Mount Luigi di Savoia, was again reflected shimmering in the lake, I could not but agree with the old Ruwenzori explorers who claimed that Kitandara was the most beautiful spot in the entire range.

To regain the Uganda watershed and the headwaters of the Mubuku, the circuit route must now cross the 14,000 ft (4,270 m) Freshfield Pass − an easy col between Baker and Luigi di Savoia.

Above – It is customary to issue socks to the loyal Bakonjo porters before venturing above the snowline. John Temple supervises the sizing on a rocky ledge below the Scott Elliot Pass.

Left – Plastered with the characteristic Ruwenzori ice-rime, the summit tower of Moebius (16,134 ft/4,918 m) is a short and easy scramble from the crest of the great Stanley Ice Plateau. John Temple and Jim Slade stand on the mist-shrouded summit, after making the first ascent of the long Zairean Face of the peak.

On the crest, the morning sun gilded the ice on moss-ringed pools and a cloud-sea cloaked the Zairean foothills to the west. An easy mile leads down to the celebrated Bujongolo Rock Shelter, at 12,400 ft (3,780 m) the site of Abruzzi's 1906 Base Camp. We, however, struck up the ridge northwards from the pass, intending to traverse the beautiful crest of Mount Baker, a classic, many-summited alpine ridge, aiming to descend the awkward Moore Glacier to Bujongolo before dusk. Within an hour it was snowing but we eventually achieved our objective, only locating the rock shelter well after dark by the large fire the porters had built in its mouth.

Bujongolo is only some three hours from Kitandara and trekking parties may prefer to camp in the Kabamba Cave lower down the Mubuku Glen. But we had enjoyed a long day and we relaxed round the roaring fire beneath the jutting overhang, downed our last drams of precious whisky, and dried our socks while our brave porters sang their songs in the shadowed starlight.

It would be misleading to describe the Mubuku Valley as 'downhill all the way home'. Even more exotic than the Bujuku Valley, it is certainly fierce country. My diary records '. . . indescribable . . . extremely impressive . . . but how come the bog remains bog when most of it is so steep? Can it be possible to ascend by this route? . . .' But some people do! We sloshed down boggy terraces, we slid down moss-covered glacis and we elbowed through tangled thickets of giant heather. Delicate waterfalls plunged over cliffs beneath hidden valleys and time and again we waded the widening Mubuku. First it rained and then the sun shone. It was a regular Ruwenzori day.

A final steep ascent led us towards the Nyabitaba Hut and the completion of the circuit. On the hillside the ground was dry for once and on the trail lay the distinctive droppings of a leopard.

"Lucky that leopards don't like wet feet!" chuckled Temple.

"We've suffered enough recently without having to worry about their attentions!"

"Sure," I replied, "but suffering is relative. It's the price you pay for the Ruwenzori – but what an incredible place! It'll take me years to recover but one day I'll be back . . ."

Seasons
So-called 'Dry Seasons' are mid-December to mid-March and May to September but unsettled weather and rainfall can still be expected during these periods.

Times/distances
While the basic circuit as described is only some 40 miles (65 kms) on the map, the journey is better measured in days.
Road head – Bujuku Hut: 3 days
Bujuku Hut – Kitandara Hut: 1 day
Kitandara Hut – Road head: 2½ days
Most parties will wish to make side trips from Bujuku or Kitandara and a total of 10–12 days would allow for a worthwhile expedition.

Difficulty
Some sorts of track exists round the basic circuit but the going is often damp and boggy and typically rough and strenuous. There are several straightforward river crossings. Off the main track, route-finding experience on rocky hillsides is useful. Several worthy summits are accessible as side trips but involve ascending easy snowslopes and crossing straightforward but potentially crevassed glaciers.
Highest elevation on basic circuit: 14,350 ft (4,370 m)

Bases
Currently Nairobi (Kenya) is the most practical starting point, driving from there to Ibanda road head via Kampala. Fuel shortages in Uganda can create problems, not insurmountable, but allow plenty of spare time. Nearest international airport – Entebbe (Uganda) – 310 miles (500 kms), with flights from Nairobi.
Nearest city – Kampala, Uganda's capital – 280 miles (450 kms).
Nearest large town – Fort Portal – 60 miles (100 kms).
Nearest town – Kasese – 15 miles (25 kms), is served by thrice weekly overnight train service from Kampala on which cars can sometimes be carried. Also in normal times by regular internal flights from Entebbe.

Accommodation
Mountain Club of Uganda built seven small, simple huts in the central part of the range. While now in a ruinous state they still offer some shelter but are bug-infested and thus tents are preferable for sleeping. A special feature of the range is an abundance of convenient caves and rock shelters.

Equipment
Cold frosty nights and frequent wet days necessitate warm and weatherproof clothing, more 'Scottish Winter' in style than 'High Altitude Himalayan'. Proper trousers

Giant Lobelia at Kitandara Lake with McConnell's Prong and Mt Luigi de Savoia in the background.

and long-sleeved shirts are useful in the 'jungle'. Constantly wet feet suggest plenty of spare socks. Camping stoves are essential as any fire wood is bound to be damp as well as rare at higher altitudes. If trips above the snow line are contemplated, ice axe, crampons and rope are necessary and dry boots are welcome.

Medical
Normal tropical injections and anti-malaria medication are necessary, and a supply of antihistamine ointment useful. Much of the circuit lies above 10,000 ft (3,000 m), so usual altitude acclimatization precautions should be taken.

Logistics
It is usual but not essential to hire local porters. Their employment makes longer and more comfortable journeys feasible. While in no sense 'mountain guides' they will know the main routes and their local knowledge is useful. They will understand Swahili and possibly a little English.

There is an 'official' scale of porter rations and equipment agreed with the old MCU which includes a blanket and pullover. January 1988 porter wages, at the official exchange rate, were US$1.70/day, double for the non-load carrying headman and extra for wet or long days, carrying on snow, etc. Allow also for watchman to guard car left at road head. Porters now carry about 40 lb/18 kgs.

The key man is the local trader John Matte who should be contacted beforehand at: Ibanda, PO Box 88, Kasese, Uganda He runs *Mountain Services*, a cooperative for headmen and porters and will organise requirements for a fee or perhaps payment in kind with locally unobtainable items such as mattock heads or plastic hose pipe, etc. He will supply basic porter rations except for sugar – currently unobtainable in Uganda – and can sometimes supply kerosene. All other supplies, including porter blankets and such porter 'goodies' as ball-point pens, aspirin, sticking-plasters and socks should be brought from Nairobi where most things are obtainable. Highly specialized supplies must be brought from abroad.

Access
The Ruwenzori Mountains are close to – but not part of the Rwenzori (sic) National Park (late Queen Elizabeth National Park) which is a game park. There are no access restrictions from the Uganda side though problems exist on the Zaire flank, in what was once the Parc National Albert.

Reading
Literature:
Guide to the Ruwenzori – H. Osmaston & D Pasteur (Westcol, London, 1972) Contains useful sketchmaps. *Ruwenzori* – F de Filippi. (Constable, London, 1908)

Fountains of the Sun – Sir Douglas Busk (Parrish, London, 1955) *The Way to the Mountains of the Moon* – R M Bere (Barker, London, 1966) *Mountains of East Central Africa* – Clive Ward (forthcoming from The Bodley Head)
Maps:
1:50,000 *Central Ruwenzori* sheet No 65/11 (DOS 1957), or the extremely rare 1:25,000 '*Central Ruwenzori*', provisional map for mountaineers (DOS 1950s). The former may still be obtainable from Edward Stanford Ltd, 12/14 Long Acre, London WC2E 9LP or Dept of Lands & Surveys, PO Box 1, Entebbe, PO Box 7061, Kampala, or PO Box 32, Fort Portal.

John Cleare is a freelance photographer, writer and lecturer – besides being a mountaineer, adventurer and wilderness traveller of wide experience. He has been climbing actively since his early teens and has expeditioned and trekked among the mountains and wild places of six continents. A member of the 1971 International Everest Expedition, he has made 16 expeditions to the Himalaya and Karakorum and, as a recently converted ski-mountaineer, he led the successful 1982 American ski ascent of Mustagh Ata in China.

Once engaged largely in 'mainstream' professional photography, in advertising, editorial, fashion and industrial work, he made several notable films and TV broadcasts about climbing including the acclaimed *Matterhorn Centenary*, *Old Man of Hoy*, *Eiger Sanction* and others – and now works with both camera and pen largely in the field of travel, adventure and mountaineering and consultancy, often among the world's wilder places, beside operating his own picture library – 'Mountain Camera'. This is his eighth book.

He is married with one daughter and lives in rural seclusion in deepest Wiltshire.

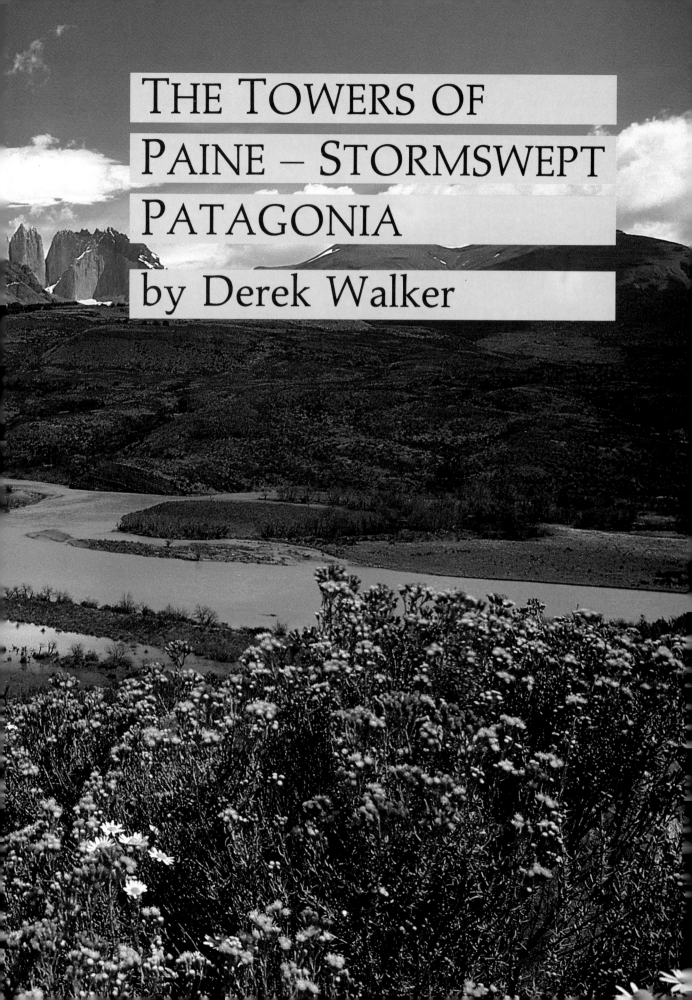

THE TOWERS OF PAINE – STORMSWEPT PATAGONIA

by Derek Walker

'Patagonia! She is a hard mistress. She casts her spell. An enchantress! She folds you in her arms and never lets go.'
Bruce Chatwyn, *In Patagonia, 1977*

'The Paine massif is unrivalled . . . it rises . . . like an impregnable fortress, crowned with towers, pinnacles and monstrous horns surging boldly to the sky. In its colours and form it is without doubt one of the most fantastic and spectacular sights that human imagination can conceive.'

Padre Agostini, the great Salesian priest who explored the length and breadth of Patagonia, and wrote about his journey in *Andes Patagonicos* in 1945, leaves us in no doubt that the Paine range is the most magnificent part of this vast land.

Patagonia is indeed immense, forming the final 1,000 miles (1,700 kms) of the South American mainland. Much of this territory, to the east of the Andes, lies in Argentina – an endless land of wide open skies and rolling brown pampas, inhospitable and deserted save for lonely *estancias* and millions of sheep.

In stark contrast much of the Chilean side, to the west, is narrow, wild and rugged, an archipelagic sponge with icy fjords and innumerable islands, great ice-caps and remote rock peaks, glaciers flowing to the sea and dense forests. It is notorious as a land of tempest, with atrocious storms, driven by the 'Forties' from the Pacific, which bring continuous rain and savage winds for long periods.

The appalling weather has proved the main obstacle for mountaineers and explorers, and most peaks so far climbed have been snatched in brief periods of settled weather, often only after long sieges. However for the tourist or trekker there are regions in southern Patagonia easier to get to, with a more reasonable climate and unsurpassed beauty. The finest of them all is the Cordillera del Paine. Indeed the Paine National Park has become one of Chile's major tourist attractions. Surprisingly it boasts more hours of sunshine per day than Great Britain!

I was fortunate enough to be on the first British expedition to visit this remarkable area in 1960, after a faded photograph of the Towers of Paine in the British Museum had inspired our young leader, Peter Henry. No doubt on that trip I ate heartily of the calafate berry which, traditionally, is said to ensure a return to Patagonia, for I was to come back to climb again in the Paine, and later to live and work in the most southerly city in the world, Punta Arenas, the capital of the Magallanes Province, and the

starting point for all exploration in South Patagonia or Tierra del Fuego.

The 1,500 mile (2,400 kms) scheduled flight from Santiago to Punta Arenas follows the whole spine of the southern Andes and must be one of the most spectacular in the world. I can vividly remember one particular occasion when, after flying over the snowy wastes of the ice-cap in perfect visibility, we were suddenly directly over the icy spire of Cerro Torre, perhaps the most inaccessible summit in the world. Approaching Punta Arenas, the pampas looks brown and arid, and the waters of the Magellan Straits dark and gloomy, the long, low shores of Tierra del Fuego stretching to the far horizon.

After boarding the plane in the balmy warmth of the capital, you will almost certainly be aware of the temperature drop and the gusting wind as you land, for rarely in spring or summer is it calm.

Punta Arenas, originally a penal settlement in the 1850s, is now a thriving business and commercial centre, an oil town and an important strategic base for the Chilean armed forces. The British were instrumental in the development of the area, for they began sheep farming on a grand scale in the 1890s, and in time, out of the wilderness, established the largest sheep-farming company in the world, with huge *estancias* producing vast quantities of wool and mutton for export to Europe.

One of the best books I have read about the early days of exploration contains line drawings and the first descriptions of the Paine Towers. It is *Across Patagonia* by Lady Florence Dixie, written in 1880. With her brother, the Marquis of Queensbury, and a few friends, she travelled on horseback north from Punta Arenas for 250 miles (400 kms) along bleak, dusty trails, hunting wild 'ostrich' and guanaco for food. She claimed that her party were the first Europeans to see the 'Cleopatra Needles', her name for the Towers. They camped in the 'Wild Horse Glen', watched the smoke from Indian encampments and marvelled at the scenery they beheld.

Sadly there are now no traces of the original Indian inhabitants. Within a few years of the arrival of the white men, the Teheulche Tribe had disappeared, killed by TB, influenza, or measles, or more shamefully, hunted down by white settlers anxious to clear their lands for sheep. The same sad fate befell the Onas and the Yaghans of Tierra del Fuego.

Having travelled so far you should not leave Punta Arenas without seeing some of the sights. You cannot miss the impressive statue of Magellan in the main square, the Plaza de Armas, and for luck you should touch the toe of the

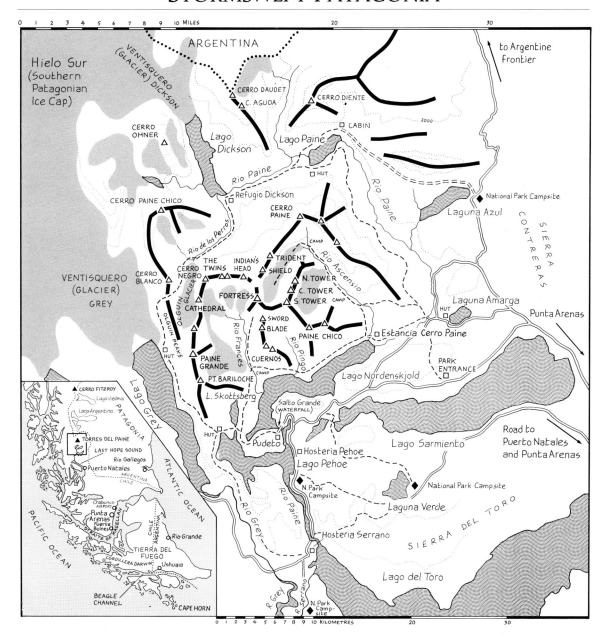

Patagonian Indian on the same monument. There is another superbly evocative statue half a mile out of town, the Ovejero, the lonely shepherd with his horse and dogs, straining against the relentless wind. And visit the Patagonian Institute and the Salesian Museum to gain some insight into the history and development of the region and the tragic fate of those remote natives. If time permits, spend half a day at Fuerte Bulnes and Puerto Hambre, one hour's drive to the south. Here was the original Spanish settlement on the Straits, founded in 1584 and called the 'City of King Philip', but rediscovered and renamed Port Famine a few years later by the English corsair Thomas Cavendish, who

found an abandoned stockade and no sign of life. It was at Puerto Hambre that I first sampled centolla, the delicious king crab, caught by local fishermen only here and in Alaska.

It would also be tempting to take a trip through the channels of Tierra del Fuego should time and opportunity allow. To follow Darwin's route along the Beagle Channel towards Cape Horn, accompanied by shoals of dolphin, and see those icy, Fuegian peaks rise dramatically from the sea is yet another experience of a lifetime.

But our main objective is 250 miles (400 kms) to the north, a journey that is now so much easier and more pleasant than in my day. Then the tarmac stopped at Chabunco Airport, 15

miles (24 kms) from town, and one was faced with a long, bumpy, dusty drive which choked up throat and nostrils, through windswept, flat grasslands, unrelieved save for the occasional distant *estancia*. Now a paved road leads for 160 miles (260 kms) to Puerto Natales, the unpretentious capital of Ultima Esperanza Province, idyllically situated on Last Hope Sound, with the soaring glaciers of Mount Balmaceda behind. A brief excursion only 15 miles (24 kms) north of Natales, will take you to the Mylodon's Cave. Here the remains of a giant sloth were found in 1895 and brought to the British Museum by Captain Charlie Millward, whose distant relative, Bruce Chatwyn, retold the story in his brilliant book *In Patagonia*.

The last 80 miles (130 kms) from Natales to the Paine is along a well kept dirt road through rolling hills reminiscent of the Scottish Highlands. Soon after passing through Cerro Castillo, a huge model *estancia*, you have your first views of the three great Towers, surging dramatically up from the wind-burned pampas and the blue lakes below. I still recall how my stomach tightened in expectation each time I caught sight of these mystical mountains.

Far left — The Paine Grande on the left, the highest mountain in the massif, and the black-capped Cuernos rising on the right, are seen over the turbulent waters of the Salto Chico cataract near Pudeto. Between the mountains lies the valley of the Rio Frances. Photo: William Gardiner.

Left — The enormous 5,000 ft (1,500 m) east wall of the Fortress is perhaps the greatest rock face in South America. It overshadows the tiny campsite among the moraines of the northern cwm. Don Whillans is seen preparing for an attempt on the Central Tower. The left-hand buttress of the Fortress was climbed in a thirteen day push by Myhill, Burke and Horlov in 1979.

The whole range is little bigger than Snowdonia but the highest peak, the Paine Grande, is over 10,000 ft (3,000 m) high. It is bounded on three sides by the Rio Paine which is born high above Lago Dickson, and flows along the northern and eastern flanks of the range before turning sharply west into Lago Nordenskjold which is the southern boundary of the park. The western boundary is formed by Glacier Grey and Lago Grey. The name 'Paine' coming from the Teheulche dialect, actually means pink, and the Towers can appear either pink, orange or violet depending on the conditions when you see them.

On entry to the National Park you now have to pay a small fee to the Park Rangers and inform them of your intentions. They will give advice and maps of the area, and permission to camp outside the three main camping sites at Pehoe, Serrano and Laguna Azul. There is now a circular trek around the whole massif, which, using a series of rudimentary huts for accommodation, would take about a week. My suggestion, however, to the would-be trekker is to combine light-weight camping with the possible use of the huts. This will enable you to

make a series of excursions right into the heart of the massif as well as taking in the very best of the round trip. How much you accomplish will, of course, depend on the weather, the length of time at your disposal and your personal ambitions.

The best bases for the walker are at either Laguna Amarga in the east or Pudeto in the west. I suggest you start at Laguna Amarga, the bitter lake, from where the view of the Towers is simply superb, offering one the traditional tourist photo spots. The waters are probably the warmest in the whole province, and I have heard of people bathing here, emerging refreshed but caked with white salt deposits!

You can camp here at Amarga, or preferably, ask permission at the Ranger House to drive on towards Estancia Cerro Paine, where all the early expeditions had their base camps. After crossing the Rio Paine on the iron bridge built by an English company in 1928, the road deteriorates over the final five miles (eight kms) to Cerro

Paine Grande, the highest summit in the range, is seen from Pudeto.

Paine. The farm is in a marvellous, sheltered situation, nestling under the Paine Chico, close to the Rio Ascencio. It is a simple, two-storeyed, stone-built house, with red-topped, corrugated iron buildings and wooden sheep pens. In a sheltered copse nearby was our base camp for the summers of 1960–61 and 1962–63.

In those far-off days we enjoyed the typically wonderful Patagonian hospitality of the owners, Juan and Pedro Radic, who were great and colourful characters. They spoiled us with delicious lamb *asados*, washed down with gallons of red Chilean wine, as we relaxed in base after hard days battling against the elements high on the mountains above.

The map issued by the Park shows the trail to the Towers, from Laguna Armaga, passing north of Cerro Paine and up the right bank of the Ascencio River. The most direct way, and the one we always used, is past the farm and across the river by a simple bridge a short distance away. From here we climbed steeply up the left bank as the river dropped through a deep, black shaley gorge beneath. This slope up the lower flanks of the Paine Chico was always known as 'the Grind' as, inevitably, we were staggering under huge rucksacks laden with climbing gear and supplies. The hillside is littered with dead trees, burned down years ago by settlers and blown into incongruous shapes. At the top of 'the Grind', perhaps 1,500 ft (500 m) above the farm, cairns and faint tracks lead across steep, black scree slopes back towards the river. As you continue through the dense forest and glades, you may come across the remains of campsites used by other climbing expeditions. Sadly I have read recently of piles of trash disfiguring the hillsides here-abouts, a sad reflection perhaps of growing popularity and lack of respect. After a further half an hour through the trees, you emerge onto a huge, boulder-strewn slope, the top of the Central Tower appearing high and invincible on the left.

On my first expedition we had our Camp 1 at the far end of this boulder field, close to the river and directly below the gully leading to the Towers. I well recall, all these years later, the first time we scrambled up those boulders into the eastern cwm. As we reached the top of the scree-covered gully, the three great Towers surged into view and we were amazed, chastened and horrified by the sheer size and scale of these stupendous peaks. The Central Tower, or 'Big Ned' as we affectionately christened him, dominated the scene, his 4,000 ft (1,200 m) east face rising steep and sheer from the glacier and tiny turquoise lake beneath.

It will always be for me the most incredible,

magnificent mountain scene I have ever contemplated – quite simply a view to wonder at. The air was still and crystal clear, the towers red and orange against the brilliant blue background, the only sound made by icy fragments dropping into the glacial lake below. We young climbers collapsed in almost hysterical laughter at our presumption that we could actually attempt such impossibly steep and ferocious faces.

At that time only the smaller North Tower had been climbed, by Italian millionaire Guido Monzino's team in 1958. We were to reconnoitre and attempt the South Tower unsuccessfully for several weeks in appalling weather, before conceding defeat. But two years later we returned with a stronger team. Then, in January 1963, the two finest British mountaineers of that era, Don Whillans and Chris Bonington reached the summit of the Central Tower after a six week siege, claiming the greatest prize in the southern Andes just one day before a competing Italian team. These same Italians climbed the South Tower soon afterwards while Ian Clough and I made the third ascent of the North. Since then new routes have been made, the most remarkable climb being directly up that great east face of the Central Tower by Paul Fatti's South African team in 1974.

You will often find yourself pausing to take photos and reflect on the history of these early ascents as you gaze on this incredibly beautiful and awesome panorama. From here you may wish to scramble back down to the lush greenery of the valley and the comforts of base, but if the weather is good, stay high and venture further up the Ascencio into the heart of the massif, the valley behind the Towers, where you will find scenery of similar grandeur and savagery.

Barrie Page and I were the first British climbers to enter this northern cwm. We had continued beyond our Camp 1, picking our way through the dense beech forest in an exploratory mood. Just as we were murmuring to ourselves such sentiments as 'where no man has trod', we were astonished to come upon a little log cabin in a clearing with about 30 signatures carved on the walls, dating from 1928! Pedro Radic later told us that his *gauchos* would have been up there hunting for pumas. Although we sometimes followed their tracks, we were thankful that we never actually saw one of these great cats near our camps. In contrast, we were plagued at times by thieving wood mice!

It was cold and blustery as we emerged from the tree line, scrambled up the steep riverbed through a chaos of boulders, and looked up the valley. At its head were two more enormous and

unknown mountains whose sheer granite walls seemed even to dwarf the Towers. Nearer, and to the right, was a triple-buttressed, black, sedimentary peak. Looking for a British flavour to name these 'Torres Innominatas' we called the nearest peak Britannia's 'Trident', and the other two became her 'Shield' and her 'Fortress', and so we put these now famous mountains on the map. Shortly afterwards we were to make the first ascent of the 'Trident', which must be the only relatively easy major peak to climb in the area, being mainly a long snow plod, followed by some easy but loose rock pitches to the shaley summit.

To be in this desolate cwm is a fantastic experience. As you walk up the glacial moraine you will see the approach we found to reach the Central Tower. We had our camps beneath the North Tower, surviving for weeks in snow holes and under boulders as our tents were destroyed by the relentless winds, at times so strong we had to lie on the ground clutching boulders to stop being blown away. It was up here that the concept of the Box Tent was brilliantly conceived by Don Whillans. Using fence posts from Radic's farm and an I.C.I. tarpaulin, the original 'Whillans' Box' was created by Don and Vic Bray far below in Base. We then carried it up in sections through the twelve miles (20 kms) of forest and moraine to erect it high on the flanks of 'Big Ned'. The Brittania Hut or 'Hotel Brittanico' was our 'secret weapon' in the competition against the Italians and the starting point for the successful ascent. It enabled a pair of climbers to survive in reasonable comfort and security the full fury of the Patagonian storms while waiting for a good day to arrive. Similar purpose-built box tents were to play a major role in Patagonian and Himalayan expeditions for the next 15 years.

Camping up here beneath the Towers, Vic and I often used to joke about our recurrent nightmare of being stranded, alone in the middle of the great Fortress wall. 5,000 ft (1,500 m) high and completely sheer, it is probably the greatest rock face in South America and it was an outstanding achievement when three young British climbers, Keith Myhill, Phil Burke and Mick Horlov made a route up its left-hand buttress in a continuous 13 day push in 1979.

The Towers of Paine rise dramatically from the glacier and tiny lake in the eastern cwm above the Ascencio Valley. The Central Tower — one of the greatest mountaineering prizes in the Andes — was first climbed by Don Whillans and Chris Bonington in 1963 from the col on its right — the 'Notch' — that separates it from the North Tower.

If the weather is calm you may decide to camp on the moraine up here among the peaks. An alternative is to retreat below the tree line, where we pulled back our Advance Base in 1963. Even here on New Year's Day, at the height of the Patagonian summer, we had six inches (15 cms) of fresh snow, followed by devastating storms the next day. Travelling light, you can, of course, do the whole trek into the northern cwm in one very long day from Cerro Paine and be back the same evening.

After returning to Cerro Paine or Laguna Amarga you should next consider exploring the Rio Frances Valley and the western cwm. The quickest and easiest approach to the Frances is from Pudeto at the south-west tip of Lake Nordenskjold, where there is a hut and Ranger house. From here, a three-hour walk around the western end of the lake leads to the Frances campsites. Alternatively you can walk to the Rio Frances in about five hours along the northern shores of Nordenskjold.

The drive or trek along the dirt road from Amarga to Pudeto is understandably a great scenic attraction. On one occasion I was able to film a whole family of rhea — the South American ostrich — scuttling for dear life along the road in front of my van. On the horizon a herd of guanaco were grazing, the leader, head erect, nervously sniffing the air, sensing danger. Shortly afterwards we stopped again to film a pair of black and white skunks gambolling in the scrub by the roadside.

You pass tiny green lakes teeming with wildlife of all kinds, including pink flamingoes and black-necked swans. Meanwhile a magnificent mountain panorama is gradually unfolding, the rugged, black-capped Cuernos, those 'monstrous horns', and the massive, ice-encrusted Paine Grande. Rounding a final bend you see the suspension bridge and the corrugated iron shack of Pudeto. It is a marvellous spot, close to a spectacular waterfall, the Salto Grande, where the waters of Nordenskjold flow into Lago Pehoe.

The walk along the northern shore of Nordenskjold passes directly beneath the great bulk of Paine Chico and the Cuernos, sometimes following the waterline and sometimes a few hundred feet higher on the rough hillside. Nordenskjold is a deep, cold, forbidding lake, and very dangerous, because of the sudden squalls which can whip the waves into swirling water spouts — the treacherous 'williwaws'. Tragedy overcame our first expedition in February 1961 when our young leader, Peter Henry, was drowned when his small boat capsized during a crossing from the Frances campsite back to base at Cerro Paine. Despite searching for days, ironically in brilliant sunshine with the lake mirror calm, we never found Peter's body or the boat. Small items of wreckage were washed ashore in a lovely bay halfway along the lake and near here, on the highest point of a peninsula, we set up a cross with Peter's name inscribed and his ice axe firmly attached.

The last time I trudged past here was when Barrie Page and I made a lightning weekend trip from Punta Arenas to attempt the smaller, right-hand Cuerno. The rain began as we pitched our tent at its foot and continued all night. With snow falling on the high peaks we switched our objective to the 'Little Nobbler', the 'baby' Cuerno just above. By next morning, even this was out of the question in the continued downpour, so we packed away our sodden gear and tramped back to Cerro Paine. I wonder if they've been climbed yet?

The Frances campsites offer good shelter and have been well used by numerous climbers since the '50s. It was from here that the first attempt on the Paine Grande ended in disaster in 1954, when two Argentine climbers were avalanched from high on the enormous, complex face above. I remember this camp as a rather gloomy place, perhaps there were too many storms while I was there, too many rumblings of avalanche far above, too many disappointing retreats from the South Tower or Cuernos. On my expeditions this was always a 'dump' camp, a staging post on the way to attempts on the west ridge of the South Tower or the Fortress higher up the valley. But, as always there is an abundance of wood for campfires and attractive bird life – bright green parrots and glossy black woodpeckers – inhabits the beech woods. There were three groups operating from this valley in 1968, all of which were successful in achieving major first ascents. Ian Clough's British party climbed the Fortress in January while a few weeks later, Italians climbed the Shield and the Chileans the Cuernos Principal.

The trek from the Camp through the dense, twisted forest up the Frances Valley can be heavy going, but you are well rewarded with magnificent views as you gain height. High on your right is a whole new range of jagged Aiguilles stretching from the Cuernos towards the South Tower. We gave them evocative names like 'Hot Alf', 'the Blade' and 'the Mummer' from the racy American detective novels we were reading at the time, but we later reluctantly changed 'Alf's' name to the more acceptable 'Sword'. All were climbed for the first time in the '70s. The massive five mile (eight kms) snow and ice wall of the Paine

Grande dominates the opposite side of the valley. After a couple of hours you will pass through our Advance Base of 1968 and, soon afterwards, emerge above the trees into the remote, boulder-strewn upper basin. Directly ahead is the huge monolithic wedge of orange-grey granite that is the Fortress, showing the ascent route of '68 up the left skyline. Beyond is the Shield and then the head of the valley terminates with the Indian's Head, the Twins and Cerro Negro which are all more conventionally shaped peaks of black rock. Further left, a series of grey granite peaks run northwards from the Paine Grande forming the west wall of the upper Frances basin. The most elegant of these we called the 'Cathedral', for it rises high above the others and looks for all the world like the dome of a great medieval church. Its superb 3,000 ft (900 m) sheer wall drops straight to the valley floor. Up on the right, a high glacier leads to the west ridge of the South Tower which we had hopefully, but mistakenly, thought would be a reasonable climbing option back in '61.

After yet another photographic extravaganza, retrace your steps through the forests, pick up the gear at the campsite, and carefully cross the river by the camp, perhaps with some difficult boulder-hopping and wading. It is always important to carry a rope for security in case the rivers are in spate. Continue now along the western end of Nordenskjold then follow the path east to Pudeto.

The Salto Grande, or Great Waterfall, at Pudeto is a major attraction of the Park, offering spectacular views of the Cuernos and Paine Grande across the green waters of Nordenskjold. The most famous visitor to our Base Camp there was the Soviet poet Yevgeny Yevtushenko who chatted for half an hour, then signed his autograph adding 'From Russia with Love'. A few miles further south by the official campsite, there is excellent fishing at the Salto Chico and it gets even better along the Rio Serrano, where even a novice fisherman like myself managed to land a five pound ($2\frac{1}{4}$ kgs) salmon trout. In this area the needs of more affluent visitors are catered for by two guest houses, the Hosteria Serrano on the northern shores of Lago Toro, which is reasonably priced, while the Hosteria Pehoe is in the luxury class.

After suitable rest and relaxation at Pudeto prepare yourself for the final stages of your walk around the Paine. If you have time, are ambitious, and are fortunate with the weather, this will lead you right around the massif in four or five strenuous days back to the starting point at Laguna Amarga. If, however, you have been battered by the wind and forced to endure too many 'rest' days, you may prefer to stick to the classic and deservedly popular trek to the Ventisquero Grey (Grey Glacier). You start by retracing your steps along the shores of Nordenskjold, pass between the northern tip of Pehoe and Lago Skottsberg, then stop for midday break by the first shepherd's hut. You will soon see Lago Grey and the glacier six miles (ten kms) ahead. Continue above the lake, through the trees and scrub, passing the base campsite of Guido Monzino's expedition which made the first ascent of the Paine Grande up this great west face in 1957. I first made this trek to the Grey with some Czech mountaineers, returning the same way the following year to attempt the Cathedral from the upper Olguin Glacier. On several occasions we were shadowed by enormous condors with twelve foot (3.7 m) wingspans, which hovered gracefully on the air currents above our heads. The unforgettable opening sequence of the TV series *Flight of the*

Condor brought memories flooding back, for it shows the dramatic slow movement of these majestic creatures against the stark, ethereal backdrop of the Paine Towers.

As you walk along the lake, you will see bluish-white icebergs which have broken off the ice-cliffs at the neck of the glacier slowly floating down. A primitive, two-roomed log cabin is situated at the end of the lake near the glacier snout and I well remember the pleasant evening I spent there in the company of my friend, Miroslav Rozehnal, a veteran of many Czech expeditions to different parts of the world.

The route next day is really memorable as the rough path, only faintly marked, climbs from a few hundred yards beyond the hut above the true left bank of the great glacier, a creaking, tangled maze of shattered ice, towards a pass leading over the shoulder of Cerro Blanco to the Paine Valley, on the northern flank of the massif. Once the trees thin out, there are stone cairns to mark the way up to the col — an ascent of five or

In the corral at Patagonia Estancia.

Above *– The Calafate bush (Berberis empetrifolia)*
grows throughout the region and is seen here growing
close by the snout of the Glacier Grey.
Photo: Colin Monteath.

Above right *– The Grey glacier meets the lake in a*
tumbled and tortuous mass of bizarre ice shapes. This
is a perfect place to pause and consult the map, close
to the Rifugio Grey. Photo: Colin Monteath.

six hours – an imposing place with incredible views that might just as well be the end of the world. The descent leads down the shaley slopes and through patches of bushes, almost eastwards now, into the beautiful and remote glen of the Rio de los Perros, hung with waterfalls and surrounded by glaciers and a jumble of moraines. Apparently the name commemorates some sheepdogs drowned while crossing the river.

Follow the river into a fine forest where, eventually, you will find a rough trail which leads down to the little refugio at the southern end of Lago Dickson. According to the Park information brochure, this is a 14 hour trek, but that assumes the track is in good order and that the couple of river crossings involved present no problems. In any case, it is a long, hard day. There are several possible campsites on and near the pass should you decide to break it up. It would be advisable to consult the rangers as to the state of the trail and other potential difficulties before setting out as this is very remote country and no place to hit trouble.

Another enormous, glinting glacier, the Ventisquero Dickson, flows down southwards from the ice cap into Lago Dickson and a visit to its snout, complete with ice caves, via the pretty western shore of the lake, makes an interesting side trip, probably taking two days. The ice cap that births the glacier is the renowned Hielo Sur, some 200 miles (320 kms) long and the larger of the two vast ice sheets that crown the continental divide in Patagonia.

From the little Refugio Dickson, the trail continues intermittently, but over easier ground, generally following the river – now the Rio Paine itself – towards Lago Paine. From this side the great rock spires look very different, but still recognisable are the Cabeza del Indio (Indian's Head) and the Shield Wall. Here, between these two lakes on the sunny northern flank of the massif, the magical calafate bush, heavy with berries, grows in abundance and perhaps this is where, having eaten your fill, Patagonia will finally seduce you ... if it hasn't already done so!

It is possible to reach Laguna Amarga in one ten hour day, but this is a place to linger and a more enjoyable plan is to stop over at the more elaborate ranger's cabin at the eastern end of Lago Paine, a hike of around five hours from Lago Dickson. One can then complete the journey along the trail beside the Rio Paine or by the dirt road via Laguna Azul – the 'Blue Lake'. Either way, the route leads through meadows bright with foxgloves and other flowers from where the three Paine Towers are seen from a new angle, strikingly handsome, and ever awesome.

It is unlikely that Patagonia will ever achieve the popularity for European trekkers enjoyed by many of the other great ranges. The distance is too great, the cost too high and the weather too uncertain to attract visitors in large numbers. And long may this be so. But if you are one of the discerning few who decide to travel to the Paine you will be rewarded with mountain scenery as dramatically beautiful as any in the world. You may also be fortunate and enjoy several days of superb walking in balmy sunshine and light breezes. Personally, I can't wait to go back.

Difficulties/dangers

There are no altitude or acclimatization problems. The usual trails are quite well marked by the Park Rangers, but the treks up the Ascencio and Frances Valleys involve strenuous walking and boulder scrambling. You should seek advice before you decide to go north of the Grey Hut towards Lago Dickson.

Crampons and ice-axes are not necessary unless you intend to go onto a glacier or/and ice-cap.

River crossings can be difficult, especially crossing the Rio Frances by the campsite. Carry a short, light (60 ft/20 m) rope for security.

There are no porters available but you may be able to hire horses at Laguna Amarga or Pudeto.

Pitch camps in sheltered locations.

Season/weather

The best time to go is during the summer, from late November to early March. Temperatures can be as high as an average northern British summer, but are often moderated by the wind. Laguna Azul on the eastern side of the range has its own micro-climate with temperatures up into the 80s°F (30°C). Cold is not really a problem unless you are caught in a storm high up in the valleys. The major weather problem is, of course, the wind which can reach in excess of 100 mph (160 kph).

Equipment

Normal warm mountain clothing, fully wind and waterproof, such as one would use in Scotland, is essential. Strong walking boots, good quality sleeping bag and light weight mountaineering tents. Normal food supplies can be bought in the supermarkets and corner shops in Punta Arenas but no food is currently available in the Park itself, save the meals served in the *hosteria*.

Access/permits

The Paine National Park is under the care of CONAF (*Corporation Nacional Forestal*). A small fee is payable on entry to the Park. Friendly and helpful rangers offer advice and guidance information, but there is no trekking service available.

Foreign climbing expeditions require a prior permit from DIFROL (*Direccion de Fronteras y Limites*).

How to get there

Regular daily flights by Lan Chile or Ladeco from Santiago to Punta Arenas.

Approx. cost (1987): US$132 single $268 return

Daily Bus Service from Punta Arenas to Puerto Natales. Bus and truck services from Natales to the Paine Park do exist but currently seem to operate on a weekly basis.

The little log cabin discovered in a clearing beyond camp 1, used by gauchos on hunting trips.

Car rental is available in Punta Arenas from Hertz or Club Automovil de Chile. Assistance with bus services and other transport problems can be obtained from Turismo Paine, Calle Eberhardt, Puerto Natales.

Where to stay

There are plenty of hotels in Punta Arenas – from the luxury 'Cabo de Hornos' at US$57 daily for a single room, down to more basic accommodation.

Hotel 'Eberhardt' in Puerto Natales and guest houses at Estancias Dos Lagunas and Cerro Castillo.

In the Paine – luxury Hosteria Pehoe and more reasonably priced Hosteria Serrano.

The main campsite at Lago Penhoe is equipped with toilets and running water and there are hot showers at the Park Admin. Centre by Lago Toro. There are other official campsites at Serrano, Laguna Azul and Laguna Verde, but you can ask CONAF for permission to camp in other places.

There are a number of basic huts or bothies in the Paine including those at Pudeto, Glacier Grey, Lago Paine, Lago Dickson and Laguna Amarga.

Medical considerations

There should be no real problems. The Ranger bases offer first aid facilities and they are in radio contact with the Administrative Centre. There is a doctor at Cerro Castillo and there are hospitals at Puerto Natales and Punta Arenas.

Reading

Various booklets/brochures and maps are available from the Tourist Office: Direccion Regional de Turismo, Waldo Seguel 689, Casilla 106D, Punta Arenas.

The best general guide to the area (in Spanish) is *Magallanes y Canales Fueguinos* – A de Agostini (Punta Arenas, 1960). Also *Andes Patagonicos* by A de Agostini (Buenos Aires, 1945).

For descriptions of the climbs in the Paine, see *Alpine Journals* 1963, '69, '73, '75, '79 and Special Edition of *Mountaincraft* (forerunner of *Mountain Magazine*), 1968.
The Next Horizon – Chris Bonington (Gollancz, 1973) describes the first

ascent of the Central Tower.
Across Patagonia – Lady Florence Dixie (London, 1880)
Land of Tempest – Eric Shipton (Hodder & Stoughton, 1963)
Mischief in Patagonia – H W Tilman (Gollancz, 1957)
In Patagonia – Bruce Chatwyn (Jonathan Cape, 1977, and Picador)
The Uttermost Part of the Earth – E Lucas Bridges (Hodder & Stoughton, 1948) – a marvellous book describing the Indians of Tierra del Fuego.
Chilean Scrapbook – S Clissold (The Cresset Press, London, 1950)
The Flight of the Condor – Michael Andrews (Collins/BBC Publications, 1982)
The South American Handbook – Edited by Andrew Marshall (Trade & Travel Publications Ltd, annual)
Backpacking in Chile and Argentina plus the Falkland Islands – Hilary Bradt and John Pilkington (Bradt Enterprises, Chalfont St Peter and Boston, 1980)

Derek Walker's love of the mountains began in the Lake District and Snowdonia while still at school. During National Service he began climbing seriously as a member of the RAF Mountain Rescue Team in North Wales. He then became President of the University of Bristol Mountain Club, and soon after graduating in History in 1960, was invited to join the South Patagonia Survey Expedition. Two years later he organized a second expedition which climbed the Central Tower of the Paine. From 1966–70 he was Headmaster of the British School in Punta Arenas, during which time he took part in the Fortress expedition and attempted other peaks including the Cathedral.

He now teaches in Cheshire and his love and enthusiasm for the mountains remains unabated. He was President of the Climbers' Club from 1984–87, and is chairman of the Don Whillans Memorial Fund.

ROYAL ROAD
OF THE INCAS

by Christopher Portway

ROYAL ROAD OF THE INCAS

'. . . the roads of the Incas were the most useful and stupendous works ever executed by man.'
Alexander von Humboldt, 1769–1859

The Royal Road, in spite of its grand name, is more than ever, an adventure trek. Except for some remote portions there is no set path, even in the most rudimentary sense, since, for much of it, the exact location of the historic road is unknown to this day. Thus a great deal of preparation and pre-departure research is vital and much of the itinerary is open to conjecture and whim.

Of all historic roads, those built by the Incas of the Andean lands must rank as the most evocative. The coastal route is now buried under tarmac and a welter of excruciating South American traffic, leaving only the parallel trans-Andean Royal Road as an extended artery of historic significance that one can attempt to follow in the fastness of the mountains. Lateral roads, linking these two main highways, there are in plenty and one of them, the Inca Trail to Machu Picchu, is itself a well-known hiking route that can be traversed in three to four days.

All who go to Peru today find their way to Cuzco. It breathes its Inca history as can no other place throughout the Andean countries. Founded by Manco Capac about AD 1100, it has become a shrine to the Incas, where the visitor can do the rounds of exciting museums, memorials and edifices. Almost every street holds a remnant of Incaic wall, a miracle of construction, that is shown to perfection at Sacsahuaman, the massive fortress standing guard above the northern outskirts of the city. This amazing structure is a third of a mile long and includes terraced walls of monolithic blocks, some weighing up to a hundred tons. Yet, without benefit of the wheel or mortar, each fits together so perfectly that even a razor blade cannot be inserted between them.

The Royal Road is forgotten at Cuzco. It creeps out of the back-side of the city to begin its mammoth 1,200 mile (1,900 km) journey to Quito, its departure marked by nothing more permanent than a refuse dump. Clear of the tightly-packed slum dwellings, not shown in the tourist brochures, it becomes the hard core for a dust road that wanders lamely towards the great panoply of mountain ranges shining white in the sun. As David and I strode buoyantly towards their straining peaks our footsteps rang out like those of Fransico Pizarro's Spanish *Conquistadores* – even if they were going the other way.

There were any number of civilizations in South America before the 15th century but none made so great an impact as the Inca. Until its conquest in 1532 little was known about this incredibly advanced civilization. It is now only legend that tells how Manco Capac, the first Inca leader, emerged from the Land of the Sunrise carrying a wedge of gold which, periodically, he laid upon the ground as if in anticipation of a sign. Arriving in the valley of the River Vilcanota the wedge sank abruptly out of sight, signalling that Manco had reached the centre of the earth. With the help of the local Quechua tribe he raised a city they called Cuzco.

For at least a century the first Inca and his descendants lived peacefully in their valley. But then marauding penetrations by envious neighbours grew increasingly serious and forced the Inca onto the offensive. It was the formidable Pachacuti who began the great military expansion of the empire in the mid-15th century and his successor, Topa Inca, who finished the job by conquering or bringing into subjugation all the lands from the equator down to what is now modern Chile and from the Pacific shore to the Amazon jungle. Their territory now covered nearly half a million square miles and they called it *Tahuantinsuyu*, the Four Quarters of the Earth.

In order to hold the huge realm together and convert great territories of mountain, desert and jungle into the close-knit empire it became, communications had to be of the highest order. The result was the Inca Road. The only comparable systems ever built have been the Roman and Persian highway networks in Europe and the Middle East. Though the Roman roads, mile by mile, could claim to be longest, the Andean Royal Road, with its extensions south of Cuzco and north of Quito, was the longest continuous artery, a mind-boggling 3,250 miles (5,200 kms) in length. Roughly parallel to it ran the coastal road beginning at Tumbes in present-day Peru and ending at the River Mawle in Chile. Today, time and modern roads – especially the Pan-American Highway along the coast – have obliterated much of what has gone before, except in the remoteness of the Peruvian Andes. Even at Cuzco, where the great road construction programme started, there is little to see, though a bannister of relics marks the early stages of the Royal Road north.

Limatambo is the first such landmark. Here, hidden from the shameful little dirt road that carries today's sparse traffic, is all that remains of the Inca temple of Tarahuasi, which also served as a resting place – or *tambo* – for Inca travellers. The ruin is a fine one, another good example of the shaping and placing of those huge stones,

100

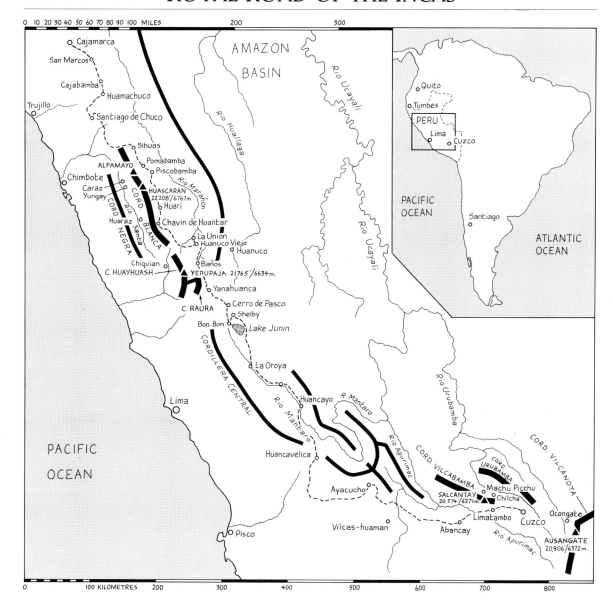

and amongst them David and I put down our sleeping bags for the night.

The *tambos* were official posthouses built at intervals along the Inca roads at, to quote a traveller of the period, '*every four to six leagues (12 to 18 miles, 19 to 29 kms) each with a great abundance of all provisions that the surrounding districts could supply*'. Some, especially those not adjoining temples, were strictly utilitarian, consisting of a low structure of adobe or rough field stone. Others were larger, containing several rooms, and opening out onto a corral for llamas and other beasts of burden.

In spite of our heavy packs we made light of the first 70 miles (110 kms). The ground was level and the little road led straight and true so that all we had to do was follow it to the Apurimac Gorge which, for centuries, held the

northward Inca conquests in check. The ancient supports of an Inca suspension bridge offered mute evidence that the Royal Road had come this way. Its stone foundations, together with the later colonial structure, remain to be immortalized in Thornton Wilder's novel, *The Bridge of San Luis Rey*.

Near Abancay we took a clapped-out bus that crawled along a snake of a road that was certainly not Incain, through country that reminded me of England's Northumbria, until near Ayacucho, the vehicle gave up the ghost and us the impetus to take to our feet once more. In this manner we came upon Vilcas-huaman.

The ruins of Vilcas are far more dramatic than those of Tarahuasi. Not for nothing was it styled the 'Hawk's Sanctuary' standing, as it does, at

As we progressed northward, village dwellings became more substantially constructed from worked stone taken from ancient ruins and, possibly, the Royal Road. Most were roofed with grass thatch but the living conditions in these hovels were still surely worse than those in the time of the Incas; entire households sleeping in one room.

11,000 ft (3,400 m) on a plateau above the Vischongo River. The temple, or what is left of it, consists of a truncated pyramid, impressive in its massiveness, that is gained by a set of dignified steps and a stone doorway of imperialistic hauteur. From the top of the steps the outlines of the immense plaza can be discerned, but the drama of the place stems, as at Machu Picchu, from its loneliness and isolation, though the surrounding countryside is very different and Vilcas has no visitors.

It is not until Lake Junin, beyond the industrial town of La Oroya, that the Royal Road becomes apparent to any substantial degree.

Some ten miles (16 kms) from the village of Shelby, and close to the modern dam that holds in check the Mantaro River as it flows from the north end of Lake Junin, are the ruins of Bon-Bon. Together with the remains of another suspension bridge of Inca origin, this one-time administrative centre was the hub of three roads, though we were able to see only one, etched into the grass of the flat Pampa de Junin with its distant walls of sharp-toothed mountains. The stone foundation of what is left of the huge plaza, a collection of what might have been Inca council houses, and a reviewing platform bright with wild flowers offered an idea of the scene 500 years ago. The only inhabitants today are grazing sheep.

An altitude in excess of 12,000 ft (3,600 m) did little to encourage our plodding footsteps as we made for the township of Yanahuanca. We had spent two nights in and around Bon-Bon, investigating the ruins and trying to adjust to our excruciating loads. That we had overestimated our strength and underestimated the effect of altitude was fast becoming apparent, while the way had become stonier and less positive. We found temporary relief for our shoulders from Carlos, a youth possessing a heavy-framed bicycle, who had befriended us on the *pampa*. Our bags strapped insecurely to his machine the three of us processed towards Yanahuanca, by-passing the centre of Cerro de Pasco, and in three days reached the township huddling under storm clouds.

From Yuanahuanca the Royal Road stomps northward towards Huari for well over 100 miles (160 kms). Plain to see, it is even marked on two sheets of the large-scale Lima Geographical Institute maps. The great artery, displaying its varying construction characteristics to suit the differing terrain makes no bones of the gradients it meets. Tunnelling through outcrops of rock or changing its grass surface and stone paving for well-laid steps it goes where no other road dares to tread. Efficient drainage systems to deal with every rivulet or stream – for in the Andes rivers shift their banks with callous ease – are still in use today. A width of 16 or more feet (4.8 n), the road only reduced itself to less where geography decreed.

At tiny Huarautambo, utterly exhausted – for Carlos had left us at Yanahuanca – we remained three days, sleeping at night on the floor of the wretched little village school. By day we explored the Inca and pre-Inca ruins which dotted the hillside. Guided by the village schoolmaster we looked upon mysterious cave paintings and a cavern-tomb full of deformed skulls never before seen by foreign eyes. It was here too that we first met the rumours of buried treasure which haunt those who live along the road. Assuredly there is much buried gold still to be unearthed though only *gringos*, it seems, are immune from the wrath of the Gods if a search is made. David and I promptly got involved in a search, keeping a midnight tryst with a wild-eyed Peruvian who had allegedly seen the tell-tale 'money-light' high in the hills above the village. Alas, we still had to run the risk of more potent earthly jealousies and village wrath but, though we dug all night, we unearthed nothing.

Sometimes behind convoys of itinerant horsemen moving from village to village, but more often following a single pack horse, its owner enticed and bribed into carrying our loads, we trekked on into the mountains suffering the ravages of heat and cold, hunger and fatigue. It was the potato season and we had to compete for our four-legged carriers against the financial benefits of potato-haulage, a situation that frequently left us stranded for days near tiny hamlets like Huarautambo, our small tent perched on the inhospitable mountainside. In the days of the Inca, relays of runners – or *chasquis* – were able to run an average 250 miles (400 kms) a day, relaying messages between Cuzco and Quito within a week. This recorded feat of physical fitness was ever in our minds as we stumbled up rugged slopes, gasping away our last reserves of strength.

The Inca ruins of Tunsucancha, the hot springs near Pilocancha, and the enormous complex of Huanuco Viejo marked the road to the small town of La Union which became, after days of constant discomfort and a diet of potatoes, a mecca towards which we dragged our weary feet. Starvation and exposure were very real dangers in this remote and desolate region in which the incredible majesty of the countryside is the one saving grace. As we were nearing La Union, below the *pampa* on which Huanuco Viejo stands, we almost succumbed to hypothermia when our eagerness to attain the town overcame our sense of caution. Soaked and frozen following a day-long downpour, we attempted to ford a stream by night. In pitch darkness we floundered into the water, not realizing that the rain had raised the level, and were swept downstream in the seething torrent. Gasping and struggling, we eventually gained the opposite shore and took refuge for what was left of the night in the shell of a farmhouse upon which we stumbled, by the grace of God.

La Union, for all its shortcomings, was a balm for three days and, refreshed and rested, we set out again for Huari. No longer was the Royal Road so obvious to the eye, which made the offer from a local horseman to accompany us to a village along the way very welcome indeed.

The climb out of the valley of the River Vizcarna was steep, so steep that our new companion was forced to rein his horse back when we showed sign of lagging. This notwithstanding, David and I were beginning to make better progress, having found our second wind and, by evening, we reached some scattered adobe dwellings that rejoiced in the name of Chogolagran. The hamlet stood at the head of yet another valley, this one that of the River Taparaco, a tributary of the Vizcarra.

The sacred summit of Huayna Picchu rises beyond Machu Picchu.

It now became apparent that our man – Manuel – was a regular commuter on the route and, accordingly, had contacts along the way. Those in Chogolagran were a farming family who offered us their roof but, with five children as well as their livestock under it, we felt we would be straining their resources by accepting. However, our supper of sardines and bread was supplemented by soup and potatoes which they pressed upon us. Manuel displayed the flattened features and Red-Indian coloured face of the Andean but his eyes were more slanting than usual, giving an eastern appearance, while his hair was tinged with grey. The family were born of a younger generation; the father attired in jeans, black shirt and black trilby hat. Their children sat in a row watching our strange cooking operations, their heads cocked to one side like mystified puppies.

The Royal Road closed in towards the narrow river leading us easily along the western flank of the valley. The hamlets of Estanque and San Lorenzo de Isco produced their quota of inquisitive citizens plus a garish cemetery, oddly out of place in so poverty-stricken a neighbourhood. At San Lorenzo, a friend of Manuel's appeared with what I thought was a welcome mug of water but which turned out to be some home-brewed hooch that provided an

eye-watering aperitif for a frugal lunch.

The Road, now appearing again as a well-defined and engineered artery, took full advantage of the contours of the land; seldom was it forced to deviate from the level it first selected when entering the valley. We were walking over low hills, treeless and bare, the wind blowing in unobstructed from the Amazon jungles to set the *ichu* grass in motion. As we marched we spoke of the epic of this rural highway's construction, for only by staggering human effort and endurance could it have been built. And in this particular region, with no rocky outcrops to provide material, the large stone slabs which made up the paved road had to be carried to it over dreary miles of emptiness and natural obstruction.

By late afternoon, weary but jubilant, we reached a scattering of huts called by a name – Taparaco – where a relic of some earlier age was alleged to stand. If so we never found it. But ahead lay the *tambo* of Torococha, some twelve miles (20 kms) distant, a relic of Inca durability.

Close, but not too close, to the wretched houses we bedded down, tentless, in a mound of last year's hay, strong-smelling, slightly putrid and very prickly. Even here we were invited to share in the evening meal provided by a childless couple to whom Manuel appeared to be related. The woman wore plaited hair which she modelled into a castle-like structure upon her head; not at all the usual Indian hair style of single or twin pigtails swinging free. The man constantly chewed a substance that produced a most colourful spit.

Two days of fine weather gave way, on the third, to ominous clouds, but no rain fell. We were on the right bank of the river and, by midday, came to a marshy patch of land that had us dodging between rocks and dry tufts of *ichu* attempting to keep our feet out of the water. We had swung away from the river but the swamp caught us in its slimy maw whatever direction we took. In it we found a nondescript building of ancient vintage but its stones were certainly not Incain, even to my inexperienced eyes. Any further investigation was discouraged by the depressing swamp and I wondered why anyone should choose to build a *tambo* at so moist and inhospitable a spot.

I did not have to wonder for long. Further up the valley were definite signs of road drainage stone formations of obvious Inca origin. No doubt, at some earlier stage, the whole area had been efficiently drained and dry. A ruin that could only have been that of the *tambo* stood, away from any village, dauntingly exposed to the cyclonic winds. It was a square block of a building of substantial stone without windows. Neither of us could find a reason for delaying there for more than ten minutes.

The end of the swamp brought a steady climb out of the valley and somewhere we left behind our river. The parting of the ways came around mid-afternoon, with Manuel bound for a hamlet called Manca Peque a mile off to the right. However, he suggested we accompany him there to spend the night while he used his good offices to arrange for a replacement horse. He didn't have to ask twice.

A lonelier habitation I have yet to see, with everlasting hills bucking away in every direction and not even the drama of a true mountain to quicken the pulse. The night meant a return to the tent and a diet of potatoes moistened with our own uninspiring porridge oats for, all too plainly, the silent, remote folk of Manca Peque existed at near-starvation level, their pinched faces and suspicious eyes devoid of humour and the milk of human compassion. Manuel was plainly unhappy at our reception and although I wondered what reasons brought him here we didn't like to ask. A clutch of ragged children to whom we offered some picture postcards had to be urged to accept them and not the vestige of a smile flitted across their solemn features as they gravely made off with their prize.

Manuel was as good as his word and procured both a horse and a youth to accompany us. The boy, unused to the sly bargaining of his more money-conscious brethren, was content to let Manuel fix the price while Manuel himself charged us only a one-way 'fee' of 300 *soles*.

Socially the lad was not a patch on Manuel, though he was willing enough, but communication was difficult as he spoke only Quechua. The horse was half-mule and the pace was steady as we trudged in near-silence at an altitude of about 13,000 ft, the route firmly sticking to the 4,000 metre contour on our map.

A larger village called Huacayoc, below some great bastions of rock, became the end of the marked 'Camino Incaico', the route of the Royal Road, as marked on the map. From henceforth our eyes and locally-gleaned directions alone would have to show us the way. Where the old road terminated and the modern track began we never learnt for the transfer was a gradual process. Huanacayoc was, by recent standards, a place of some prosperity, for it possessed a couple of shops, and our potato lunch was supported by biscuits that might well have been a leftover from a Spanish soldier's haversack to judge by their antiquity.

If the bigger, more prosperous, village indicated a return to civilization the environment

Right – The llama has a camel's head, large eyes, a split nose, a harelip, no upper teeth and two-toed feet which look cloven but are not. These stylized animals formed the transport on the highways of the Incas. Both photos: John Cleare.

Below – The market places set the tone. Here will be heard both the language of the pale, almost Mongolian Quechua, a sweet, flexible, rhythmic tongue, and that of the Aymara, which is insistent, rough and slow.

showed otherwise. It fast became more difficult and devious while rock outcrops, steep and black, pushed us from one miniscule hamlet to another. People and houses appeared with increasing frequency, it is true, and David, who spoke some Spanish, was forever enquiring in his demanding, no-nonsense fashion, for the whereabouts of the Inca road, although a certain savagery of countryside pinned us to its bidding. The answers received from the locals were baffling. Invariably we were given an affirmative that we were on the right road, corroborated with much head-nodding, but we were well aware that this might mean nothing. Gradually, however, we evolved a system by which we would differentiate the sincerity of an answer from the simple desire to please.

A leaden sky and an icy wind kept us walking hard for warmth and soon after we had heated our ubiquitous porridge one night a thunderstorm struck. We persuaded the lad to come into the tent with us rather than depend upon his woollen *poncho*. This made a tight squeeze but ensured we remained warm and reasonably dry while the thunder rolled among the hills and lightning licked the wet rocks with thongs of fire. Rain hissed down, forcing its way through the light nylon of the tent, finally to cease with uncanny abruptness. We lay uneasily listening to the drips falling about us.

A morning's walk brought us down from the hills past immense boulders, hoary with wet moss, and sections of eroded rock fallen from sheer cliff as if sliced by a giant cheesecutter. The steep descent led to the village of Pomachaca at the bottom of a three-way ravine where two angry rivers met head on to continue their flow as one. David was delighted when his feverish enquiries elicited the fact that, certainly, the Royal Road came through Pomachaca and a villager pointed out the steep escarpment down which we had come.

A patchwork of cultivation mottled the fertile green valley of the Huari River we now followed and the open landscape beyond made a cheerful companion. To the west, the gigantic mountain complex of the Cordillera Blanca occasionally offered a tantalizing glimpse of its highest peaks, evocative with snow and altitude.

Huari is half the size of La Union but its situation overlooking the alpine-like valley is a joy. Impatient to continue and pleased by our progress we had no thoughts of a prolonged stay. Ahead lay another hurdle in the obstacle course of the Andes and it was all too likely that, added to the exertions of walking the Royal Road, would be the exasperations of trying to find it.

Our assumption was all too correct. Hardly had we left Huari before we were searching wildly for signs of the old road. Physical investigation, the questioning of locals, the tracing and identification of ruins was expensive in time and effort and made progress excruciatingly slow. We located sections traversing the crests of high hills above the towns of Piscobamba, Pomabamba and Sihuas as well as a complex of pre-Inca fortresses. At each of these towns we came down from the hills to question their citizens and taste the fruits of urban living while, at Pomabamba, we were dined royally by the chief of police and his North American wife on portions of hard-to-digest guinea-pig and a never-ending supply of luscious oranges and sweet honeycomb from their orchard and beehives.

Three days we remained in Pomabamba, such were its attractions. During this sojourn we were witness to the funeral of our hostess's uncle, murdered by cattle-rustlers who, together with the embryo cells of the Maoist terrorists, the *Sendario Luminoso*, or Shining Path, who are currently troubling Peru, haunted the mountains through which we were passing. This sombre event was a far more effective warning of the danger than the police chief's admonitions.

Between Sihuas and Huamachuco lay more than 60 miles (100 kms) of savage wilderness and our passage across it would, in the light of these unwelcome revelations, have to be made with a maximum of caution. With eyes alert for more than signs of a historic road, we returned to the ridge.

Another town, this one going by the name of Santiago de Chuco, off to our left, drew a rash of tiny villages along a route where the royal highway was nowhere to be found. Here we remained a couple of days, our billet being the local agricultural headquarters where we slept on the floor of one of the offices. Here too we met another unpleasant facet of modern Peru the P.I.O — or Secret Police, who wanted to know why we were staying in their town. Their attentions were as unpalatable as they were alarming and we were happy to escape back to the rustler-infested hills.

Draw a straight line between Pomobamba and Huamachuco and you have, very approximately, the route of the Road. For some 80 miles (130 kms), it traverses a mountain fastness marked a stormy dark brown on our map and crossed by only one rough and rugged dirt track. Somewhere here we hoped to find the royal route.

Whether we ever did over the first half of that line remains inconclusive. Everywhere great ranges hemmed us in, sometimes driving us in any direction except the one we wanted to go.

The pattern of those days amongst the straining peaks changed little. We had already ditched many of the contents of our rucksacks, retaining only those items we deemed vital to survival. There were no villages in sight for days on end and, therefore, no horses. Our switchback progress made it clear that we were moving against the 'grain' of the mountains, crossing valleys and not following them. The path we had found initially petered out and our route became no more than a succession of ridge saddles, each selected by the demand of the compass. The weather remained dry, more by good luck than judgement, for we frequently observed rain falling elsewhere — heavy squalls deluging the peaks within grey mantles of waterlogged cotton wool. Not another living soul or animal did we come across; it was as if we were alone and fortuitously alive in a dead world. Only the great condors, gliding effortlessly overhead, assured us that life still breathed in the universe.

It was while we were atop one of the interminable crests of an afternoon that we *did* spot some fellow beings. There were five of them; five men riding horses or mules, leading pack animals. They were a good mile away and had not seen us, but were coming across our path. There was something about them that prompted caution; a suggestion that these fellow-creatures might not be so glad to see us as we had, initially, been to see them. A grassy ditch offered cover so we crouched down in it and watched the band as they moved nearer. Two of them had rifles slung over their shoulders and, from the direction they were riding, we judged they would pass no nearer than 500 yards (450 m). We remained in position, silent and thoughtful.

As soon as men and beasts were out of sight we moved on again, feeling a little foolish. Maybe they were perfectly innocent riders on legitimate business between villages. Alternatively, we may have avoided having our throats cut.

A while later we came upon some isolated sheep, a sure sign of proximity to human habitation. And not a false sign either, since a ragged, desperately poor little community hove into view with the onset of evening. We camped well away from and out of sight of the place, our suspicions unabated.

In the morning we entered the village warily but the suspicions now belonged to the villagers. The first we saw took hasty refuge in their houses and even the children — usually more inquisitive than timid — took to their heels. It was impossible to get near enough to any of them to attempt a conversation; they just squealed and ran. It was, again, the village schoolmaster who was to inject some sense into the situation.

He was awaiting the arrival of his young charges at the corrugated iron-roofed schoolhouse when we appeared. He spoke a little Spanish and, after words of greeting, David probed his knowledge of Incain matters. The man pointed to the east, to a low range of hills, grass-covered, almost homely in their gentleness. So we were not as far off course as we had feared. We thanked him, a gaunt figure whose round, smiling face contrasted with his angular frame, and shook his hand with exaggerated fervour.

Two hours later we stood on the new crest. And, sure enough, a grass track of familiar straightness probed into the distance. We followed it for many miles until the clarity weakened and faded altogether.

We were reminded again how deceptive are distances in these parts. Sihuas to Huamachuco may have been 60 miles (100 kms) as the crow flies but as two hikers slogged it — weaving about looking for landmarks and avoiding the more impossible walls of granite — it must have been double that. The 20 to 22,000 ft (6,000 to 6,700 m) peaks of the Cordillera Blanca occasionally swung into view, but even at our average height of around 13,000 ft (4,000 m) we were buffeted and half frozen by a succession of high winds, bitterly cold nights and stinging downpours in the days that followed. Only during the late morning did the sun hold any warmth, the ground in the shadows remaining firmly frozen. The thin, stony soil gave a minimum of sustenance to the defiant clumps of coarse, yellowing grasses and alpine plants — some bearing minute flowers — that hugged the ground. There were no trees, only tall ferns or the slow-growing, cactus-like puyas.

In such an environment animals are rare, although many rodents, lizards and birds find cover in the low vegetation, among boulders or in burrows. Yet there are others. We never saw a puma but they exist here as do the guanaco and the fast-running vicuna. These we had seen as we had Andean condors, the largest bird of prey in the world.

How we envied them the freedom of the sky. Our way ahead stretched into infinity, a horrific yet stirring panoply of mountain ranges and eternal escarpments that, we were only too well aware, would give us no respite — even after negotiating those we could make out in the far distance. But there was beauty too, beauty on a gigantic scale coupled with the compelling drama of isolation. Together they offered a compilation of emotions that, on occasions, swelled into a kind of claustrophobia in reverse.

Food, or the lack of it, was an ever-present concern. Whenever we came upon the smallest hamlet we would make efforts to top up with bread and potatoes, all too often the only

We stood on the new crest, our eyes searching the rolling land, and sure enough, a grass track of familiar straightness, softened by a few nature-formed indentations and clusters of flowers, materialised before us, stretching into the distance. Photo: John Cleare.

choices on offer. Our emergency provisions — oatmeal and soup powder — were exhausted by the time Huamachuco began dotting the hillsides with more prosperous villages and a chequerboard of cultivation.

Then gradually the countryside relented, its harsh outline and vast horizons turning to picture-postcard valleys. Remnants of battlefields long ago haunted the slopes north of Huamachuco, into which town we almost ran with relief and gratitude. And on the further long slog to Cajamarca our activities were enlivened by brief sojourns in townships such as Ichocan and San Marcos, where life had more to offer than mere existence. More often than not we spent nights in village police cells or on the earthen floors of private houses to fulfil a craving

to be among our fellow men. Close to Cajamarca, the Royal Road appeared again to lead us by the hand into this remarkable town.

The story of how the small Spanish army under Francisco Pizarro enticed Atahualpa, the Inca chief, into their treacherous ambush at Cajamarca is one of history's great tales. Held to ransom for a roomful of gold, Atahualpa was murdered even while more gold was on the way. Pizarro and his 180 Spaniards then began their march on Cuzco.

For us there was suddenly an abundance of food and the experience was exhilarating. For a while we couldn't believe it as the notion sunk in that we had stumbled nearly 1,000 miles (1,600 km) along the spine of one of the greatest barriers on earth.

The author was to continue his journey on foot, local bus and lorry northwards via Tumbes and, into Ecuador, to Cuenca and Canar, along the Valley of the Volcanoes – ascending nearby 20,561 ft (6,267 m) Chimbarazo en route – and finally to Quito.

The material for this chronicle was abridged from part of the author's book, *Journey Along the Spine of The Andes* (Oxford Illustrated Press).

Huamachuco definitely lies astride the Royal Road of the Incas. The town is frequently mentioned in the chronicles of the Incain conquest. Pizarros's Spanish army having rested here for four days during their southbound march of conquest in August 1533. Its traffic today wears a less martial overtone.

Difficulties/dangers

The Andean Inca Road in the north of Peru passes through extremely savage mountain territory. Travellers are advised, therefore, to take full precautions against starvation and exposure. There is also some risk of attack by cattle rustlers and aggrieved local peasants, particularly in the present climate of unrest and occasional terrorist activity.

In the main, walking is not too difficult, particularly where the old road can be followed. Usual altitudes are around 12,000 ft (c.3,500 m) so an acclimatization period is crucial prior to commencing the trek.

Distances/times

For the full Cuzco to Quito distance measurements are best made in time rather than miles. The most interesting section Inca road-wise is that between Yanahuanca and Huari – about 190 miles (150 kms) as the crow flies – which can be covered inside a fortnight. The whole journey took me three months but this included some side excursions to the coast, a number of prolonged sojourns along the way and a considerable amount of searching for the old highway.

Season/weather

The climate of the Andean highlands is varied; the west side is dry but the northern and eastern parts receive very heavy rains from October to April. I made my journey from the end of this rainy period, commencing in May – a good time for alpine flowers. The prime 'dry' season in the Peruvian Andes is later, from June until mid-September, but some rain and mountain storms are possible at any time. On clear days temperatures even at the height of this trek may rise above 70°F/20°C while frosts can often be expected at night. During the dry season the nights last some eleven hours at this latitude.

For the high Sierra warm clothing should be taken; the difference between day and night temperatures is considerable though it is seldom very warm at high altitudes.

Equipment

Good comfortable trekking boots are essential as well as warm clothing. However, at sea level or lower altitudes the heat can be intense, so some light clothing, shorts etc., should also be carried. A cooking stove and all survival accessories are vital as well as reserves of food, since village sources of provisions are few and far between and, even then, pretty basic. When packing a rucksack a compromise has to be made between what can be reasonably carried and the choice of what one considers to be the vital necessities of life. A compass is a must, as are good maps though even the best of the latter are far from accurate.

Access/permits

There are frequent police checks in towns along the way and foreigners are not permitted close to the Peruvian–Ecuadorian border except at the official crossing points, of which there are few – near Tumbes on the coast is the main one.

Logistics

Both Yanahuanca and Huari are accessible by road and bus services run between the larger townships along the route. Lorries carry passengers, for which their drivers ask a similar fare to those of buses. Such is the wild abandon of the drivers and the state of some of the minor roads it is recommended that the back of lorries is the safest place in which to ride in rural areas – one can jump for one's life when/if the vehicle plunges over a precipice – no rare occurrence in highland Peru. There are good roads from Lima to Cuzco with frequent bus services and also rail links. There is an excellent, regular and not over-expensive air service linking Lima to Cuzco.

Medical considerations

Altitude sickness is the main scourge so acclimatization is vital. Exposure and its result – hypothermia – must always be borne in mind; when soaked by rain *keep walking* and so stay warm – even if exhausted. Local food can cause problems but there is little enough of it to cause them. The nearest hospital could be hundreds of miles away – and anyway will probably be terrible. No vaccinations are required by the Peruvian authorities but typhoid and gamma globulin (against hepatitis) shots are recommended. Although malaria does not occur in the mountains many travellers in Peru do take precautions against the disease which is prevalent at lower altitudes on the Amazon side of the mountains. Water above the village line is safe – there is plenty of rain.

Language

The local tongue is Quechua though some of the inhabitants – especially the schoolmasters – of villages and townships speak and understand a little Spanish.

Reading

Maps:

Large scale map sheets of the region between Cuzco and Quito are difficult to acquire. I purchased mine from the Military Geographic Institute in Lima, but Stanfords in London may well stock the required sheets from time to time, and can obtain them to special order. Two of the sheets – those titled *La Union* and *Huari* – were the only ones to show the route of the *Camino Incaico* (Inca Road).

Guide books:

South American Handbook – (Trade & Travel Publications, annual)

Fodor's Guide to South America (Hodder & Stoughton)

Backpacking & Trekking in Peru & Bolivia – Hilary & George Bradt (Bradt Enterprises)

Literature:

Highway to the Sun – Victor von Hagen (Gollancz)

Realm of the Incas – Victor von Hagen (New American Library)

Conquest of the Incas – John Hemming (Macmillan)

Tears of the Sun God – J H Moore (Faber)

Journey Along the Spine of the Andes – Christopher Portway (Oxford Illustrated Press)

History of the Conquest of Peru – W H Prescott (Weidenfeld & Nicolson)

Eight Feet in the Andes – Dervla Murphy (John Murray)

The Rucksack Man – Sebastian Snow (Hodder & Stoughton)

Half a Dozen of the Other – Sebastian Snow (Hodder & Stoughton)

Four Faces of Peru – Byford Jones (Robert Hale)

Collin's Guide to Mountains & Mountaineering – John Cleare (Collins)

Peru – H E Mellersh (Plata Publishing, Chur, Switzerland)

Other Classic Treks in the Peruvian Andes

The native people of the Andes – like those of the Himalaya – have created over the centuries a network of interconnecting trails linking village to village, to pasture and to market, practical routes over which they have always gone about their daily business. Only in recent years have rough roads and motor vehicles started to usurp the more important of these rugged links.

As in the Himalaya there are also more formal and probably even older highways among the mountains, but whereas in the Old World these are ancient trade routes linking the Indian sub-continent to the bazaars of Central Asia, those of South America are the arteries of a sequence of vanished civilisations, royal roads, military roads, the sinews of long forgotten empires. And nowhere is this more apparent than in Peru whose highlands, once the centre of the Inca civilization, still support a not-inconsiderable population of mountain peasants. Peru also boasts the most impressive scenery and the most beautiful mountains on the continent – with the possible exception of Patagonia, where the weather is as rugged as its mountains – and with easy access from North America and Europe, and comparatively stable politics, the Peruvian Andes have become in recent years a trekkers' paradise.

Obviously one can trek almost anywhere in the Peruvian mountains, but travellers with less time and less of an urge to break new ground should perhaps start with shorter and more classic routes. Certainly the best centre is the charming city of *Cuzco* standing at 11,000 ft (3,300 m) in southern Peru, where any trek in the three great mountain groups that ring the ancient capital – the *Cordilleras Vilcanota, Vilcabamba* and *Urubamba* – can be combined with a heady dose of Inca culture, for this was its very heart and its traces abound on every hillside, in every valley.

The other prime trekking areas are the *Cordilleras Huayhuash* and *Blanca* which lie some 400 miles (650 kms) further north. Unfortunately up here there is no characterful centre like Cuzco and very little added 'piquancy' in the way of Inca remains, while access to both ranges is by a day's long and gruelling road journey from sea-level at Lima.

Cordillera Vilcanota

Seen from Cuzco, the great ice-hung peak of *Ausangate* – at 20,906 ft (6,372 m) the giant of southern Peru – hangs on the south-eastern horizon. A day's journey by bus or truck leads over rough dirt roads to the little town of *Ocongate* and beyond to *Tinqui* village at 12,250 ft (3,730 m), below the northern foot of the forest of considerably smaller but equally spectacular ice peaks that surround Ausangate. The classic trek in the Vilcanota is the circuit of the mountain from this road head, a delightful journey best completed for acclimatization purposes anti-clockwise in about six days, although side trips or climbing diversions can pleasantly extend the trip to a fortnight. There are trails the whole way, the going is never difficult though the two high passes, the *Palomani* and *Pacanta* – both above 16,500 ft (5,050 m) – must be treated seriously. The especial beauty of this area is the contrast between the glinting ice spires and the swelling golden pampa dotted with turquoise tarns and grazed by herds of llama and alpaca. Guides and pack-animals can be hired from Tinqui or from Oconogate.

Cordillera Vilcabamba

Despite being the most famous and popular trek in South America, the so-called *Inca Trail* is a '*must*' – and is a very different trip from the high mountain routes. It follows what is known as the '*brow of the jungle*', keeping well away from the eternal snows of the Vilcabamba and close by Cordillera Urubamba, usually visible in the distance. Basically it follows an ancient Inca road, engineered through extremely rugged country, that links a series of incredible forts and watchtowers to the magnificent ruins of *Machu Picchu* perched above the profound gorges of the Rio Urubamba, and now a National Park. Though longer approaches can be made through the high mountains, it is usual to start the trek at the road head at *Chilca* (9,250 ft/2,820 m) or the lower

'*Km 88*' request halt on the Cuzco – Machu Picchu railway, and the 35 miles (55 kms) or so can be completed easily in three to four days, crossing a couple of 13,000+ ft (4,000 m) passes en route. Tents and cooking stoves are essential and environmental consideration at a premium. A train journey of some 3½ hours returns one to Cuzco with the Machu Picchu day-trippers.

Cordillera Huayhuash

This is a compact knot of mountains whose six 20,000 ft (6,100 m) summits include *Yerupaja* (21,765 ft/6,634 m) – Peru's second highest. An awesome range, it is noted for the savagery of its peaks, for its tortured glaciers and for its wealth of spectacular lakes and tarns, several of them laying claim to be 'The Source of the Amazon' – though that river's *hydrographic* source properly lies in the adjacent Cordillera Ruara. The geography lends itself to a superb – if tough – 100 mile (160 kms) circuit of the range, crossing the continental divide twice while experiencing the subtle differences of the arid western and greener eastern flanks of the Andes. The route traverses no less than eight very high passes up to 16,500 ft (5,030 m). It would be usual to spend at least twelve days on the trek, more if several worthwhile side-trips are taken. While there are frequent lonely settlements it is essential to be completely self-contained and *arrieros* with their *burros* (mules) can be hired from *Llamac*, the last village, or from the little road head town of *Chiquian* a day lower and 20 miles (32 kms) off the main Lima road. Three buses a week link Chiquian to Lima, or a combination of bus and truck might be found for the journey from *Huaraz*, the major town in the area.

Cordillera Blanca

The most extensive of Peru's ranges is a narrow chain of high peaks over 100 miles (160 kms) long, from which rises *Huascaran* (22,208 ft/6,769 m), the second highest summit in all the Americas. Only ten snow-free passes cross the chain from the Pacific to the Amazon flanks and almost any two can be combined to give an enjoyable trek of around a week's duration. Typically the routes link two parallel *quebradas* – deep, glacially carved glens which penetrate far into the mountains and are a feature of the range – via a couple of high passes over the continental divide at around 15,000 ft (4,600 m), to a short section on the eastern slopes of the range. The main centre is *Huaraz* at 10,000 ft (3,050 m), a busy small town on the main road in the Santa Valley where climbers and trekkers are understood and catered for. The range is much more frequented than those mentioned above and lies within the Parque Nacional Huascaran which imposes no onerous regulations but requires registration at the Huarez HQ or other Park offices.

One of the best circuits starts from

Yungay, some 30 miles (50 kms) north of Huaraz, an eerie place where in 1970 an entire town was wiped out by a cataclysmic avalanche, up the profound *Quebrada Llanganuco*, immediately beneath Huascaran and over the 15,640 ft (4,767 m) pass at its head, to the green *Quebrada Huaripampa* on the Amazon flanks. The return leg crosses the rocky *Punta Union* pass to descend the beautiful *Quebrada Santa Cruz* beneath *Alpamayo*, surely one of the world's most shapely mountains, to *Caraz*, back on the main road again. The total distance is about 65 miles (105 kms).

Christopher Portway was born in 1923 in Essex and was educated at Gosfield, Abbotsholme and Felsted schools. At 17 he joined the army and fought in the North-West European Campaign of World War Two. Taken prisoner in Normandy he escaped from camps in Poland, Czechoslovakia and Germany.

A member of the British Guild of Travel Writers, Fellow of the Royal Geographical Society and travel editor of a family magazine, Christopher Portway manages to mix his holiday travel assignments with those of a more expeditionary nature.

Married to a Czech girl whom he spent many years attempting (finally successfully) to extricate from behind the Iron Curtain, he has a son and a daughter and now lives in Brighton. In addition to books, he writes on travel subjects for many newspapers and magazines.

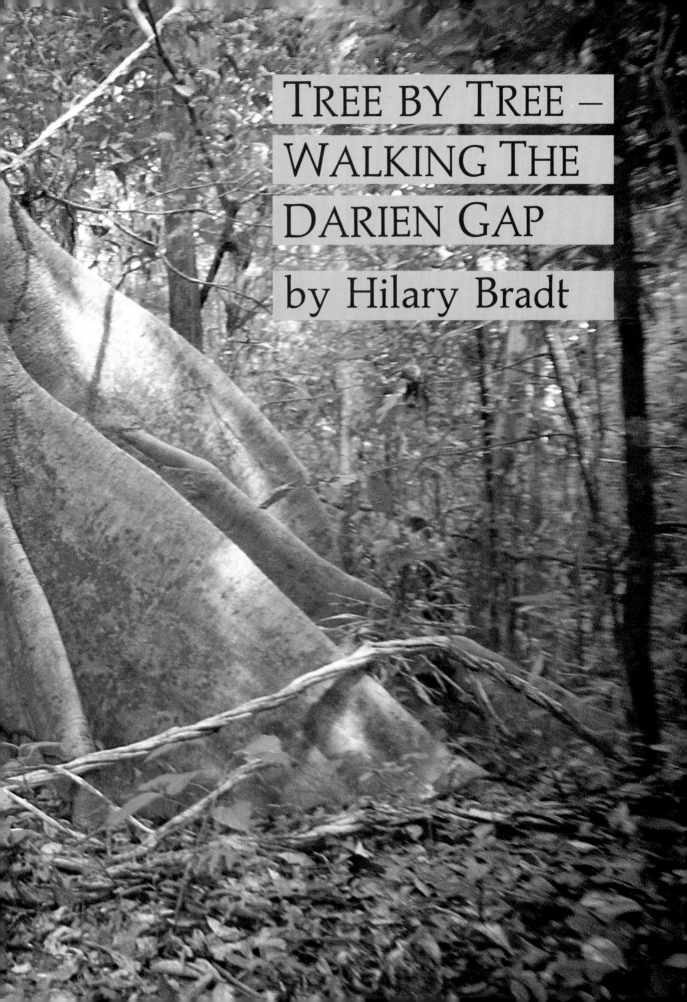

TREE BY TREE – WALKING THE DARIEN GAP

by Hilary Bradt

'In 1972 a team of thirty-three British scientists and soldiers crossed the Darien Gap which took them ninety-nine days. They had to haul their two trucks by rope when the going was too rough, and raft them across the rivers.

At some points they had to hack their way tree by tree through some of the most treacherous territory on earth. The savage jungle has thousands of poisonous snakes lurking in foul swamps, enormous black ants whose sting could make a man numb all day and tarantulas the size of a dinner plate.

The $260,000 expedition was supplied by air drops with food and gasoline. The team lost five men who were sucked to their death in an oozing mud swamp.'

Ernst Jahn, *The Latin America Guide, 1976*

How sad that the jungle is so often seen as an adversary, to be confronted, fought and subdued. Appreciation of the rainforest has increased since Colonel Blashford-Snell's expedition, described above, but few journalists resist the temptation to add 'impenetrable' in front of jungle, and

'fearsome' before most of the creatures that inhabit it. In fact, the rainforest is only impenetrable near rivers or roads where sunlight has caused an unchecked abundance of undergrowth. Within the forest the trees grow tall and straight towards the light, and the jungle can be one of the most beautiful and exciting places on earth.

The Darien Gap links Central America to South America. It was not always thus: about 160 million years ago South America was part of a huge land mass which included Africa and Australasia but not North America. The volcanic activity that gave birth to Central America linked the two Americas much later. Now, that firm land bridge has disappeared and the Atrato Swamps impede the progress of the Pan-American Highway — an otherwise continuous road from Alaska to Tierra del Fuego — and protect one of the last remaining expanses of virgin rainforest north of the Amazon basin.

George and I knew the Darien Gap by name only when we set out to journey from Colombia

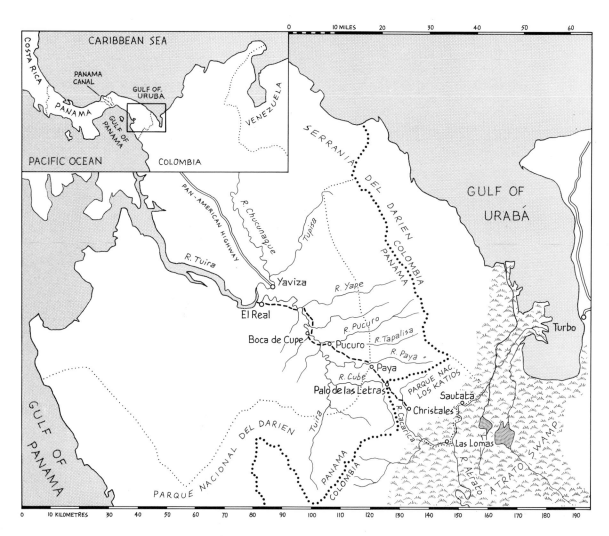

to Panama. An afternoon at the Royal Geographical Society had yielded little information. No map showed any path across the Gap, only the proposed route of the Pan American Highway. We could find no one who had crossed the Darien the way we planned – on foot and by canoe – so in the true tradition of exploration we had to rely on local information.

The River Atrato is the gateway to Colombia's end of the Darien Gap so we flew to Turbo, at the mouth of the river, in an over-loaded ten-seater plane. From my seat in the aisle I was interested to see a notice, in red, in English, above all those complicated dials in the cockpit: 'Warning, equipment inoperative'. Instead I looked out of the window at the squiggles of brown river in the green expanse of jungle and wondered where we would find the trail that would take us to Panama.

In Turbo we wondered *how* we would find it. This is an anarchic town, even by Colombian standards, with a flourishing separatist movement, a racial mix matched only in Brazil, and a lot of dust and noise. Everyone wanted to buy us a beer, but no one had any information about the Darien Gap.

"If you want to go to Panama, take a boat," they said. Which we did, but instead of going north towards Panama, we went south on a banana boat supplying the settlements on the banks of the Atrato.

Turbo is on the far side of the Gulf of Urabá, where a raging sea bounced our little boat on its waves and threw my stomach into turmoil. After an hour the water quietened and I raised myself warily from my supine position on deck to find the boat moving peacefully along the jungle-clad bank of the river. Huge trees with buttress roots and bursts of purple blossom pushed their heads above the canopy, plants with leaves the size of umbrellas stood in the shallows, and large ungainly birds, later identified as northern screamers, flapped and shrieked at our passing. We chugged slowly past a tree with a grey trunk and vivid yellow flowers. It bore no leaves, but large reddish shapes hung like oversized fruit from the boughs. It took me a while to realize they were howler monkeys dozing in the midday sun. Some sprawled along the branches, legs and arms dangling, others hung nonchalantly from an arm, a leg or a tail. The boat made its first stop at a small collection of huts with a sign that read *Parque Nacional Natural Los Katios*. The captain suggested this would be the place to find further information.

A pet peccary greeted us enthusiastically as we landed. Having a soft spot for members of the pig family I scratched her behind the ear whereupon she collapsed on her back, grunting with pleasure.

"That's Juanita," said the park director cheerfully. "We'll eat her when she gets a bit bigger." He led us into one of the huts and I outlined our plans, my face streaming incontinently with sweat. The jungle was certainly hot. And humid. No one at the Sautata section of Los Katios knew about paths to Panama, but they suggested we continue up river to Las Lomas, an outpost of the park on the evocatively named Cacarica River (politely translated, this means 'rich in excrement').

We stayed in Las Lomas for five days waiting for ongoing transport. At last we knew that there *was* a path, and that it started above a place called Cristales. Meanwhile Las Lomas was a perfect place to start acclimatizing to the jungle. It was too hot to do much, so we lay around in hammocks, studied Spanish, spent hours bird-watching and butterfly-hunting, and played with the two baby spider monkeys that lived beneath one of the huts. These endearing orphans were named Judas and Rosita. Rosita was well behaved, perhaps because she had a surrogate mother – a pig. Rosita rode on its back or lay on its neck sucking an ear and kept out of mischief. Judas, however, was an inveterate thief and one of my lasting memories of Las Lomas is hearing an angry yell of 'Judas!' and looking up from my hammock to see a spider monkey sprint past on his hind legs holding aloft half a cooked chicken. There was also a puppy called Popeye, who loved spinach, and – briefly – an orphaned baby sloth.

Rosita – the baby spider monkey – lived with her pig foster-mother beneath the hut.

Above – *Macaws, like this scarlet one, are hunted for the pot, so are usually shy. But they are often seen in screeching pairs, silhouetted against the sky as they fly back to their roosts at dusk.*

Left – *Clouds formed by warm air rising from the humid jungle provide some splendid sunsets. This is the best time of day – until the mosquitoes come out and drive you into the tent.* Photo: Roger Sampson

The boat trip to Cristales was the most spectacularly beautiful of the whole trip. After a short stretch of open water our *motorista* suddenly turned the dugout canoe into a seemingly impenetrable carpet of mauve-flowered water hyacinths. Cutting the motor, he poled quietly upriver through a sun-spangled tunnel of dark green. Tangled vines hung into the water, giant leaves brushed the sides of the canoe, and birds – gallinules and kingfishers – flashed ahead. *"Culebra!"* called the crew at intervals, their sharp eyes accustomed to picking out snakes from their camouflaging background.

There were other reptiles too. Huge double-crested basilisks, looking like mini-dragons, basked on the river banks and plopped into the water at our approach, while their smaller cousins, nicknamed 'Jesus Christ Lizards', scurried across the surface of the water on their hind legs. The river was seldom more than twelve feet wide, and sometimes so shallow we had to jump out and haul the canoe over boulders or submerged logs. I can't remember how long it took us to reach Cristales, but it certainly wasn't long enough.

We were greeted warmly at the ranger station and shown a place to pitch our tent. At dusk we cringed inside our tightly zipped home, being careful to let no part of our bodies touch the mosquito-netting. The mosquitoes thronging the outside seemed as noisy as an orchestra and as big as bats. And bats were also a danger: there are rabies-carrying vampire bats in the Darien. Many people keep cats, not as mousers but as batters.

Our imaginations were heightened by the anticipation of our trek. The Cristales staff were the first Colombians we had talked to who actually *knew* there was a path into Panama, and they had promised to find someone to take us further up the river to the trail head the next day. We were both very nervous, having no idea how long, arduous or dangerous the walk would be.

At dawn we fought off the mosquitoes, sprayed ourselves with repellent, and packed the tent. Already we were sweating. The park guard emerged from his hut as we were finishing breakfast and walked to the river bank.

"Jesus!!" he bellowed, gazing across the water to a bamboo and thatch hut the other side. A young boy, coal black, emerged and spirited bargaining began. The price was reduced from 20 *balboas* to eight, and Jesus started baling out his canoe.

The path to Panama begins at a Choco Indian settlement. Two Indian groups live in the Darien,

the Choco and the Cuna, and it is they who will be most affected by the building of the Pan-American Highway. For centuries they have lived in harmony with nature, but they are ill-equipped to cope with the assertive *Choleños*, black descendants of slaves, who form part of the mixed population of this area. The Chocos we met all shared a serenity and beauty that personified 'the noble savage'. The men wore only loin cloths and kept their hair bobbed, with a straight fringe. The women's long hair hung over their naked shoulders and breasts which were partially covered by heavy necklaces of beads and silver coins. Both men and women decorate their brown skins with black dye from the plant *Genipa americana*. They are supremely handsome people.

Jesus poled the canoe in to the river bank by a large palm-thatched hut on stilts. Father was squatting by his canoe, mending the holes in its sides with pieces cut from a tin can. He smiled briefly and gestured for us to enter his house. This we did precariously, up the notched pole that is the traditional Choco 'ladder'. The house, in Choco style, had no walls, so no door, but the overhanging thatch kept out most of the rain, and the interior was light and airy. His wife and children gazed at us and said nothing; it was left to a pet parrot to break the silence. After sharing a drink and admiring each other's possessions, we were led to the start of the trail.

After about an hour George caught me up and said "I like this!". My sentiments exactly. Instead of the oozing black swamps of our imagination, we were walking along the spine of a sharp ridge past bushes of bright crimson flowers. Mighty trees with buttress roots stretched towards the light, and strange shiny fungi on slender stems gave brightness to the shady forest floor. Caterpillars like walking Christmas trees worked on the greenery, and leaf-cutter ants made their well-disciplined march across the trail to tend their fungus gardens below the topsoil.

It was very hot. At our first river crossing I pulled off my sweat-sodden clothes and floated in a deep pool of cool water, gazing up at the jungle canopy overhead. Then a toothy fish bit my bottom. I decided to wash instead of swimming, and found the soap devoured in a few minutes. There's no accounting for fishy appetites. Something made me look up to meet the rapt eyes of a group of Chocos. They had probably seen few white people before, and certainly not naked ones. It was some time before they could tear themselves away from such an enthralling scene.

We walked on for some hours, crossing and recrossing the river, until the light faded. The tent was set up in an open area by the edge of the river under an evening sky full of squawking macaws and parrots flying home to roost. A pile of bright feathers by the remnants of a fire showed where a local had supped on grilled macaw — a sharp reminder that not everyone regards these birds as exotic beauties. The inhabitants of any jungle love hunting, and in Latin America almost all now have rifles. Hence there is little wildlife to be seen outside national parks or very remote areas.

Our first night in the forest was extraordinary. Our lightweight tropical tent was made entirely of mosquito netting and we didn't bother to pitch the rain fly. It rained — not water, but a perpetual patter of flowers, twigs, and other debris from the canopy above us, as monkeys and birds nibbled and dropped their evening

meal. Dusk had brought mosquitoes, so we lay in the tent and listened to jungle sounds. A chorus of frogs piped up. 'Clever' they seemed to croak, in perfect American accents. With the night came nocturnal animals, howling, croaking, squeaking and buzzing. Large objects splashed into the river or crashed near our tent. It was quite terrifying. With my imagination working overtime I thought a tree would fall on us, or a tapir would trip over the guy ropes and trample us in a rage. And perhaps there were jaguars . . . or more likely, bandits. I slept very little that night.

Day Two was the longest and toughest of the trek, taking us up over the watershed and into Panama. Our goal was *Palo de las Letras* which is marked proudly on maps as though it were a town. In fact it's a concrete marker, with a

A woman from one of the Choco villages, visited by the Malaria Control Boat, engaged in the traditional craft of basket weaving.

scratched inscription *Carrera de Darien, Colmbia* [sic]. So this was the Darien highway, and we were entering Panama! Years ago the border was marked by a huge tree whose trunk was covered with the carved initials of passers-by, hence the name 'Tree of letters'.

During the early part of the day we frequently crossed bends of the river which steadily became wider and its shores sandier. Once I rounded a bend to see that the water was rimmed with a band of shimmering green. As we approached hundreds of butterflies rose in an emerald cloud, then settled again on the shores to drink from the damp, mineral-rich sand. We always saw butterflies in the sunlit clearings. The most spectacular were undoubtedly the *Morphos* whose four inch wings were the most brilliant metallic blue imaginable. Nature has compensated

Cuna Indian girl and her young brother. She is wearing a mola, *the reverse appliqué blouse traditional to this tribe; her brother's necklace of monkey teeth ensures wealth in the afterline (and probably, in a young boy, strength and health in this one).* Photo: George Bradt.

for the sombre dark of the jungle with brilliantly coloured inhabitants. That Morpho blue is echoed in the feathers of tanagers and other tropical birds, and all the colours of the spectrum are found in the butterflies.

The climb up to *Palo de las Letras* was exhausting. In the shade of the rainforest it was not particularly hot, but the humidity, the weight of our packs, and the gradient of the trail ensured that we sweated copiously. Our second night, camped near a trickle of water (it's

Keeping boots dry while fording the river between Paya and Pucuro. In the rainy season, crossing this river can involve a chest-deep wade through fast, debris-filled water.

surprising how dry a rainforest can be when you're thirsty), was as restless as the first. This time it was not the mosquitoes that pestered us, but ticks. I've never concerned myself much with ticks since they greeted George with such joyful appetite that I apparently came a poor second. However, the Darien ticks were hungry and perhaps a little bored. They were also tiny 'seed ticks' which were all the more irritating in that you could hardly see them but could feel them wandering around looking for those nice clammy places so dear to their hearts. Once they've dug in they can only be removed with difficulty and leave a long-lasting itchy spot. You need to know your Darien companion rather well; tick-seeking is an intimate pastime. George and I took it in turns with the masking tape and

removed hundreds of the little blighters.

Next day we descended to the Paya River, a broad, sunlit expanse of water that had us excitedly washing our clothes. With only one change of dry clothing, we had to put on our damp, smelly clothes each morning, retaining the others for evening and night wear. Nothing dries in the sunless damp of the jungle. When everything was laid out on the rocks to dry, we turned our attention to the problems of getting across the river, but before we had time to realise that there was no obvious way across,

Cayman crocodiles are among many species of reptile to be found on the banks of the Atrato.

Alberto appeared, paddling a tiny dugout canoe, and offered to take us to his village, Paya.

Alberto was a Cuna Indian, and Paya was once the Cuna centre for learning. Although the majority of the tribe have always lived around the Gulf of Urabá in Colombia, and – in recent times – in the San Blas Islands off Panama, bright young men were sent to Paya to learn magic, medicine, history and folklore. In those days, about 75 years ago, Paya was a thriving town. Now it is a small, peaceful village of bamboo and palm-thatch huts, the carless 'streets' kept clean by foraging chickens. Learning is now in the hands of the local missionaries and it is doubtful whether the Cuna culture in Darien will long withstand the Christian influence. Listening to

the missionaries describe the Cuna religion, it was hard to see that following Christ would be their salvation. In broad terms, we learned that Cunas believe in an eight-tiered 'heaven'. Those who have led good lives will take their place in the upper levels. What makes a good life? Honesty, hard work, faithfulness.

Cuna women are as beautiful as the Chocos. Their gold nose-rings and *molas*, make them instantly recognisable. *Molas*, a type of reverse appliqué blouse, have gained great popularity in recent years and may be found in chic boutiques all over the world, but their geometric designs may have had their origin in body painting. When the missionaries told the Cuna to cover up, they transferred their designs to fabric.

Animal and bird motifs are common, with the introduction of new-fangled objects such as aeroplanes (seen in the Darien whereas cars are not). Women also wear broad anklets, made from a long strand of beads, painstakingly calculated to form a design when wound round the ankles. Bracelets are made up in the same way.

Most men wear Western clothes, but many wear handsome necklaces of animal teeth. These will often be from the white-faced capuchin monkey, which is considered the banker of 'heaven'. The more monkeys a man kills in his lifetime, the more flowers – the currency of heaven – the animals will be able to gather. Presumably they then loyally hand over the cash to the soul that dispatched them!

We planned to spend only a few hours in Paya. This being the first settlement in Panama, we knew that we must have our luggage inspected by the Panamanian 'customs officers' who live near the village. We thought it would take, maybe, half an hour. Two hours later Donato, Flako and Abril were still at it. This was no mere inspection of luggage; they made it clear that their role in Paya was to prevent the spread of foot and mouth disease from Colombia to Panama. This meant dunking everything that looked like leather (even if it was plastic) into a bath of disinfectant. Our tent was examined and some traces of mud found on the bottom: 'Colombian Earth!' they cried triumphantly, dropping it with a splash into the bucket. Then came the turn of smaller items. All were examined minutely and with great interest ("What's this for?" asked Donato, dismantling a Tampax) and written down on their list. Then came the money count. It seemed necessary to lay all our money on the ground, sorted in piles by denomination, while the men laboriously calculated our wealth then proclaimed it to the large group of onlookers. We were not happy at the knowledge that everyone now knew that two unbelievably wealthy *gringos* were about to walk the lonely path to Pucuro.

Three hours after telling the hospitable missionaries that we'd just check with the border officials before going on our way, we accepted their invitation to stay the night. A new seat of learning was established in Paya – in the arts of cat's cradles and Frisbee throwing.

The path to Pucuro, linking the two Cuna villages, was well used and easy despite the wide rivers we had to ford. We took our time and camped one night on a river bank to have our last experience of being alone in the jungle. From Pucuro we would be looking for a boat to Panama City. We used the solitude to have a competition for the most insect bites. George

won with 368 on one leg. But then he had insisted on wearing shorts throughout the trek.

In Pucuro we introduced ourselves to the delightful old village chief and asked permission to camp. He was fascinated by our possessions and particularly in the picture postcards of London. Explaining the Queen trooping the colour was difficult. I pointed out that Buckingham Palace was her house and that she was sitting on a horse, while his brow furrowed in puzzlement. Possibly he had never seen a horse, let alone a palace.

We were lucky in our river transport, a Malaria Control boat was visiting the area and gave us a lift. Not only did we move speedily with a cool breeze fanning our faces, but we stopped at various Choco villages so the team could take blood samples. Most of the women were engaged in their traditional craft of basket weaving and broke off reluctantly to co-operate. We marvelled at the stoicism of the little children, who allowed their fingers to be nicked with a razor without so much as blinking. It was all done with great efficiency – samples were taken, mounted on slides and packed in a cool box, and the particulars of each villager written in a note book. Ages were guessed – Indians don't celebrate birthdays.

We were dropped at Boca de Cupe, where we were assured that there were plenty of boats to El Real and a plane from there to the capital. The first person who found us was Maria. She appeared, rotund and black, from the shadows of a wooden shack (the only 'hotel' in town) and beamed up at us.

"Dumplins?" she asked.

"What?"

"Dumplins, dumplins!" and she rubbed her belly and smacked her lips. Yes, on reflection, we could do with some dumplings, so we sat down at her rickety table and gazed out at the first real houses and bustle we'd seen for two weeks.

Boca de Cupe seemed like the end of our trip, but of course it wasn't. There were still no cars, but at least there were plenty of boats and it was not difficult to negotiate our passage to El Real, where, after several chaotic days, we flew to Panama City. And of course the concrete jungle was far more dangerous than the one we'd walked through – within hours my handbag had been snatched. Trying to retrieve luggage that had been air-freighted from Colombia we ran up against bureaucracy denser than the rainforest: it was during the time of negotiations between the United States and Panama over the Panama Canal.

"OK", said George. "If you won't give me our parcel, I won't give you your canal!" It worked.

125

Panamanians using the only transport available in the jungle – canoe. If the Pan-American Highway is finally pushed through the Darien Gap, this way of life – for Chocos, Cunas and others – may disappear forever.

Difficulty/dangers

An adventurous, but not difficult trek. Heat, humidity, and biting insects make the going uncomfortable, and sections of the trail are arduous. Deep river crossings can cause problems; in the rainy season the water can be chest high, but warm and slow moving. The path is not always clear, and those unaccustomed to way-finding will be happier with a local guide. Because of the isolation of the jungle paths it is inadvisable to travel alone. Trekked in dry season, with sufficient time, the Gap presents no major hurdles to healthy and physically fit people who can carry their own backpacks. (Porters are not normally available because the route crosses an international border.) The greatest difficulty is negotiating for boats and dealing with awkward border officials.

Distances/times

The actual walking time for the Darien Gap is three to five days. With no delays the whole trip *can* be done in six days. This is an unrealistic time frame, however, since transport is unreliable or at the whim of the boat owner, and those in a hurry will have no bargaining power. Ten days to two weeks is a reasonable time-allowance.

Route

Most travellers do the Darien Gap from Panama to Colombia.
Panama City to El Real:
(boat – 12–36 hrs) or plane ($\frac{1}{2}$ hr).
El Real to Boca de Cupe:
(boat – 4 hrs).
Boca de Cupe to Pucuro:
(boat – 6 hrs).
Pucuro to Paya: (foot – 1–2 days).
Paya to Cristales via Palo de las Letras: (foot – 2–3 days).
Cristales to trail head: (canoe/boat – 1 day + +, depending on canoe availability and bargaining power).

The route described earlier, from Colombia to Panama, has the advantage that it's far less popular so chances of finding a boatman willing to take you up river from Bijao (which is on the main Turbo – Atrato – Cacarica route) or Los Katios National Park to Cristales for a reasonable price are greater. In either direction, this is the stretch that causes most delays.

Seasons/weather

The Darien Gap receives from 80 to 200 inches (2,000 to 5,000 mm) of rain annually. The best month for the trip is January, with a good chance of reasonably dry weather between December and March. Towards the end of the dry season the rivers are very low and sometimes impassable. July and August are possible, though likely to be quite wet. The torrential rain and flooded rivers of other months should be avoided.

Equipment/provisions

Equipment needs to be chosen with care; jungle conditions are very different from those in the mountains. In the heat, it is essential to cut down on weight wherever possible.

Boots

Jungle boots or canvas sports boots are better than leather hiking boots because of all the river crossings. Cheap canvas boots shrink in the constant damp so buy half a size too large.

Clothing

Pure cotton is cool but rots. Mixed cotton and synthetics are more practical. Shorts (men only) are only suitable for the most stoical. Baggy, lightweight trousers (not jeans) and loose, long-sleeved shirts are best. Long socks, worn outside trousers, give some protection against ticks and chiggers.

Tent/hammock

A hammock with a properly fitting mosquito net and rain cover is ideal, although a well ventilated tent is perfectly satisfactory.

Miscellaneous

Large plastic bags are essential for keeping gear dry in canoes, and everything should be packed in separate plastic bags within your pack. A compass is necessary. (See *Jungle Nasties* for other items for your protection.)

Food

You cannot rely on food being available anywhere between Bijao, on the Cacarica, and Boca de Cupe, so travellers must carry supplies for at least six days: dried food, not tins, and powdered drinks to make

heavily treated water taste more palatable. All water should be sterilized. Although there is plenty of firewood it is often damp so a stove is necessary.

Language

Spanish is the second language for the two Indian groups in the Darien, but most speak it reasonably fluently. Although the American presence in Panama means that many people speak English in the city, only Spanish is understood in the Darien, and since the trip depends on skilful negotiating for canoes, and includes many dealings with officials, a reasonable command of the language is essential.

Jungle nasties

There is little danger from the larger animals: jaguars and pumas keep well away from man. The only dangerous mammal is the vampire bat, because it carries rabies, but your mosquito net will protect you. Snakes do not make unprovoked attacks and are only likely to bite if stepped on or disturbed in some way, so use care when clearing your campsite, and always check where putting your hands when dealing with obstacles across the path. By far the most dangerous creature in the jungle is the mosquito. These are a problem between Turbo and Cristales – terrible around Cristales – but not at all bad elsewhere. Malaria is common in the area so get medical advice on the most appropriate prophylactic. Use insect repellent and closely woven clothing that cannot be penetrated by the mosquito's proboscis in the evenings. Ticks can be deterred somewhat by repellent and should be removed with masking tape before they have dug in. An anaesthetic cream, or even toothpaste, can ease the itching of insect bites. Aspirins also help.

Always shake out your boots before putting them on as they are a favourite hiding place for scorpions and small snakes.

Now for some good news: there are no leeches in the Darien!

Other medical considerations

Apart from the insect-borne diseases mentioned above, heat exhaustion may be a problem, although the temperature in the shady rainforest is rarely over 85°F (30°C). The humidity makes it feel much hotter, however, and extra salt should be taken to compensate for mineral loss due to sweating. Heat problems are best prevented by adopting a slow pace with plenty of rests and immersion in rivers.

Fungus infections of feet or crotch are common. Medicated powder does much to prevent or alleviate the problem. Bring medication for traveller's diarrhoea.

Minimum impact

Increasing numbers of travellers are threatening to change the way of life of the Darien Indians, and thoughtless adventurers in jeeps are doing untold damage to the main path and fragile rainforest. Those crossing the Darien Gap have a responsibility towards the people and nature that have existed in harmony for so long. Standard considerations such as not leaving litter (even buried rubbish will be dug up by forest animals) and not disturbing the wildlife are easier to comply with than protecting the culture of the Indians. Do not give presents, however much they are appreciated. It is an artificial intrusion and can cause hostility towards those who arrive empty-handed. However, carefully chosen trade goods can be used in exchange for food or *molas* instead of cash. Do not succumb to outrageous prices (for canoe transport) or attempts by border guards to procure a bribe; your compliance only increases the corruption which is a relatively recent phenomenon in the area.

In an Indian village, first introduce yourself to the chief. Find out the local attitude on photography. Interact with the people, rather than staring and photographing. A frisbee, football or other games are far better for gaining your acceptance than handing out trinkets.

Reading
Maps:
A poor map of Panama's section of the Darien Gap is available from the Geographic Institute in Panama City. The best readily available map is the inset of the Darien Gap in *South America – North West* published by International Travel Maps of Vancouver and distributed in Britain by Bradt Publications.
Guide books:
Backpacking in Mexico and Central America by Hilary Bradt and Rob Rachowiecki (Bradt Publications) contains a chapter on the Darien Gap.
The South American Handbook (Trade and Travel Publications) contains a section on the Darien Gap and is updated annually.
Literature:
Very little has been written about the Darien Gap; almost all of it is of the 'confrontational' variety.

The following can be studied in the library of Canning House, London (The Hispanic and Luso-Brazilian Council):
Operation Drake – Voyage of Discovery edited by A W Mitchell (Severn House Publishers Ltd, 1981). Contains a chapter called Darien Disasters.
Darien Breakthrough by Col J Blashford Snell. A report on the 1972 expedition (can be seen at the Royal Geographic Society). (There is also said to be a book, *Ninety Days in the Darien* about this expedition, but I've failed to find the author or publisher.)
A New Voyage and Description of the Isthmus of America with Wafer's Secret Report (1968) and Davis's Expedition to the Gold Mines (1704). Published by the Oxford Hakluyt Society, 1934. Historical rather than practical interest!

Hilary Bradt has written four backpacking and trekking guides to South America, along with others on Africa and Madagascar. She also works as a leader for an American Adventure Travel company, leading treks and jungle excursions, and estimates that in the course of her travels she has walked 2,000 miles in Latin America. Between trips she runs her own publishing company.

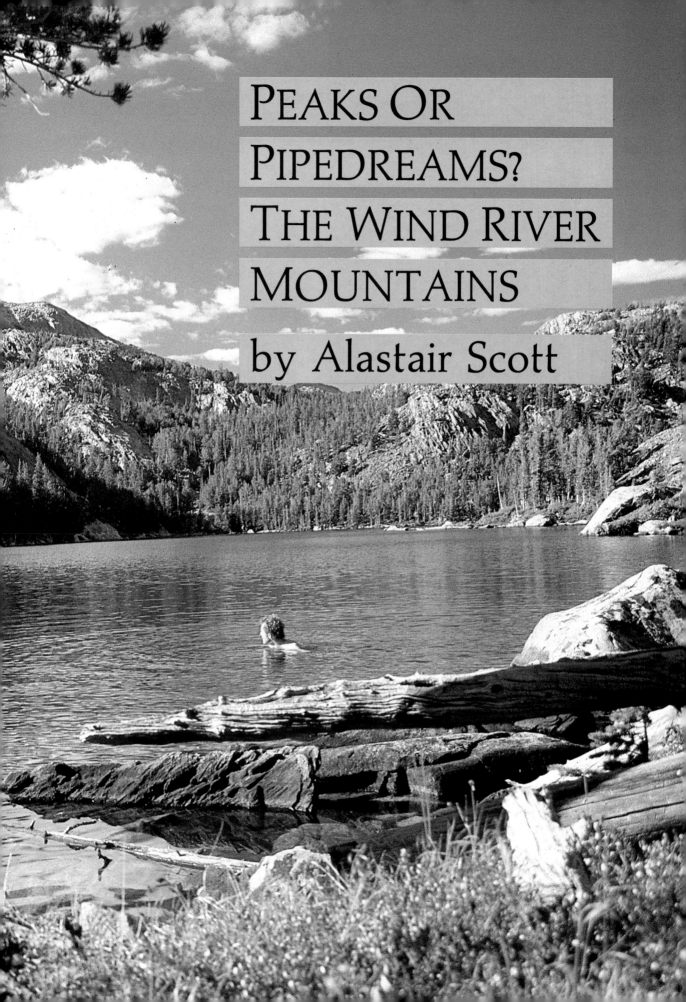

PEAKS OR PIPEDREAMS? THE WIND RIVER MOUNTAINS

by Alastair Scott

'Where man is so small and insignificant, the world knows not of his presence.'
Finis Mitchell

By the time it enters the Gulf of Mexico as part of the Mississippi, the Wind River has changed its name four times and travelled 2,500 miles (4,000 kms) from its source in Wyoming. It flows down the eastern flank of that charismatic backbone of North America, the Rockies, passes the century-old cowboy settlement of Dubois and bleeds through a wound in a region of semi-desert where the air is seldom still and which the Shoshone Indians called the 'Valley of the Warm Winds'. To anyone looking up from this region for the namesake range of mountains – the object of my quest – they do not appear to exist.

I was travelling north through the valley towards Dubois. Rounded hills undulated against the skyline on both sides, at first presiding over fields of hay and corn straddled by spider's legs of irrigation pipes and later over gas pumps which pecked rhythmically at the arid ground. Then came the badlands of rocky desert where the view was a wash of pink, white and cinnamon hues – the sedimentary rocks of the sea that had covered this region for 500 million years. Nearer Dubois the hills rose higher, a sparse growth of grass turned them yellow and sporadic groups of antelope nibbled sage bush, but the painted desert continued to dominate the landscape. There was still no sign of the Wind River Mountains, the geological site of one of the most massive vertical displacements to have occurred on this planet. They show no hint of themselves. Nothing prepares the trekker for what is to come.

Dubois (pronounced 'Du-boys') spreads out from one broad main street to accommodate its population of 1,200 and its meticulously contrived 'Wild West' image – hitchin' posts and wooden shops and walkways – evokes a lighthearted charm. The abundant game of the region had long attracted Shoshone, Crow and Blackfeet Indians, then came white trappers and early explorers searching for a convenient pass across the Continental Divide. The first white settlers arrived in 1886 and Dubois grew up as a centre for their cattle ranches and later for 'tie hacks' – tough foresters, mostly Scandinavian immigrants, who felled trees and cut ties (sleepers) for the great age of railway building. Ranching and timber (though the latter industry is declining) continue to form the basis of the local economy along with tourism, particularly during the hunting season.

I bought provisions for ten days at Welty's Store, still run by the first family to open up shop here, and followed a jeep track south for nine miles (14 kms) to look for my elusive mountains.

The trek starts at an altitude of 7,500 ft (2,300 m) near Trail Lake, on a hillside liberally sprinkled with red granite boulders etched with Indian petroglyphs. City-dwellers once used to holiday here at a dude ranch to experience for a week or so the lives of working cowboys, but the cluster of cabins now situated in the valley is an Audubon Camp (named after the ornithologist and artist) where summer courses are held on the region's flora, fauna and geology. In late September it is deserted except for the flashy pick-ups of early hunters. Cottonwoods and aspens are ablaze in orange and yellow at this time and among the snow willows by the river, moose are turning their thoughts to mating. They chase each other through the shrubs and emit lugubrious, high-pitched whines which, to a non-moose, sound absurdly comical and most unbecoming for such large animals. The wildlife of the region was to prove one of my constant delights.

The route that I had planned headed first to Dinwoody Glacier, 25 miles (40 kms) away on an out-and-return trail, then looped round a central group of mountains in a rarely visited region, and finally completed an arc back to Dubois through forests which the map showed to be less densely contoured. I decided to leave half my provisions at Audubon Camp to avoid carrying unnecessary weight, with the intention of returning to restock at some stage of the journey.

The hill formations at the trailhead were called hogbacks, rounded crusts of limestone which sloped up from the grass valley, pine-clad except for rose-tinted cliffs that scarred their sides and inclined towards the skyline. I picked the Old rather than the New Glacier Trail as the climb is less steep and the path less used (mainly because it has officially been closed since a rockfall in 1976! – it is nevertheless safe). It twisted upwards through the sweet tang of pine forests and eventually emerged in a high altitude meadow of dry grass. In the distance was grazing a flock of bighorn sheep, their white rumps betraying their otherwise perfect camouflage. The Sheep Eaters, a poor branch of the Shoshone tribe, used to hunt these ranges. They built traps similar to cattlegrids and funnelled the wild sheep towards them, looked down upon by their buffalo-hunting relatives of the plains. Despite the Sheep Eaters' predation, the largest population of bighorn sheep in the

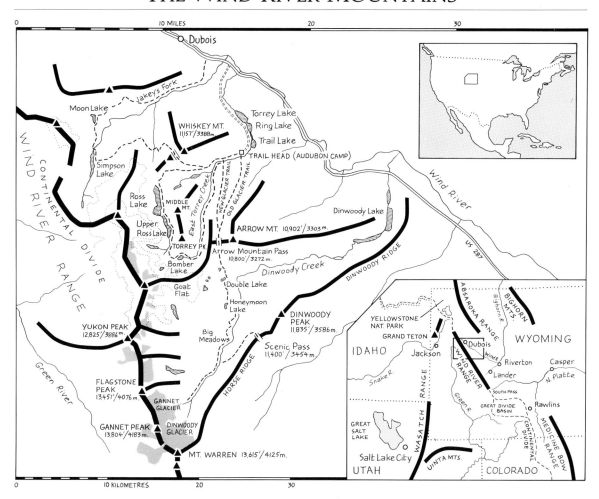

USA is still to be found in the Wind River Range.

Grasshoppers disturbed by my boots took off like flying castanets as the trail led me to the convergence of the Old and the New near a meadow pass at 10,800 ft (3,300 m), between Arrow Mountain and a colossal pile of rubble. Beyond this was a different world, a granite testimony to the violence of creation. The view is best appreciated from Scenic Pass (a worthwhile sidetrip for the following day) but from Arrow Mountain Pass and above Honeymoon Lake it is still an awesome sight. The Wind River Mountains at last reveal themselves and stand proud. They are a magnificently scabrous assembly of ice- and weather-honed peaks; arêtes, spires, sawtooth ridges, buttresses and crag-edged plateaux form 100 miles (160 kms) of summits, a glacier-encrusted divide that splits the nation and determines whether water is sent to the Atlantic or to the Pacific. Among them are sweeps of scree and ice-burnished cliffs, hanging corries, lost valleys and a myriad lakes in evergreen forests. Because of the high foothills, this majestic region was long considered to be

Wyoming's best-kept secret, its peaks referred to as the 'roof of the state'. To the Indians they were the 'Shining Mountains', revered as the crest of the world.

As geological athletes, the 'Winds' are exemplary. Motivated by as yet undetermined forces they thrust upwards through 20,000 ft (6,000 m) of sedimentary rock, spilling debris into their valleys, until they reared tall above the surface. They completed this energetic feat about 55 millions years ago. Then came an intense period of volcanic activity in a neighbouring region and lava buried the range, leaving only the summits protruding as small hills. The Winds quickly shook themselves free and rose again. Streams gradually eroded the lava bed and excavated the valleys shortly before the arrival of the ice age when glaciers crushed, smoothed and gouged the final touches to the current topography. Forty-five summits in the range extend above 13,000 ft (c.4,000 m). Around them rests a cold mantle of 63 glaciers, remnants of this former ice sheet, and seven of them are listed among the ten largest glaciers in the Lower 48.

It was late afternoon by the time I forced myself away from the view and followed the trail on its descent to Dinwoody Creek. A succession of captivating lakes appeared, each set in a natural amphitheatre among crags. Double Lake, placid blue and reflecting its domineering cathedral of rock, tempted me in for a swim which ended as a lightning plunge when I felt the temperature of the water. A chill invaded the valley as the sun sank and shadows crept higher up the steep slopes. By dusk my tent was pitched beside a whitewater torrent and I was sipping tea before a lively fire. I kept the flames low, mindful of the wildfire that had killed the older trees around me. Their ghostly white trunks held out twisted branches and, in the half-light, they seemed grasping with sinister, Grimmsian intent. Darkness robbed me of my confidence and a snapping twig returned the one fear I had about this walk. Nights are hard when you are alone in bear country.

Animal noises woke me early the next morning but they came from a moose and her calf splashing through the shallows. I made this camp my base for two days to explore Glacier Trail and its side paths. One day took me to the aptly named Scenic Pass and the other to Dinwoody Glacier, the most popular destination in the Winds. A coyote stalking voles in Big Meadows was startled by my approach and fled, glinting as the sun caught the winter sheen on its russet coat. I climbed 1,000 ft (300 m) with the towering walls of Horse Ridge as companion, crossed the moraine-laden nose of an old glacier and entered the numinous atmosphere of the high peaks.

The trail ends among the boulder fields of a huge cirque. To the left, beyond a milky-green meltpool, is the jagged skyline of Dinwoody Peak, Doublet Peak, the statuesque Dames Anglaises and Mountain Warren

Right – *Gannet Peak and its glacier, above Dinwoody Creek, taken from the Ink Wells Trail. Gannet Peak is the highest point in Wyoming at 13,804 ft (4,207 m).*
Below – *Bighorn sheep, taken on the Whiskey Mountain Trail. The crags in the background are just above the Old Glacier Trail. The trail head lies two miles to the left. This area is a geologist's paradise of granite and limestone, the product of intense land upheaval and glaciation.*

(13,722 ft/4,182 m), draped by their dirt-stained but ever-bright expanse of ice. To the right is a dark rock face with a perpetual cowl of snow, the rounded crest of Gannett Peak (13,804 ft/ 4,207 m). This, the highest summit in Wyoming, was named in 1906 after an eminent geographer, Henry Gannett. He was not the first to reach the summit but he brought the mountain to the attention of the public by writing an account of his ascent. A 37 year-old explorer, Captain B. L. E. Bonneville, claimed to have climbed Gannett as early as 1833 using the more scenic but less practical approach along Horse Ridge although this is today considered unlikely by local experts. To reach the top it's advisable to have crampons, ice axe and rope – and a pencil for writing your name in the register rolled up inside a copper cylinder. For those without, it is one effortless bounce to the fissured glacier that creaks and sparkles in a cradle of rock directly below. A quiet moment in this panoramic splendour convinces you that except for Bonneville, Gannett and Finis Mitchell – the 'Lord of the Winds' who walked the range for 70 years – you might be the first to chance upon this spot. To recall the sentiments of Mitchell, the Shining Mountains make you feel serene, small and terribly insignificant. And appropriately so.

On the fourth day a flurry of storm clouds blew in low as I retraced my steps along Glacier Trail, turning the hills into dark menacing shapes. By the time I reached the turn-off to Bomber

Basin the sun was once more supreme in a faultlessly blue sky. ('If you don't like the weather in Wyoming,' they say, 'wait a moment.') The Bomber Lake circuit was to be my deviation into the wilds, where no trails were marked except a dotted pencil line on the Forestry HQ wall map with the word 'Difficult' written alongside. During World War II bombers used to practice low-level flying over this area and one particular crew were well known as avid moose spotters. The wreckage of their last flight is still visible scattered over the ground.

Bears were on my mind at first and I sang while walking through the wood to scare them away. I have a good voice in this respect. Then the terrain became steep, then crotchety, and bears became the least of my concerns. The way sloped up the floor of a deep canyon, wide at first but narrowing as it billowed round the side of Torrey Peak. My choice of ground was between swampy sedgeland, woods full of blown-down trees and treacherous expanses of scree. By alternating from one to the other I made slow progress. Soon my feet felt bruised by the scree and tiredness dulled my appreciation of this incredible fault line. Dried grass stuffed under the inner soles of each boot helped enormously and I reached Bomber Lake, my intended camping place, an hour before dusk. It looked a gloomy spot in the fading light, though attractively cupped in the crumbling split of the mountains.

Camp among the pines at Downs Fork.

With difficulty I found a flat patch of ground for my tent among boulders and hastily cooked soup, rice and sardines. The latter caused me immediate regret for there is probably no finer bear lure then the smell of sardines. My campfire purged the tin – but had the damage already been done? Again the darkness brought suspense as I lay mummified in my sleeping bag, and yet it was totally unexpected noises that disturbed me. The wind had been increasing steadily during the evening and now it came in powerful gusts. They roared somewhere far off in the canyons, growing louder until the blasts strained against the boulders above my campsite, finally seeming to shred themselves in the nearby trees. Roars, moans and whistles were followed by small eddies that rattled my tent. I have never heard the wind perform such a repertoire of sounds. I hoped the gale would not bring snow, for the walking was hard enough without an additional hazard. Sleep soon claimed me. I wouldn't have heard a bear even if the love of sardines had caused one to trip on a guyline.

Snow did not fall that night but the temperature dropped well below freezing. Ice crusted the inside of the flysheet and, worst of all, my leather boots were frozen solid and inflexible. They were like plastic skiboots that did not fit and it took ten minutes of clumping around as if in high-heeled shoes before my feet thawed them sufficiently to make the leather malleable. This ritual was to be repeated each morning for the remainder of the trek, but I refused to let my boots share the comfort of my sleeping bag.

Beyond Bomber Lake lies a T-junction in the clefts between the ranges. Even on large-scale topographical maps the brown contour lines here frequently bunch together so closely that it appears the cartographer added them at a stroke with a broad paintbrush. A short climb through a scattering of trees takes the trekker over a spur and allows a glimpse of the astonishing desolation that lies beyond Turquoise Lake. The visible tops are only 2,000 ft (600 m) above head level now but the sheer walls of these monolithic obstacles, cracked and friable, make them appear no less invincible. Swaths of grey scree cling anywhere a hold is possible and trickle into the moraine through which East Torrey Creek splashes and tumbles. Every view here might illustrate a page of a geography textbook and although the impression is not one of beauty, there is a certain savage grandeur about this natural quarry.

My direction lay to the right where a U-shaped valley dropped through woods to Upper Ross Lake, passing a mitre of rock called The Guardian, which has been polished smooth by ice, streaked by run-off or strata and which, each morning, is set alight by the first rays of sun. Upper Ross Lake was hemmed in on both sides and neither looked pleasant walking. An inflatable boat would have been just the thing. Without one, I chose the east bank, which was formed by a steep talus of boulders emerging from the water and running up to the precipitous walls of an escarpment. 'Difficult' walking – it struck me as being murderous. Every fifth step seemed to require precise placing on a sharp rock and there were thousands of seesaw stones waiting to cause an upset. Visibility was often obscured by boulders the size of caravans and it took two and a half hours to gain just over one mile. Towers of loose rocks poised high above me and it looked as if the slightest sound would bring them crashing down. But in the brief moments of resting, what little breath I had left was taken by the views.

At the northern end of Upper Ross Lake is a small patch of grass which must rank among the finest campsites in the Winds. Sheltered by woods and amply supplied – in September – with ripe blueberries and fragrant juniper, where dozens of monarch butterflies flashed orange, it is a matter of feet from the water's edge and offers a clear view up the lake. Trout were feeding even under the midday sun, and moose and elk had left their hoofprints in soft ground by the shore. Once, high above, a golden eagle wheeled over the skyline crags. Bighorn sheep grazed the heights (I was told later), but I never saw any for the terrain above the treeline was one immense flock of rocks.

As it was only midday I decided to carry on and crossed the narrow neck of land separating Upper Ross from Ross Lake. Both were named for Nellie Taylor Ross, governor of Wyoming (1925–27) and the first woman in the country's history to govern a state. To my mind Ross Lake is the most beautiful in the range and a gem among the world's inland waters. Its eastern bank is fir-clad below the abrupt heights of Middle Mountain while its western bank starts dramatically with a buttress, a hanging icefield, a spire, a pap, a waterfall and then continues as a ragged scarp 600 ft (200 m) tall. A reasonable path appeared along the eastern side and made the going easy but the vistas through the gaps in the trees removed all incentive for speed. My pace faltered and lazed, but had eventually to revive for there were still seven miles to go in order to find some supper. Only that evening did I feel the weariness of the day's walking, having crossed over the mountains and returned to my cache of food at Audubon Camp. I slept in the

Taking a rest at Mile 2 on the Old Glacier Trail, looking north towards the Whiskey Mountain Trail. Red is not my favourite walking colour — except in hunting season, which was about to begin. The trees are quaking aspens (tremuloides).

open under a sky excessively crammed with stars. Though strenuous, this was the most rewarding day of the trip.

The final two days were less spectacular in terms of scenery but among the most enjoyable on account of wildlife. For three miles I retraced the previous day's route, up the switchbacks on Whiskey Mountain. An old-timer once set up a still in the jumble of red boulders near the top of this mountain and perhaps, while the brew was bubbling, he used to gaze at the central tooth of the Tetons which is visible 60 miles (100 kms) away to the west. Whiskey Mountain is covered by meadows and forest, although a devastating fire swept one side of it in 1976, burning so fiercely that the vegetation has not yet recovered. The view from the trail shows a dead forest of charred trunks. This section of the Winds (which comprises the Fitzpatrick Wilderness and the Glacier-Whiskey Mountain Primitive Area) is part of the Shoshone National Forest and it is modern policy to let fires that start naturally burn freely as long as human life is not threatened.

In designated Primitive and Wilderness areas travel is only permitted on foot or horseback. I met two horsemen near the highest point of the trail (11,000 ft/3,300 m) and except for the liferaft orange hats, they were silver screen cowboys; leather waistcoats, spurs, holster-slung rifles and coiled lassos. They nonchalantly smoked cigarettes between the fingers of leather gloves and said they were after bighorn sheep. I looked at them incredulously. A large group of bighorn sheep were grazing quietly not 80 yards away. But it transpired that these were ewes and lambs and the hunters' permits were for rams with a three-quarter or better curl of horn – and the day before the hunting season begins, without fail, rams mysteriously disappear! I wished the cowboys well, but out of politeness because I couldn't condone this system whereby permits were put up for 'general sale'. Granted that game management might be necessary and that wildlife experts calculated the number of permits to be issued, it still seemed irresponsible to issue these permits on a lottery basis when inexperienced hunters might win and, unaccompanied, demonstrate their ineptitude with bows and arrows, muzzleloaders and high-velocity rifles on live animals. Neither did I relish the thought of returning to Dubois with an arrow sticking through my pack.

The cowboys brought the total number of people I had met on this walk to seven, and they were the last. Spruce hens, large grey birds of the partridge family that are loathe to fly, were marginally more common. Magpies, grey jays and red-breasted pine grosbills glided silently from perch to perch with rapid bursts of wing movements but the only ones to sound were small chickadees with vivacious chatter. Red squirrels were constantly in view, easily the most abundant species, and some bold individuals disputed my intrusion by holding ground and uttering chiding clicks while twitching their tails. My fear of bears had diminished by this time and now I desperately wanted to see one but on the undulating forest trail to Simpson Lake, none appeared. Only mule deer with their long ears held erect as they cautiously kept their distance. That evening, beyond the fire of my final campsite, the silver reflection of a crescent moon danced and shattered repeatedly on Lake Simpson's ruffled surface.

The seventh day led me away from the granite peaks, through pine, spruce and fir to the fringe of hogback hills with their pink and yellow scars. Two thousand feet (600 m) below the last one lay Dubois, a speckled cluster on the pale shades of the desert. Desert stretched on all sides, to the dark horizon of the Owl Creek Mountains – created by the same volcanic surge that once buried the Winds – and to the right, south-east, to a strange tabletop cone, Crowheart Butte, which was the scene of an epic fight.

The Shoshone and Crow Indians were often in contention over hunting rights in the area and hostilities climaxed around the year 1860. Chief Washakie, one of the greatest and most respected of Indian chiefs, led his Shoshone and allied braves against the Crows, led by Chief Big Robber. After three days of fighting without any decisive result, Washakie and Big Robber agreed to resolve the issue in a personal duel to be fought on the tabletop hill. Washakie descended as the winner, some accounts saying he held Big Robber's heart high on the tip of his spear, others that he ate it to acquire his enemy's strength. The Crows departed and never invaded the Wind River Basin again.

Crowheart Butte slipped from view as I descended a steep, ankle-grinding path into the sage and prickly vegetation of the desert. The sun's heat was reflected by the dry earth and it seemed incongruous to think that glaciers existed a matter of miles from this scorching air. I looked hopefully for a bear as the last trees disappeared behind a ridge, but there was none. Not a single bear on the whole journey. In retrospect this was to be expected and in fact it was perhaps surprising that I had seen any wildlife at all. I had been walking for seven days, and the only thing I'd forgotten to pack was a bar of soap.

Glacier Trail running alongside Dinwoody Creek, looking towards Dinwoody Peak. Horse Ridge is on the left.

My feet felt heavy on the last mile. The warm wind that gave the river and ultimately the mountains their name was blowing dust into my face. There was no sign of the peaks I had just left, no sharp outline and hardly a tree to be seen. The trick of disappearance was complete. The secret was safe. Were it not for the pictures in my mind, vivid and large as life, I might have suspected that the Wind River Mountains were no more than a Shoshone pipe dream.

Right – Indian petroglyphs are easily visible on the hillside to the west of Trail Lake. They are very common here and can even be seen from the jeep track.

Left – Unnamed crag above Double Lake, on Glacier Trail, looking west. Beyond this is Goat Flat, a plateau at 12,000 ft (3,650 m).

Below – Dinwoody Creek. Looking back down the Glacier Trail towards the Ink Wells Trail. The Ink Wells are a serious of small lakes in the shadow of Gannett Peak. Horse Ridge is on the right.

Difficulty/dangers

The trails are all maintained and well-marked, with the exception of the wild country along East Torrey Creek (via Bomber Lake) to the northern end of Ross Lake. Congested woods, sedgeland and vast boulder fields make the going very hard and at times offer only treacherous footholds. Great care is required here, but the scenery amply rewards the effort. 3,500 ft (1,000 m) is the maximum stretch of continuous climbing to be encountered on any part of the trek, and zigzags in the trails alleviate all steep gradients.

Highest point: 11,400 ft (3,475 m) at Scenic Pass.

Total height gained: 16,700 ft (5,100 m).

See note below for weather danger.

Grizzly bears do not frequent the Wind River Mountains but their less volatile relatives, black bears, certainly do and deserve caution. Bears generally try to avoid man but they are attracted to food. The Forestry Service issues a leaflet with recommendations on how to behave in bear country. Most at risk are those who surprise a bear on rounding a corner, come between a mother and her cub, cook near their tent, store food in their tent instead of hanging it safely between trees and, strangely, women in menstruation. Bears are not common and you will be lucky if you see one but if you follow the recommendations, any encounter should be a pleasant one. (Making a noise as you walk avoids the risk of surprising a bear but it also scares all wildlife away and leaves the woods sterile – you must take your pick!)

The hunting season begins in earnest on October 1st, though bow and arrow hunters are let loose about two weeks earlier. During this period it is worth wearing something bright orange or red – some hunters are over-enthusiastic but most will hesitate before a diminutive, fluorescent moose.

Distance/times

The route as narrated is just under 110 miles (177 kms) on the map. Walking at a comfortable pace with plenty of stops to enjoy being scolded by squirrels, it is easily possible to complete the trek in seven days – ten hours walking each day. I recommend walking shorter days and having at least one rest day, a more leisurely total of, say, nine days.

Trail head to Dinwoody Glacier, including Scenic Pass detour, and return: 63 miles (101 kms).

Bomber Lake – Ross Lake – Trail head circuit: 20 miles (32 kms).

Trail head – Simpson Lake – Moon Lake – Dubois: 24 miles (39 kms).

Season/weather

Trekking season May/June, depending on snowfall, to September/October.

Bighorn ewes and lambs grazing at the highest point of the trail.

Generally trails are snowfree or passable from mid-June to late October, although unusual winter conditions may vary these dates by one month or more. July and August are the most popular months for walkers and certain trails become busy. September is the best month. The trails are quiet, mosquitoes and black flies have disappeared, broadleaf trees turn glorious colours and although the nights are frosty, the days can equal the best of summer.

It must be stressed that the weather in the Wind River Mountains can change very quickly and is unpredictable. Winds, of course, can be violent and snow can fall in *any* month. My trek was undertaken in superb weather but the year before I would have needed snowshoes to complete it. The weather poses no problems as long as you are prepared for its fickle temperament.

The following details apply to the township of Dubois (elevation 6,917 ft/2,108 m) and not directly to the mountain region. The temperatures were recorded in the most recent season and should be regarded as statistics of what happened one year rather than of what to expect every year.

Mean annual precipitation: 8.5 inches (216 mm)

Mean average snowfall: 13 inches (330 mm)

Mean average wind velocity: 10 mph (16 kph)

Last freeze: June 10th.

First freeze: August 25th.

Mid-month temperatures (°F/°C)

	High	Low
May	75/24	40/4
June	81/27	46/8
July	86/30	48/9
August	60/16	42/15
(4 days later 82/28 32/0)		
September	73/23	25/−4
October	63/17	25/−4
November	35/2	16/−9

Equipment

With so little rain and bogs that are avoidable, wetness is not a problem on this trek. In general your days will be hot and the nights cold. Light summer clothes suffice for walking with warm jersies/trousers and windproof cagoul/trousers for nights or storms. Boots with good

ankle support are essential. A sub-zero sleeping bag is necessary in the colder months. It is safer and wiser to take a tent but you can sleep rough – there are always rocks to give shelter. Stoves are useful but not essential as firewood is plentiful. Those who don't usually take a water bottle but drink out of streams, will need one here (see warning in health section) and some water sterilization tablets. The sun is fierce at this altitude so some protecting cream is a good idea for unaccustomed skin. Lastly, with all the wonderful wildlife, it's a pity not to have binoculars.

All provisions and most items of equipment can be bought in Dubois.

Access/permits

With the exception of a few miles at either end, this trek takes place within the Shoshone National Forest. Access and camping are free but you are requested to complete a registration card provided at wayside boxes at the Forest entrances. Vehicles and all motorised equipment are forbidden. No hunting is permitted out of season or without a licence, but fishing is allowed (and said to be good) with a permit obtainable from Dubois stores.

If you step off the described route and cross into the Wind River Indian Reservation, an entry permit *is* required. Buy it from the Reservation authorities *before* you walk their trails. Only one type of permit is available, valid for one year, and this currently costs about US$35.

Logistics

It is a paradox, and yet perhaps reassuring, that a place in the heart of Western civilization should require so much ingenuity to reach, but the fact remains that Dubois is not served by public transport. (If not ingenuity, then expense.) Frontier Air flies to Riverton, Casper and Jackson, while Greyhound and state buses pass through Jackson and Shoshoni – Jackson is the nearest alternative but is still 80 miles (130 kms) short of Dubois.

The Wind River Mountains contain hundreds of miles of trails and the possible permutations of a route are endless. I have described one trek which is particularly suitable for the lone trekker – leaving a cache of food at the trail head

avoids having to carry nine days' worth of food right at the start. I completed the journey in two stages but it could easily be divided into three (Glacier Trail, Bomber Lake circuit, Simpson Lake) or done in one. Doing it in one would require carrying all provisions but would save seven miles (eleven kms) and 3,500 ft (1,000 m) of climbing, by obviating the need to return to the trail head for food. It is incidental which way round the trek is tackled but I favour the way described in the text, ending at Dubois. You can see your hot bath from miles away. At least one company in Dubois will outfit trips and supply pack horses.

Medical considerations

It is distressing to have to note that even in this magnificent wilderness area it is *not* advisable to drink mountain water. There is no guarantee that two types of bacteria, *Giardia lamblia* and *Campylobacter*, will not be present and these can cause serious illness. A drop of water is sufficient to cause infection so don't use untreated water at all, not even for washing. Water held at a rolling boil for one minute (five minutes above 10,000 ft/3,000 m) will render the water safe, as will chemical sterilization tablets. When using tablets in extremely cold water, increased dosage or waiting time is usually prescribed – follow the manufacturer's instructions.

Those arriving suddenly in the area may experience breathlessness due to the altitude in the early stages of the trek. If so, rest for a day or two to acclimatize. Dubois has a well-equipped medical clinic.

Reading
Maps:

The excellent *USGS topographical maps* (1:24,000) are available in Dubois. Six maps cover the region described in the text; Downs Mountain, Simpson Lake, Torrey Lake, Ink Wells, Fremond Peak North and Gannett Peak. The whole area is covered in the *USGS 1:100,000 series* Gannett Peak Quadrangle. *US Forest Service $\frac{1}{2}$ inch* 'Bridger National Forest' and 'Shoshone National Forest' maps are also useful.

Guide books and books of specific regional interest:

Wind River Trails – Finis Mitchell (Wasatch Publishers Inc., Salt Lake

City, 1975)
Wyoming Hiking Trails – Tom and Sanse Sudduth (Pruett Publishing Co., Boulder, 1978)
Guide to the Wyoming Mountains and Wilderness Areas – Orrin H. Bonney and Lorraine Bonney (Swallow, Ohio University, 1977. 3rd edition)
Fieldbook; Wind River Range – Orrin & Lorraine Bonney (Bonney, 1975. Revised edition)
Wyoming Mountain Ranges – Lorraine G Bonney (American Geographic Publishing, Helena, 1987)
Seven Half Miles From Home – Notes of a Wind River Naturalist – Mary Beck (Johnson Books, Boulder, 1978).

Alastair Scott was born in Edinburgh in 1954 and now lives in Morayshire, Scotland. After gaining a BA in German and Economics at Stirling University he worked in a photographic studio before deciding to spend a few years travelling round the world. The object was both to see the world and its peoples and to gather a portfolio of photographs. Subsequently, he has written three books on his travels, the first of which was published in 1986. Since then, he has kept travelling, doing a long bicycle trek in Eastern Europe and with a dog team in Alaska.

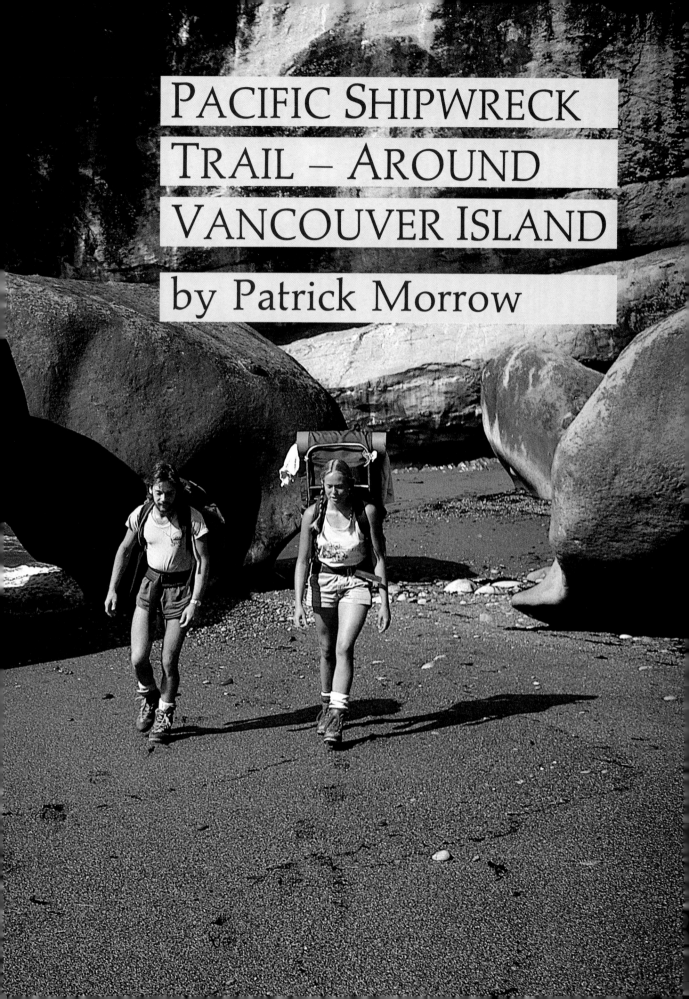

PACIFIC SHIPWRECK TRAIL – AROUND VANCOUVER ISLAND

by Patrick Morrow

'. . . the sea is all about us;
The sea is the land's edge also, the granite
Into which it reaches, the beaches where it tosses
Its hints of earlier and other creation . . .'
TS Eliot, *The Dry Salvages*

For over 200 miles (350 kms) along the
spectacular coastline of western Vancouver
Island, rugged mountain terrain blends with the
monotony of the ocean's horizon. And nowhere
else is this wild, unique combination so readily
accessible than on the 45 miles (73 kms) long
West Coast Trail, stretching from Pachena Bay in
the north to Port San Juan in the south.

Strong ocean currents and fickle marine
weather have driven more than 60 ships of all
sizes aground on this jagged headland since
1854, earning the region its nickname, 'The
Graveyard of the Pacific'. In 1906, the wreck of
the SS *Valencia*, just north of the Klanawa River,
took the lives of 126 people and convinced the
federal government that it was time to link
together traces of game paths to form what was
to become a lifesaving trail.

Until the 1950s, a muddy, precipitous
footpath and a telephone line were maintained
by solitary linesmen who were kept busy by the
erosive forces of a coastline that receives over 86
inches (220 cms) of rainfall a year, and the
encroachment of a rainforest that either grew or
fell over their attempts to tame the wilderness.

By 1970, a small population of indigenous
Indians and the few lighthouse keepers who had
replaced the linesmen started to receive
impromptu visits from increasing numbers of
recreational hikers intent on getting away from it
all, less than 60 miles (100 kms) from Victoria,
the province's capital. In April of that year,
pressure from the federal government and
interest groups such as the Sierra Club of British
Columbia convinced the provincial government
to include the trail in the Pacific Rim National
Park, resulting in the creation of the West Coast
Trail. The nearby ocean kayaker's mecca, the
Broken Island Group, and the satin-smooth sand
of Long Beach share the protection offered by
Canada's first national marine park, which differs
from other coastal parks in that it also
incorporates the marine environment out to the
10 fathom mark.

Logging companies used to having their way
in a land of seemingly infinite natural resources
have already pushed their sloppy, clear-cut
practices right up to the park boundaries at
several points along the trail, keeping
conservation groups vigilant in their attempts to
maintain the recreational and natural integrity of

the trail and the park. The easy access they
would give to the trail's most attractive sections,
such as Carmanah Beach, Tsusiat Falls and the
Klanawa River, would destroy the current sense
of wilderness, delicately preserved, and the
removal of treed 'buffer' zones by standard 'cut
and run' logging methods also jeopardises the
thin strip of primary growth left along the coast,
since wind storms will create even more
'blowdown' areas.

In the face of so serious a threat from both
the logging and mining interests, would-be
trekkers should write to the Minister of Lands
and Parks at the Provincial Parliament Buildings,
Victoria, BC to ask if the government can
substantiate all that it promises the tourist in its
'Super Natural British Columbia' advertising
campaign, writing again on completion of the
trek to urge the government to search its own
conscience on its claimed efforts to preserve this
wonderful wilderness.

I've hiked the West Coast Trail in both
directions, the first time in 1973 when less than a
couple of thousand others shared a somewhat
wilder experience than in the early 1980s, when I
joined some of the 5,000 annual visitors. Only
about half the total number of people who walk
on the trail hike it from beginning to end. Some
hike only the first six miles (nine kms) to Pachena
Point; others continue to Tsusiat Falls before
retracing their steps. Although people of all ages
and experience hike the trail, it is a relatively
serious undertaking and it is best to be prepared
with decent waterproof equipment and a
rudimentary knowledge of surviving in the west
coastal climate. The state of the trail is vastly
affected by previous weather conditions so that
even if you hike during a dry spell, you are apt
to face areas of muddy or washed-out trail and
eroding cliff.

Because transport is more easily organised
from north to south, most hikers travel in that
direction, though some prefer to tackle the more
rigorous southern section first while they are
fresh. My companion, Shirley, and I decided that
we would take the usual option, warming up to
the difficulties as we made our way south at a
leisurely pace.

In late July, 1973, we bussed from Nanaimo
on the south-east coast of Vancouver Island to
Port Alberni at the head of Berkley Sound, an
unpleasant pulp-mill town where the air was
pungent and choking. As there is a lengthy ferry
crossing from the mainland near Vancouver, the
journey took us a day longer then we had
planned, something that those on a tight
schedule should allow for.

We were scanning our tattered xerox copy of

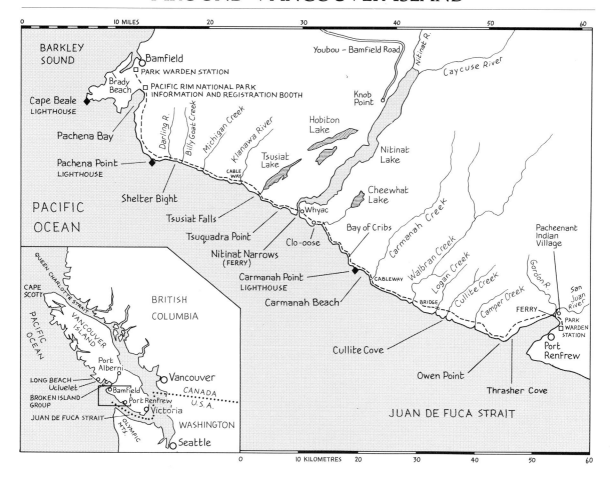

an original, typewritten, three-page trail guide at our tent door in a local camping site when a teenage Nootka Indian wandered over to see what we were up to. He spied the small treasure of smoked salmon we landlocked palefaces were enjoying with our evening meal, and looked away indifferently. When we remarked how good the rich flesh tasted, he grimaced and told us how his parents had fed him salmon as a main course from birth: baked, poached, boiled, fried, every kind of salmon. He was far more interested in the standard dehydrated hiker's fare we had brought in our 40 lb (18 kg) packs for the seven day walk. Because of the likelihood of getting wet, our seasonings and spices were carried in plastic waterproof containers, as were our home-dried cheese chips, vegetables, apples and soup mixes. Salami and smoked ham keep well in this environment but must be wrapped in wax paper and several layers of thick brown paper to protect against the dampness.

Early next morning, we strolled down to the dockside and hopped on the slippery deck of the *Lady Rose*, a foot passenger and supply ship that serves this part of the coast. The sun shone bright but comfortably cool, a harbinger of the climatic conditions we would meet during most of the trip to come.

An hour down the inlet, the captain's bullhorn heralded the sighting of a killer whale. The dozen or so passengers rushed over to starboard to catch a glimpse of the five foot tall black dorsal fin, and the small ship careened jauntily in the same direction. Everyone gasped as the six ton (6,000 kg) Orca seemed to pass right under our noses in its sweep for a meal of marine delectables. In reality it was probably some 50 yards away.

The Nootkas of the island's south-west coast call this 25 ft whale 'qaqawun', and it appears prominently in the folkloric totems their Haida cousins carve from giant cedars. Because of its peculiar role in the mythology of Coast Indian peoples, the killer whale was generally exempt from hunting. It is small for a whale, being as long as four horses end to end, compared to the two juggernaut lengths of a blue whale, but earned its name for its voracious appetite. In times of great need, they will occasionally feed on up to 25 species of whale and dolphin, as well as seals and birds, although fish, such as salmon, cod and herring are their most common fare in Canadian waters.

Organisations like the West Coast Whale Research Foundation have estimated that some 261 killer whales live off the BC coast, while the world's highest concentration lives off the northern part of Vancouver Island. They belong to 'pods' or herds averaging 10 animals, and researchers such as Erich Hoyt and John KB Ford have determined that each pod has its own dialect, and that pods in close proximity to each other often share some sounds. Only a few other species – *Homo sapiens* included – have true local dialects.

These and a dozen other species of whale that range up and down the coast of BC are at the mercy of the measures taken by the provincial government to manage their land resources. Logging and mining near the water's edge threaten to have an irreversible effect on the fisheries which provide the killer whales with their sustenance.

Whale and seal watching is one of the many perks of this trail, and a quick glance out across the Juan de Fuca Strait towards the Olympic Peninsula will often reveal a glimpse of sea life rollicking in the fertile waters of the Pacific Ocean.

When we put in at the tiny, vernal cove of Bamfield near Pachena Bay, we couldn't help but admire the beauty and compactness of the cedar-shaked houses. Here was a town that could, until recently, be reached only by sea, and perhaps because of this a sparseness of layout and design has resulted in a rare harmony with the wild surroundings.

Even though we were aware of several good side trips in the Bamfield area — to Brady Beach, for instance, or by sea to Cape Beale — we had come to do the trail proper and strode off down the three mile (five kms) road leading to the trail head at the Parks Canada information and registration booth at Pachena Bay.

Our first campsite was near Darling River, only a short walk from Pachena Point. A sign on the tiny lawn at the lighthouse advised: 'Lighthouse keepers are not lonely people — please don't try to visit us'. Here the rich, salty air of the Pacific ocean filled our lungs and stirred new sensations in bodies that had so recently left the thin, freeze-dried air of the

Atmospheric conditions along the West coast Trail vary from moody to full-scale hurricane-force winds. At the turn of the century, navigational difficulties and bad weather took a heavy toll on passing ships, earning this stretch of coast the well-deserved name of 'Graveyard of the Pacific'.

mountains. The fecundity of the sea life also amazed us. A massive pair of sea lions basked on the rocks near Pachena, and we held out furtive hopes of sighting a sea otter, a species that is slowly making a comeback to the Inside Passage area after a near extinction that began in the 1700s with capitalistic Russian fur traders who employed Aleut Eskimos and their shallow *baidarka* vessels to ply the water as far as the north coast of California.

We had brought a collapsible fishing rod and were able to augment our diet with delicious trout from numerous streams. We also found it easy to catch black bass among the kelp beds at dusk when they came close to the surface to feed. A few years before, a friend had hiked the entire trail equipped with nothing more than a knife, matches and some fishing line and hooks. He dined royally on shellfish such as mussels and a wide variety of wild fruits including huckleberries, blueberries, thimbleberries and wild blackberries in addition to young fiddlehead ferns which he steamed to include in his salads.

At the time of our hike, a 'red tide' warning was posted at either end of the trail, advising summer hikers against eating filter-feeding molluscs. The threat of succumbing to this potentially fatal disease called paralytic shellfish poisoning should be enough to encourage nature children to leave them alone and it is recommended that even if you have seen no notice, you should still avoid eating bivalve molluscs in this region. For that matter, now it is a National Park, harvesting of any sea or plant life along this trail has become prohibited.

Next morning, we were able to avoid having to pull ourselves across the strenuous cable car spanning the Darling River by skipping across upstream on a tangle of driftwood, a short cut that depends on the recent history of rain and runoff. Shortly after launching out on our second day, we came upon bits of historic detritus in the form of a capstan on the rocks at Shelter Bight which may have come from the four-masted schooner, *Robert E. Lewers*, which ran aground in 1923. There were also interesting traces of rusted wreckage in the surge channel at the outlet of Billy Goat Creek and the mouth of Michigan Creek.

We stretched our legs on the long-sections of pebble-strewn beach between Michigan and Klanawa Creeks, careful to set up our camp above the high tide mark. Because the Klanawa and the outflows of other rivers such as the Nitinat, Cheewhat and Walbran are partially salty, freshwater supplies must be sought from other sources nearby, and the slow-moving

trickles in the bogs may have high bacteria counts which could provoke diarrhoea, or worse, if not boiled. Generally, water along the trail is sweet and safe, but in areas of heavy use, we had to be sure to take drinking water from a prudent distance upstream.

A fairly well preserved linesman's cabin stands near Klanawa Creek and others in various stages of disintegration can be seen along the way. The trail left the beach at Klanawa, and took us along the undulating benchland through heavy hemlock and sitka spruce forest with few glimpses of the ocean until Tsusiat Falls, one of the gems of the trail, where crystal clear water hisses over an 80 ft (24 m) vertical drop into a dark green pool on the beach. It was wonderful for us to discover this sun-warmed water, having got used to frigid, skin-burning, glacier-born streams! We gladly took the offer of nature's shower to wash away some of the salt spray our skin and clothing had absorbed in the past couple of days.

While we were frolicking in the tepid water an anomalous canoe prow appeared at the brink of the falls directly overhead. A tow rope was thrown down and a couple of canoeists set up a kind of tyrolean traverse for their heavy aluminium craft, lowering it carefully to the sand. They had reached this unlikely spot by paddling down the Hobiton and Tsusiat Lakes on a two day journey from the road head to the ocean. Once down, the expert paddlers pushed off without ceremony into the strong ocean swell and disappeared around the corner to negotiate the treacherous Nitinat Narrows that lead into Nitinat Lake, thus completing their circuit of the Hobitan–Tsusiat watershed. This network of lakes, rivers and portages is reached with some difficulty by road from BC Forest Products' Knob Point picnic ground on the north side of Nitinat Lake and opens up a whole new dimension of the exquisite island ecosystem.

Unfortunately, the frequency of rough shelters made of driftwood and bits of shredded plastic near the Falls and elsewhere along the beach pointed to the desirability of carrying a tent and using a lightweight gas stove in an effort to minimise human impact on what was once pure wilderness. Park officials and conscientious hikers have gone a long way towards cleaning up after the heavy hiker traffic, but anyone who embarks on this journey of discovery should keep in mind their own role as a keeper of the land.

One of the journey's more delightful sections of beachwalking came soon after we left the Falls and headed for Nitinat Narrows. There's nothing quite like walking along at sea level with the fresh salt air swirling in your nostrils, skipping around playful waves as they heave themselves against the beach. We paused to explore the self-explanatory 'Hole in the Wall' at Tsusiat Point and the sea caves at Tsuquadra Point. These solution pockets, carved by the ocean in the soft sandstone shelves, held a treasure-trove of marine life. Camouflaged sand crabs scuttled past bright-coloured starfish and flower-like anemones. An even more impressive marine display exists at Botanical Beach, reached from the highway just south of Port Renfrew, where we were so absorbed by the action in the foreground that we almost missed a pod of six Orcas cruising by. The sociable mammals frolicked in the powerful ocean currents, unaware they were giving us the show of our lives.

It was dusk when we came to the most serious crossing of all, Nitinat Narrows. The village of Whyac slumbers on the east side of the channel in which tides, rushing in towards the lake at speeds of up to eight knots, create powerful whirlpools. There was no question of wading or even swimming across for we knew that even using a boat, many people have drowned here. An Indian, on retainer for Parks Canada, answered our cries and ferried us across in his motor-driven freighter canoe for $3 apiece. As we passed his small frame house, held together by cedar shakes, we spied a rack of freshly smoked sockeye salmon and managed to buy one for an additional couple of dollars.

Whyac, which consists of only a few moss-covered buildings, is considered to be one of the oldest settlements on the west coast of North America. A few years after this hike, I met Betty Carey, a middle-aged housewife who, as a student, found a twelve foot dugout canoe washed up on the beach in Oregon. She installed a set of rowlocks in the tiny vessel and launched out from Seattle, with little more than a bag of gorp (a climber's snack of nuts, raisins and Smarties-type chocolate buttons) and a great dollop of faith, following the tides up the entire

Inside Passage 1,600 miles (2,500 kms) to Alaska. She so enjoyed herself on that voyage that once her own children were at university, she kissed them and her husband goodbye and repeated it, relying on food handouts from friendly fishermen and Indians. Later she was able to trace the canoe's origins to Whyac, where it had apparently been set adrift during a notoriously fierce winter storm.

Just past Whyac, we passed a long beach decorated with petroglyphs, blowholes and a barnacle-encrusted anchor. The palmated branches of the lush raincoast forest hung out over the sand, framing the white-capped ocean and a beach where glass fishing floats occasionally wash up on shore all the way from Japan. We spent a cosy night at a delectable little camp spot near here.

We picked an arduous way along the beach next day, until forced up by a rocky headwall halfway to Clo-oose. On this headwall, we could make out some petroglyphs, historical graffiti left by the ancestors of the three groups of Indians that live along the trail; the Ohiat Band at Pachena Bay, the Nitinat Band in the Nitinat Basin, and the Pacheenaht Band at Port Renfrew. Our map marked the reserves along the trail, and we knew that we could camp on or use firewood from these areas only with special permission from the Indians themselves.

We found more mementos from the past in the village of Clo-oose. Early white settlers came to the area in the 1880s, and in 1912 a land development scheme brought several dozen optimists to set up home next to the original residents. A series of economic setbacks over the ensuing years saw the last of the original white families leaving in 1952. The former United Church chapel, a white hut, now serves as a home for a caretaker, and stands amid vestiges of houses that have been abandoned to the weather and vandals.

A Japanese glass fishing float found on the beach near Whyac.

Above — *One may seek refuge in the numerous caves along the trail, like this one near Tsusiat Point. However, it is more comfortable to bring your own tent, which can be easily moved in the face of incoming tide — something that must be remembered if ensconced in a cave camp.*

Left — *Spectacular campsites abound, like this one at Cullite Cove. If one campspot is already occupied, you can simply push on until you find the privacy you are looking for.*

Midway to the lighthouse at Carmanah Point, we climbed up a rocky promontory and gazed out across the Strait of Juan de Fuca towards the United States, at the Olympic mountains rising from the peninsula of the same name. Glancing down at the beach below, I recalled the horror story a friend told me about a mishap that occurred when he was hiking on a similar trail in the Olympics. He was forced to circumvent the high tide by scrambling up onto a grassy slope, and in doing so, slipped and became airborne.

After a 30 foot (ten metre) fall, he landed on his feet with sufficient force to shatter bones in both legs and one arm. Lying in agony on the sand, just before losing consciousness, he remembered wondering if he had landed far enough up the beach to escape the incoming tide. Miraculously he was soon discovered by other hikers and shortly afterwards was on his way to hospital by medivac helicopter — a close-run thing! We tried to be especially careful near similar dangerous dropoffs. Access routes from the beach to the main trail running through the woods above are usually marked by old buoys hanging in the trees, though towards the southern end of the trail, access is often by long, steep wooden ladders that demand a cautious footing on muddy rungs.

By this time we were getting in good shape and the continuous ups and downs of the trail, and the often steep side trips onto the beach were nothing but sheer pleasure. While searching for a source of fresh drinking water, we passed up the cedar bark-stained tidal water of the

Cheewhat, named by the Indians 'River of Urine' – for reasons which were obvious. Nevertheless, we located a tiny spring of sweet water a few hundred yards upstream where we managed to fill our water bottles. We never ran short. Although this jagged coastline and the vagaries of the seasons result in a multitude of different route variations, we were always able to obtain useful and up-to-date information about the best routes, good campsites and sources of fresh water from fellow trekkers we passed travelling in the opposite direction.

From here, nearly all the way to the Bay of the Cribs, we followed a straightforward trail that led through a wonderland of giant douglas

Two intrepid canoeists lowered their craft over Tsusiat Falls to the beach.

fir and red cedar with occasional detours along the beach. In times past, the ropey bark of the red cedar was used by the West Coast Indians to weave waterproof basins, and even clothing, while the trunk formed the hull of their dugout canoes, sometimes over 40 ft (13 m) long and large enough to carry up to 60 people on sea journeys of hundreds of miles. A few days before, when the canoeists had pushed off to sea from Tsusiat Falls in their hi-tech craft, I had screwed up my eyes and turned them into a Nootka raiding party, decked out in war paint, stealthily riding the tides in search of booty and slaves.

The Nootka made their living almost entirely from the sea, supplemented in season with roots and berries from the forest. They dried salmon and herring roe into flat hard cakes, a delicacy much coveted during the long winter months,

while octopus, sea slugs, sea urchins and crabs complemented their main diet of whale and salmon. It was galling to recall how high a premium we had paid in a smart, ethnic Vancouver restaurant for the same fare that was the regular diet of the Nootka people!

Thanks to their ability to live harmoniously with their rigorous environment, the traditional Nootkas were able to devise technology utilizing the natural abundance of their surroundings which provided not only for their survival but also for their leisure, their ceremony and art. Life, for their northern neighbours, the Kwakiutls and Haidas was rather easier, a fact reflected in the opulence of their elaborately carved totems, ritual masks and war canoes. Unfortunately, anthropologists have tended to ignore the comparatively more austere art of the Nootka.

As we waited for a couple of hikers to pull themselves across the cable-way crossing at Walbran Creek, one of them stepped off and remarked with misty eyes that we Canadians were fortunate to have so many bald eagles. They told us they had seen more of these huge raptors in one day than in years of hiking in their native California. Rapturous over raptors.

Our one moment of drama came on the beach between Walbran and Logan Creeks when we encountered a lone hiker waiting patiently on the far side of a cleft in the sandstone shelf. One can zoom along this compact rock shelf at sea level for a mile or more, but it is sensible to consult the tide tables first to ensure that entrapment between such a cleft and an impossible rock wall is unlikely. Luckily we had brought a 30 ft length of lightweight polypropylene line for belaying over such occasional obstacles and I threw an end over to the luckless fellow. Then we hauled each other's packs across before Shirley, with some trepidation, started clambering over. It was only a couple of awkward moves but the rock was covered in slippery sea-weed. Without warning, a sneaky wave swept in, knocked her footing away and sucked her, head first, into the water swirling in the gap. In an instant I took up the slack in the rope and held her secure while she sputtered and grabbed onto wet handholds on the far side. My own crossing lacked the drama, but my heart was still pounding with the thought of what could have happened had we tried this manoeuvre without a rope.

There are several similar places along the beach route, but if one is not up to leaping, climbing or crawling around them, you can always backtrack and bypass the difficulties on the headland above. Of course, one can avoid these technical sections of beach by following the forest trail the entire way, but this only

works in theory because the lure of the sea's edge is too strong for one to stay in the shadow of the trees for very long.

The relative popularity of this trail at least gives the illusion of safety should something go wrong, whereas on the really isolated beach walks further up the coast, which must be reached by inflatable from Tahsis, or on those round Cape Scott at the extreme northern tip of Vancouver Island, it is painfully obvious that great care must be taken both in selecting routes and controlling risks. Even so, the Shipwreck Trail can be more serious than it appears.

It is towards the southern end of the trail that the handiwork of the Parks Department is most evident. An attractive suspension bridge over Logan Creek is followed immediately by a steep series of ladders up the east bank. Most of the creeks in this area have cut their way through dozens of feet of topsoil down to sea level and the trail must cross the creeks at right angles – against the grain of the country. Traversing this type of up-and-down terrain is arduous but a mountaineer's gait, moving slowly and steadily, will ensure that one's energy reserves last throughout the hike.

Between the Logan and Cullite Creeks a sturdy boardwalk now protects a fragile, boggy surface, and keeps the hiker's pant legs clean into the bargain. Not so long ago they risked plunging into the rich humus mud up to their hips. But these boardwalk or cedar-round paths can be treacherously slippery when damp and on this occasion we met a family of four from Victoria whose youngest member, a boy of twelve, had tried unsuccessfully for the first few hours to keep his jeans clean. It was only a matter of time before both he and his clothes took on the colour of the land. Boys will be boys, of course, and once he realised his parents were resigned to it, he probably enjoyed the mud!

At Cullite, we found a luxuriant campsite, bemoaning the fact that now we had finally warmed up to the vagaries of travel in this up-and-down world of trail and beach, we were approaching the journey's end. However the experience stood me in good stead for hiking on both the east and west coasts of the Queen Charlotte Islands a few years later where other, more remote beachwalking possibilities traverse an even wilder world. It was not all plain sailing from here, though. Especially in wet and slimy conditions, the blowdown area just east of Camper Creek will stimulate the old adrenaline. Here the wind has knocked down a swath of giant conifers, which lie tangled across each other, and the trail literally takes to the trees.

The trail builders, forseeing a strenuous, chain-saw wielding epic, simply walked along their suspended horizontal trunks, lopping off branches. In some places, this 'trail' is up to twelve feet from the ground.

Our final campsite was near the spectacular Owen Point. Eons of storms have drilled a cave right through the prow of the headland, and the coarse surface of the shelf has mixed with pebbles and sand to create a lovely moonscape. Thus far on our trek we had received not so much as a drop of the fabled west coast 'liquid sunshine', and had been pitching our small tent every night out of habit. This night we looked up at the darkening sky and thought 'may as well just roll out the mats and sleep under the stars'. At about 2am, the goose down in our bags started to absorb the first drops of what turned into a torrential downpour that left me, and all our kit, a sodden mess. By the time the first light seeped through the heavy cloud ceiling next morning, my body core temperature had plunged and I was bordering on hypothermia. Only with a great effort did I fight with our small gas stove and get a flame going under a pot of porridge. Even after downing several cups of hot tea and forcing myself to eat, I was still shaking. Luckily Shirley's bag was waterproof, but she was in only slightly better form.

On this occasion, we covered the last few miles of the trail far away from the sea, but when I next hiked the Shipwreck Trail several years later, I started from the south – from Port Renfrew – and caught a ride from the Pacheenat Indian Village all the way to Thrasher Cove near Owen Point, completely by-passing this relatively uninteresting final – or initial – section.

Eventually we reached the Gordon River and were about to yell across to the Pacheenaht Indian Band village for a lift when a brief flurry of motion near the water's edge caught my eye. I thought it was a heron at first, but when my eyes focused in the gathering darkness, I saw the sinuous form of a mink. Intent on securing a delectable meal of minnow or frog, the sleek animal dived into the water, leaving hardly a ripple. We sat in our soggy clothing waiting to return to the hurry-up world, hoping we too had left only a ripple on this lovely stretch of serrated coastline.

Wild winter storms toss up logs torn from log booms further up the coast as well as exotica such as fishing floats from the Sea of Japan, and the occasional whale carcass. A beachcomber's delight.

Difficulties/dangers

Difficulties can be found if desired by keeping close to the tide line but all problems can be avoided – see main text. The sea, its currents and tides are always potentially dangerous and should be treated with respect.

Distances/times

The wilderness track from the **Northern Trail Head at Camp Ross on Pachena Bay**, some 3 miles (5 kms) south from *Bamfield*, to *Port San Juan* on the Gordon River, 2 miles (3.5 kms) from the **Port Renfrew Southern Trail Head** is a distance of 45 miles (73 kms). Expect to take between four days and a week on the Trail, depending on one's compromise between speed and beach-combing. Allow further time to and from Nanaimo.

Season/weather

The season is summer, mid-May to mid-September. At other times access may be difficult, ferries inoperative, Park facilities closed, and the weather severe.

The climate is that of temperate coastal rainforest with cool temperatures and high rainfall. Though summer is the driest season, rain, fog and wind are not uncommon and may persist for several days.

July averages are: temperature 57°F/14°C, rainfall 2 in/6 cms. *Annual average rainfall* is 89 in/227cms.

Equipment

Be prepared for possible cold and wet conditions. Standard backpacking equipment should include tent, warm sleeping bag, warm clothing and waterproofs, besides firestarter and waterproof matches, insect repellent, 50 ft (15 m) of light 'confidence' rope, a small shovel, biodegradable soap and plastic garbage sacks – both for keeping kit dry and packing out garbage.

Permits

The West Coast Trail lies within the Pacific Rim National Park. Registration is recommended but is not compulsory and may be made between 9am and 5pm (or by self-registration after hours) at Northern Trail Head, Pachena Bay/Camp Ross (phone (604) 728–3234) or Southern Trail Head on Parkinson Ave, Port Renfrew (phone (604) 647–5434). Both Trail Head Centres provide up-to-date information on trail conditions as well as maps and tide tables.

Park Rules are for Low Impact, Environmentally Conscious Camping and Hiking: all garbage must be burnt or carried out, human waste must be burnt or buried well away from fresh water sources. Only dead or drift wood may be burnt – and that only with special permission on the several small Indian Reserves crossed by the trail (marked on the map). Heavy boots are discouraged and dogs are not permitted. It is prohibited to damage or kill any sea or plantlife.

Logistics

There are two water obstacles on the West Coast Trail which necessitate ferry crossings – the Nitinat Narrows and the Gordon River. Ferry services are provided across both by local natives for a small fee, the former is sponsored by Parks Canada and operates from mid-May to mid-October, the latter is private and operates on request.

The town of Nanaimo on the south-eastern coast of Vancouver Island is reached by ferry or by air from Vancouver or by bus from Victoria. Thence regular buses run to Port Alberni from where a 2½ hour bus ride on gravel logging roads leads some 60 miles (100 kms) to Bamfield on Pachena Bay. Alternatively take a leisurely half-day boat trip down Berkley Sound on the *M.V. Lady Rose* which operates three times a week, four times in July/August.

If you use your own vehicle it is best to leave it at Port Renfrew and reach the Northern Trail Head by public transport.

Hitchhiking is not recommended as traffic on these roads is light.

Medical considerations

Hypothermia is a potential hazard for improperly equipped or unlucky parties in prolonged rainy periods. Trekkers should know how to deal with this condition.

Fresh water should be selected with care and if its origin is in doubt it should be boiled.

Besides being protected, bivalve molluscs may be fatally toxic.

Reading

Maps:

Most useful is *'West Coast Trail, Port Renfrew–Bamfield'* at 1:50,000 with 100 ft contours.
Other relevant maps are:
National Topographical series 1:50,000 sheets 92 C/9, 92 C/10 and 92 C/11 and *Vancouver Island* 6 miles/inch.
These are available from:
Province of British Columbia, Map Production, Surveys and Mapping Branch, Ministry of the Environment, 553 Superior Street, Victoria, BC, V8V 1X4 (phone 387–1441) or local map dealers.

Also essential is a copy of the *Canadian Tide and Current Tables*, Vol 6, which is obtainable at most marine stores or Canadian Govt. Publications Centre, Ottawa.

Guides and other books:

Parks Canada publish a useful leaflet, *West Coast Trail*, available – as with other relevant information – from Pacific Rim National Park, see address below.
The Birds of Pacific Rim National Park – a leaflet listing the 249 bird species known to occur in the Park – is also published by Parks Canada.
The West Coast Trail and Nitinat Lakes (Sierra Club, San Francisco)
A Guide to Shipwrecks along the West Coast Trail – R E Wells (Sooke, BC, 1981)

Further information

Pacific Rim National Park:
PO Box 280, Ucluelet, BC V0R 3A0
M.V. Lady Rose schedule:
Alberni Marine Transportation Inc, PO Box 188, Port Alberni, BC V9Y 7M7
Parchena Bay Express bus service: Mr Chester Clappis, phone 604–728–3448
Pacific Rim Tourist Assoc: 4586 Victoria Quay, Port Alberni, BC V9Y 6G3
Tourism British Columbia: 1117 Wharf Street, Victoria, BC V8W 2Z2

Pat Morrow, at 35, is one of North America's leading mountaineers and professional adventure photographers. He reached the summit of Everest with the first Canadian expedition in 1982 and subsequently went on to climb the highest summits of all seven continents. He is author of several books, a Contributing Editor to *Equinox Magazine* and a partner in *Adventure Network* – the first adventure travel company to operate on the Antarctic continent. He was awarded the highly prestigious *Order of Canada* in 1987.

ROCKY SPINE OF GREECE – THE PINDOS TRAVERSE

by Tim Salmon

When God created the world, Greeks will tell you, he found he had a bucket of stones left over, tipped them out and the result was Greece.
Traditional Greek myth

A look at the map will show you that a goodly proportion of these stones fell and formed a broad, continuous backbone of mountains running from the Gulf of Corinth to the frontiers of Albania. Though strictly speaking the name Pindos only belongs to the northern two-thirds, the range is one and it is with the whole of it that this trek is concerned.

It is perfect country for mountain walkers, wild and rugged enough to give a sense of adventure without ever being really daunting. The typical landscape is deep ravines flanked by forested slopes rising to stony alpine pastures and bare limestone crags. Rivers and streams run all summer through and there are abundant springs to cool the cockles of the sweaty traveller's heart. All but the highest peaks and ridges are free of snow from May to October and the weather is largely trustworthy, except for the occasional mountain storm. Even at the height of summer, the air stays pleasantly cool above 3,000 ft (1,000 m). And the wild flowers are among the loveliest and rarest in Europe.

For me the greatest pleasure lies in the fact that these are working mountains. There is no tourism of any kind, there are no organized facilities even for the ecologically undisturbing walker. The few remaining inhabitants still pursue their traditional activities, cultivating their tiny plots of beans and maize, mowing their hay with scythes and pasturing their sheep and goats on the uplands. They are also incredibly friendly and welcoming, and will always provide you with bed and food if you do not want to camp all the time. The rhythm of life is so different that within a day or two the world you normally inhabit seems to belong to another planet.

There are other rewards too, for these mountains are full of history, not the kind that fills the school books, but the stuff of legend and folk song. For during the long night of Turkish rule, from the fall of Constantinople in 1453 until 1912, these inaccessible regions of the northern Pindos were the strongholds of Robin Hood bandits who kept the spirit of Hellenism alive by force of their outlawed arms. It is a tradition which continued into the 1940s, when the powerful Greek Resistance movement kept the mountains free from the occupying Italian and German forces. And the Greek Communist partisans made their base here during the 1946–49 civil war. When people know you are British, you will certainly hear about both these events. You will be blamed, albeit good-humouredly, for causing the civil war, then asked confidentially if you have got a metal-detector in your rucksack to search for the caches of gold sovereigns dropped by the RAF for the wartime Resistance.

But of most interest to the walker is the extensive network of footpaths that, until the 1950s, were the only lines of communication between the mountain communities. Though many have been partially obliterated by new tracks constructed in the decade or so I have been walking these mountains, and all are much less frequented than formerly, they are still easy enough to follow and form the basis of this trek.

My internal compass tells me the logical way to travel is up the map, and that is what I did on this journey, starting at the little market town of Amfissa near Delphi on the shores of the Gulf of Corinth and working my way north to the summit of Mt Grammos just a stone's throw from the Albanian border.

There is no gentle run-in. The first three or four days are a cruel test of character, when the muscles are still flabby and the spirit untried. Starting from near sea-level you have to switchback over two passes more than 6,000 ft (2,000 m) high. It is practically the only stretch I have done with a companion. Within an hour of leaving the relative fleshpots of Amfissa, conversation had dried on our tongues. But morale improved as we encountered the first *élata* (Greek firs) around the 3,000 ft (1,000 m) mark and our first village, Prosilio, forerunner of so many others, with its huge plane trees, copious springs and sturdy, stone-tiled houses backing up the ridge in a gilded evening mist of greenery – walnut and cherry, bramble and Old Man's Beard.

We stopped at the *magazí* – the café-cum-general-store that is the only commercial establishment you find in the mountains – for refreshment and directions. Heated discussion broke out on our behalf. Which was the best route? We were forgotten, until suddenly, compromise achieved, we were presented with a scrap of paper on which was traced a single looping, wiggly line – totally unintelligible. We decided to stick to the classic route, up the Reka ravine.

It is a dramatically deep and narrow trench, precariously hung with trees and shrubs, that cuts into the east side of Mt Ghiona. We had been promised bones from a wartime ambush but saw nothing so ghoulish. Two hours in we made

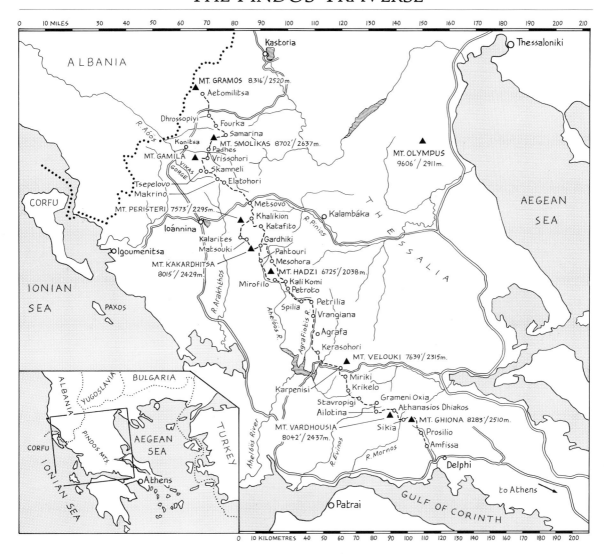

our camp. All memory of weariness and ill-temper vanished as we lay by the fire listening to the night sounds and watching the blue spaces above our heads fill with millions of stars and the ghostly stragglings of the Milky Way.

Morning found us toiling clear of the treeline into flower-bright meadows beneath the high wall of the summit ridge, where patches of still unmelted snow set off the brilliant blue of the sky. A shepherd and his family insisted on spreading a gargantuan lunch for us, which considerably slowed our afternoon climb up the steep scree to the Skasmadha Col below Ghiona's highest peak, Pyramidha (8,225 ft/2,510 m). Chatty shepherds were thick on the ground that afternoon.

"What's the matter with the men in your country," asked one, "that you let yourselves be governed by a woman? They're unstable." We could only grin sheepishly. By the time we stumbled into Sikia, guided by the elusive dance

of fireflies, and with knees still quivering from the 5,000 ft (1,500 m) descent, it was well after dark.

Next day we crossed the Mornos Valley, pausing to bathe in streams and stirring clouds of butterflies from the brambles and wild roses that are slowly engulfing the tiny fields, abandoned since the massive post-war depopulation of the mountains. The heat in the enclosed valley bottom was stifling and it was a delicious relief to reach the fir zone again and the village of Ano Moussounitsa, shaded from the evening sun by Vardhousia's beetling summit, Korakas (7,995 ft/2,437 m).

Ano Moussounitsa, now officially renamed Athanasios Dhiakos after a native son roasted alive by the Turks, is typical of mountain villages. It hangs off the mountainside at around 3,000 ft (1,000 m), well-watered and wooded, with enough fertile ground to make small terraced plots of vegetables, and extensive

165

summer pastures two to three hours' walk away on the mountain. In winter it is semi-dormant with just a handful of old people staying on. Life begins again in May with the arrival of the flocks from their lowland winter pastures, reaching a peak in the summer holidays when the emigrés return briefly from the cities. The centre of life is the *platía* or square, with its giant plane trees, fountain, church and coffee-shops — largely the men's domain still, for etiquette forbids the appearance of women in such a public place.

A really early start saw us into the middle of the mountains not long after dawn, the hour when the sheep move down to their folds to be milked and the air is full of the chimes of their bells. They have to be milked twice a day by hand, and the milk taken down to the nearest village, by mule if there is no jeep track. As we passed the last fold we were summoned imperiously in to breakfast on a bowl of fresh milk and bread mushed together like a broth. The hardest thing always is to leave, for the shepherds love to talk, especially about sheep, how we rear them in England, why we do not milk them when, after all, ewe's milk is God's greatest gift to humanity.

On our way again at last, we clambered up the springy turf towards Vardhousia's western col, following the line of a stream, where orchids and Lady's Smock grew in the seepages and tiny frogs watched with periscope eyes from the safety of their slime. From the col, invigorated by a stinging wind, we threw ourselves down the other side in a mad scree race, trying to keep a weather eye for the treacherous bedded rock that would send us sprawling. And then it was a steady plod westwards down through the resin-scented woods, with occasional dips in green pools between boulders of the stream, until we came to the once large and thriving village of Artotina, facing back towards the alpine skyline of Vardhousia, a view that justly earns it the title of 'Little Switzerland'.

From Artotina onwards I have travelled alone and at different seasons of the year. As far as Karpenisi the going is easier, for although you are still crossing the grain of the land, you seldom have to climb above 4,000 ft (1,200 m). But it is remote and wild for all that, especially in the autumn when the scattered villages are nearly deserted and the weather begins to break.

Agrafa: a bewildering maze of peak and ravine. Prosperous in the days of the Turkish conquest, when its inaccessibility offered security from the oppressor, it is now the poorest and most neglected region in Greece.

I found it decidedly spooky to be alone in that big country with black clouds roofing the valleys, wind soughing in the trees and the ever-threatening roll of thunder. It caught me twice in fact, once at Mandrini, where I would certainly have got lost if it had not been for two old men grinding maize flour in an ancient watermill, and again the next morning approaching Krikello. That was an experience literally much too electrifying. I arrived in the village with my hair standing on end in sheer terror, feeling I had been used for some sort of malevolent target practice.

But Greek mountains are nothing if not full of surprises. When I reached the plateau where Karpenisi stands, the rain overtook me again and this time it was getting dark. As I sheltered under a tree, thinking,

"Well, it's a cart track. Should be able to find my way even in the dark," a pick-up truck came splashing along.

"So you're English, eh?" said the driver. "When I was a boy of 13 ..." He had been minding his father's goats one night in 1943, when the RAF came over and missed their dropping zone. All night the Italian garrison and the partisans had fought for possession of the drop, this one small boy crouching petrified in the dark beneath the lines of tracer bullets. On the strength of it, I was taken home and wined and dined.

Karpenisi, with its 4,000 inhabitants, tavernas and tarmac streets, seems a giddy metropolis after a week in the hills, though its physical charms are few. Its chief attraction for the starving walker is food, and you need a double blow-out, one to assuage the pangs of the previous week, another to prepare you for the way ahead, for the next square meal is a week and more away to the north.

It is a fantastic stretch too, this next one, through the mountains of Agrafa and Tzoumerka, a complicated geological jigsaw, its pieces cut by the rivers. It was here that my original initiation into Greek mountains took place. I had chosen the area because it was the largest tract of trackless brown on the map.

On that occasion I started in from Kerasohori, a two hour bus ride north-west of Karpenisi. It is walkable, but a bit tedious following the road. Besides, the boneshaking local bus is an experience in itself, dropping off parcels and

In the Pindos the wild geranium subcaulescens *flowers from May till October.*

people at houses, crossroads and plumb in the middle of nowhere.

A track took me down into the gorge of the Agrafiotis River and stopped by a handful of tumbledown shacks enveloped in greenery. A train of mules flicked their tails in the shade. Four or five men sipped coffee in the lee of the *magazí*. On either side the mountains rose steeply, the lower slopes thickly wooded with oak, giving way to the ubiquitous fir higher up. No sound could be heard above the roar of the river. As it was getting late, I had just decided to stay there for the night, when one of my companions said,

"Come to my house. It's only an hour up the gorge."

We set off, following the riverside path at first, then, as night came on, going down into the riverbed, where it was easier to see the way against the glimmer of the white stones. We had to wade a few times and were delayed by the tying and untying of boots. It was well after dark when we arrived at Christos's house.

In the kitchen his barefoot wife squatted on her haunches cooking over an open fire by the light of an oil lamp. The only furniture was a bed, two or three homemade stools and a rickety table. The rough stone walls and rafters were blackened with smoke and I could see the stars through chinks in the tiles. "*Fái*," they urged "*fái*. Eat, eat," and set beans, salad, cheese and great doorsteps of bread in front of me.

"Poor food, but it's all we have." When I left in the morning the children hid.

"They're not used to strangers," Christos explained.

I climbed steadily all day, sometimes close to the river, sometimes high in the woods above it. I made a detour to the village of Agrafa, which has given its name to these parts, and sat in the *magazí* for a rest, where I made the mistake of giving in to the insistent "*Ti na sas kerásoume?* What can we offer you?" and ended by downing three or four glasses of *tsípouro*, the characteristic mountain drink, a fiery, colourless alcohol distilled from the grape stalks and skins after the wine has been made. My bacon was saved by a man with a mule who gave me a lift for a couple of hours.

By nightfall I had reached Vrangiana, a beautiful place close to the headwaters of the Agrafiotis at around 4,000 ft (1,200 m). Today no more than a scattering of houses in a green amphitheatre ringed by peaks, this was a thriving centre of learning in the 17th and 18th centuries, with a population of 3,000 souls.

Once over the watershed I turned west down the valley of the Petriliotikos, with the wind rising and the firs darkening to a menacing black. The storm broke just as I reached the gates of the Spilia monastery, perched on the brim of a crag. There are no monks any more, but the caretaker let me in, fed me and gave me a cell, where I slept only fitfully, wrapped in shaggy *flokáti* blankets, listening apprehensively to the violence of the storm.

When day broke at last the sky was washed a pale duck-egg blue. The woods were dripping and black with damp. The caretaker assured me his recommended route up the riverbed to Petroto would be perfectly passable. And indeed all was plain sailing for an hour or so, until I had to start fording the stream. The level had risen in the night and the water was angry and red with mud. It pushed and frothed at my thighs threatening to pull me down every time I waded into the current. It never did more than wet my shorts, but it was enough to make me extremely apprehensive. I thought of turning back, but after five or six crossings that made no more sense than continuing. It was beautiful down there, cocooned by water and trees, as I was able to appreciate once I had relaxed a bit. But my troubles were not over. For when, after five hours, I came in sight of Petroto, I found the way completely blocked by a lake of liquid mud and had to claw my way out up the steep and unstable mountainside.

Below Petroto, where, in 1987, a bulldozer accidentally uncovered some 3rd century BC graves, the Petriliotikos joins the Ahelöos, one of the loveliest rivers in Europe, now sadly in imminent danger of being ruined by a Greek Electricity Board project to create two huge artificial lakes and divert its waters to the plain of Thessaly. The wanton disfigurement of the mountainsides is already under way outside Petroto.

A morning's walk to the north, above the narrow trench of the Ahelöos, I came to the village of Kali Komi, half-hidden on the luxuriant slopes of a forgotten valley. From here I have done two routes. One follows the Ahelöos as it loops westward round the jagged bulk of Mt Hadzi (6,685 ft/2,038 m), through gorges and open valley, to Pahtouri, where I climbed over the southern ramparts of the Tzoumerka massif, swung west over Kakardhitsa (8,100 ft/2,469 m) to Matsouki and Kalarites, and north again to Peristeri (7,530 ft/2,295 m) and the village of Haliki, close to the source of the Ahelöos. The other route runs north to Moschofito, where, to my confusion one evening, a woman made the biblical gesture of bringing me a bowl of water to bathe my feet, then over a spur of Hadzi to Mesohora, and thence up the Ahelöos to Haliki.

The first route is higher and more strenuous, and you run the gauntlet of the packs of vicious sheepdogs (I bear the scars) kept by the Vlach shepherds to defend their flocks from wolves and bears. The second route, while less dramatic, takes you through the magnificent forested country of the upper Ahelöos Valley.

Villages are few and far between and scarcely inhabited in winter. Haliki, for instance, is completely deserted until the flocks arrive in May. The people, as in most of the surrounding villages, are Vlachs, not ethnic Greeks, whose origins are lost in the mists of time, and whose language is a primitive form of Latin, without an alphabet. Traditionally they were transhumant shepherds, wintering in the plains of Thessaly and spending the summers up here. Though this way of life is fast being eroded, you still see both men and women dressed in the characteristic blue homespun they make from their own sheep's wool.

Right – *Kalarites, one of the wealthiest of the Vlach villages, grew rich on the products of its sheep and its goldsmiths, selling capes to Napoleon's navy and geegaws to Ali Basha, despot of Yanina and admirer of Byron.*

Below – *Aphrodite. She and her husband, both illiterate, have pastured their goats in this area of Ghiona every summer of their lives.*

The first time I came through here was in April. I had spent the night in Katafito, where only a dozen ancients had stayed through the winter. I left at dawn, under low cloud, with the threat of snow on the wind, anxious to get over the pass before anything nastier happened. Haliki was empty and as I climbed the pass I was puzzled by a peculiar mournful shrieking coming from above me. It turned out to be a lone beech tree, raked by the wind on the snowy ridge, planted to mark the 19th century frontier with Turkey. I did not see a living soul in the eight hours it took me to reach Metsovo.

Metsovo is the most attractive country town I have seen in Greece and the only one which seems to set any store by its traditions. Hanging off the mountainside like a swarm of bees, its two halves face each other across the ravine which leads to the Zygos, the oldest east–west route over the Pindos, where Julius Caesar crossed in 48 BC in pursuit of Pompey. Thanks to its strategic position and the wool-related businesses of its Vlach population, who used to trade as far afield as central Europe and Russia, it has been prosperous for centuries. Its picturesqueness has inevitably now brought the tourists, together with souvenir shops, plastic cafés and plastic music. Not that the locals are bothered as long as the tills ring . . . a familiar enough scenario.

In summer it is a relief to get back to the hills. An hour's pull up the road – the first tarmac since Karpenisi – brings you to a shallow, marshy valley where the Aöos begins its long and turbulent descent to the Adriatic coast of Albania. I camped in the valley, tucked under the western ridge, and spent a sleepless night watching the moonlight silver the mist and fighting off nosy sheepdogs. In the morning I followed the stream to Pende Alonia, where some shepherds' huts of coppery beech brash stood on the edge of a wide bowl looking over the forested hills of the Zagori. Invited for coffee, I sat rather nervously on a bench outside while the dogs continued to growl and snap despite my official status. These shepherds were Sarakatsani, not Vlachs as I had expected – another pastoral clan, ethnically Greek, who were totally nomadic until a generation ago. In fact, by their dialect and traditions, they may well be the only true descendants of the ancient Greeks.

They put me on the path to Flambourari, contouring along the rim of the Vardhas Valley at around 5,000 ft (1,500 m). For the first couple of hours I walked in glorious woods of black pine, wide enough spaced to let in the sunlight and leave room for bracken and box and wild roses to flourish. There were numerous springs and streams, with colonies of butterwort growing in the damp and thickets of thistles whose purple flowers were crawling with copper-winged fritillaries.

I lost the path eventually and had to take a well-churned logging track down to Flambourari and Elatohori, where I spent the night at the home of the telephone owner. He had a loudspeaker rigged up on a pole by the garden gate. I wondered what for, until the telephone rang and his voice boomed out across the evening depths of the ravine below the village: "Kósta! Tiléfonoooo!" And five minutes later Kostas appeared, a stout little man, panting and mopping his brow, to take the call.

In the morning I crossed the ravine and climbed through a tunnel of hazel and wild clematis, past tiny meadows where people were baling hay by hand, to Makrino. A cobbled lane led into the village beneath a trellis of vines. Beside it stood an exquisite church in typical Pindos style, stone-tiled, with an arcaded porch along one side and a separate campanile.

I fell in with the mayor and his son who accompanied me up the long, wooded ridges to the watershed dividing the eastern and western Zagori. We parted company on the top, in a flower-strewn meadow where a Sarakatsan hut stood poignantly open to the weather – the first year in living memory, and perhaps in hundreds of years, that sheep bells had not chimed in this meadow. The old folks were too old, and their children had gone off to the city.

I headed north along the ridge, through woods full of tortoises and loose-flowered orchids whose tubers are used for making salépi, a sweet, syrupy drink still sold on the streets of Athens in winter. An hour's descent brought me to the Skamneliotiko Stream, where I napped before turning west to Skamneli, at the foot of Gamila's treeless southern slopes.

This is the western Zagori, whose villages are full of imposing stone mansions built by emigré sons, driven by poverty to seek their fortunes abroad. Skamneli in fact is less interesting than its westerly neighbours, Tsepelovo, Kapesovo, Vitsa, Monondhendri and others. There are several good walking routes in the area too, both over Mt Gamila and through the now famous Vikos Gorge. It is the only part of the Greek mountains where you are likely to encounter other foreign walkers.

The most dramatic route north is via the col below the Tsouka Rossa peak (8,091 ft/2,466 m) and down to Vrissohori, some nine hours in all, starting from either Skamnelli or Tsepelovo. The two routes come together at the foot of the col. Once above the villages, the landscape is lunar and desolate, with deep-fissured tables of limestone filling the valleys. The flowers are spectacular; gentians, violets, tulips, narcissus, campanulas and hosts of others. It was the scene of John Campbell's definitive study of the Sarakatsani and his visits are still remembered.

The col is around 7,500 ft (2,300 m). If you inch to the right at the top and look over the edge, the view is fantastic. The ground drops sheer for some 1,500 ft (500 m) into the tree-filled ravine of the Aöos, with the green and forested bulk of Smolikas, at 8,652 ft (2,637 m) Greece's second highest peak after Olympus, rising on the other side, with a string of tiny villages along its southern flank. The only way down is through the moraines ahead and out through a steep, narrow gully, the only breach in the twelve mile (20 kms) frontage of cliffs. Then you are into the forest again, heading back east below the cliffs to Vrissohori, a beautiful, scarcely inhabited village not even trying any more to win the battle against encroaching nature. Streams run down the paths, hazel and hornbeam arch them over. Marsh orchids are thick in the banks. Snow brings down the telephone line, and the bus comes only occasionally.

A long and jungly descent leads down to an incongruous concrete bridge over the Aöos, followed by a steep, zigzagging climb through the pines to Palioseli and Padhes. It is all Vlach territory here and, to my mind, the finest mountain scenery in Greece.

My first ascent of Smolikas was with the village drunk. Under his guidance we set off straight up the mountainside, disdaining even the faintest path. His knapsack clinked with a fresh supply of bottles. Every ten minutes or so he lay on the ground white as a sheet and apparently stopped breathing. The first few times I thought he was dead, but as he seemed able to resurrect himself at will I stopped worrying. He sobered up as we climbed, enough in the end to find the way in the dark, which soon overtook us.

We stopped about eleven o'clock, in a night full of stars and bitterly cold. Without more ado my companion set fire to a pine tree. It certainly kept us warm, although I was too anxious to get much sleep. Environmental niceties do not cut much ice in these parts. By first light we were at the Dhrakolimni tarn, reaching the summit in time to see the sun rise way to the east over Mt Olympus. To the north-west the squat bulk of Grammos, my ultimate goal, spread along the horizon.

I said goodbye to the drunk and started down the eastern ridge, along the rim of an inhospitable cirque where a tongue of everlasting

snow is all that remains of the ice cap, and struck out along a north-easterly spur to the village of Samarina, the largest and most thriving of the Vlach shepherd communities. It is not much to look at, apart from its beautiful church, having been burnt by the Germans and the partisans, but it is full of vitality and still pastures some forty-odd thousand sheep in summer. In winter it is empty except for a single family. It is the highest village in Greece at 5,250 ft (1,600 m).

For the last three days of the journey the country is wild and lonely. It is the very edge of Greece and an ill-favoured edge at that, partly because of its remoteness, but chiefly because of its wars and the civil war in particular. It is at its most beautiful in late May and June, when the beeches are coming into leaf and the pastures are full of orchids and primulas.

From Samarina it is an easy three hours to Fourka along a sandy ridge-top track, thence over the ridge where the Greeks broke the thrust of Mussolini's invasion in 1940, and down to the village of Dhrossopiyi on the flanks of the Sarandaporos Valley. I crossed the river an hour below the village, and began the last, long climb past the abandoned village of Likorahi and up the old trail through the pine woods to Aetomilitsa, or Densiko as the old-timers persist in calling it. The last village before the Albanian border, it lies at the edge of a vast expanse of alpine meadow.

For anyone interested in Greece, climbing Grammos is a moving experience. Whatever the rights and wrongs of the case, many of the brightest and best of a whole generation of Greeks fought and died in the ranks of the Communists in the civil war. Colossally outnumbered, abandoned by Stalin and Tito, cornered by an army and air force equipped and supported by the might of the USA, they made their last stand on these heights. From Kiafa, right round the horseshoe ridge above Aetomilitsa and back along the main ridge to the 8,268 ft (2,520 m) summit and the Albanian border, they dug in on the peaks and waited, unassailable by infantry, for the planes with bombs and napalm to finish them off. You can see the remains of their trenches and foxholes still, scattered with fragments of rusting steel. On a quiet July morning, with only the sounds of the sheeps' bells and the wind whistling softly in the rocks and the grass, it is impossible not to sense the genius of the place.

The Albanians patrol their side of the frontier, which runs just a hundred yards below the summit. As I watched, I saw three soldiers unsling their rifles and stretch out on the grass for a smoke. Behind them, the western slopes of the mountain declined into a broad, peaceful-looking valley with a ribbon of dusty road and a couple of villages backed by a hazy rampart of mountains. Vlach sheep grazed both sides of the frontier, though the shepherds, some of them relatives, have not been able to speak to each other for 40 years.

There was something curiously satisfying about ending my journey here, in the air, as it were, inconclusively, looking down into this hermitic, secretive little land, unable to go any further.

Right – An old mule road. Until recently, these were the only lines of communication in the mountains. Unfortunately, many, including this one, and part of the E4 international footpath with which it connects, have been destroyed in the course of recent road building.

Below – Smolikas. The Vlachs arrive in the mountains at the end of May, when the snow retreats from the high pastures. While their families stay in the village, the men live out on the mountains tending the sheep, milking and cheesemaking.

Difficulty

The walking is strenuous, but not difficult. The only problems are likely to be route-finding where the old trails have fallen into disuse, and the ferocity of the sheepdogs, which need to be treated with circumspection.

Distances

Total walking time is around 150 hours, but the entire journey of some 180 miles (290 kms) as the crow flies divides naturally into three parts, each of which makes an enjoyable self-contained unit:
Amfissa-Karpenisi: 7 to 8 days.
Karpenisi-Metsovo: 8 to 10 days.
Metsovo-Gramos: 8 to 9 days.
Amfissa, Karpenisi, Metsovo and Yannina all have daily bus connections with Athens. From Gramos aim SW to Konitsa whence daily buses run to Yannina. Buses go everywhere in Greece.

Weather

The weather is at its most settled from the end of May to the beginning of October, though, like all mountains, the Pindos can be unpredictable. Even in mid-summer nights are cool, especially by contrast with daytime temperatures.

Equipment

You need strong, but not heavyweight, boots, for the going is rough and steep, and a combination of light and warm clothing. Shorts are essential in summer, as well as a hat and shirts with collar and sleeves if you are at all susceptible to sunburn, and it is wise to carry a waterproof/windproof cagoule. For sleeping out a bivi bag and medium-weight sleeping bag are sufficient, unless you want the extra privacy and protection from dogs that a tent gives. Camping is permitted anywhere in the mountains.

Few mountain villages boast shops or hotels but all will have a *magazee* – a sort of coffee-shop cum general-store cum local club. Ask here to buy food or a meal (basic!) or for somewhere to sleep and you will be helped. Local fare – bread, cheese, olives, sardines, spam, etc will be available. When passing through towns stock up with items such as salami, halva, nuts, dried fruit. Greeks eat no breakfast!

Camping gas is only available in larger towns but as petrol is obtainable even in small villages, petrol burning stoves are recommended.

Zagori: the 19th century packhorse bridge at Kipi.

Medical considerations

Medical treatment is generally not good in Greece. If you are concerned about anything serious happening, you should take out appropriate insurance. Facilities in the mountains are at best rudimentary. There are no chemists, for instance, in the villages.

On the other hand, there is no reason why anything should go seriously wrong. The water is unimpeachably clean. The worst that is likely to happen is mild stomach upsets from unfamiliar food.

Language

A knowledge of Greek would certainly be useful, but there is often someone around who speaks some English or German. Besides, mountain Greeks are nothing if not helpful.

Reading

Maps:

The best are the 1:50,000 series available from the *Greek Army Cartography Service*, Pedhion Areos, Athens, though sheets north of Metsovo are still classifed.
The National Statistical Service of Greece 1:200,000 series is obtainable from their Athens office at 14 Likourgou Street and, in London, from Edward Stanford, 12 Long Acre, WC2 and McCarta Ltd, 122 Kings Cross Rd, WC1.

Guide books:

The Mountains of Greece: A Walker's Guide by Tim Salmon (Cicerone Press, 1986) is the only one to give an account of this route.

Literature:

Roumeli – Patrick Leigh Fermor (John Murray, 1966).
Honour, Family and Patronage – JK Campbell (Oxford, 1964). A study of the Sarakatsan shepherds in the north-west Pindos.
The Nomads of the Balkans – AJB Wace and MS Thompson (Methuen, 1914). A study of the Vlachs of Samarina.
Flowers of Greece and the Aegean – Anthony Huxley and William Taylor (Chatto and Windus, 1977). The most comprehensive and convenient field guide.

Tim Salmon first set foot in Greece 30 years ago, thanks to a chance remark made by a teacher, and fell in love with it, like many other romantically inclined Anglo-Saxons. The passion has cooled as knowledge has deepened, but his life has remained linked to the place. He married his first wife there and met his second, who is Greek, while climbing Mt Olympus. For the past twelve years, he has spent most of his time in Greece, much of it above 1,500 m. He is now a full-time writer of travel guides and articles.

ASTRIDE THE FRONTIER –
A PYRENEAN HIGH ROUTE

by Kev Reynolds

The Basque hills of south-west France are mostly green, rolling and forest-covered. Damp mists flood in from the Atlantic to keep their slopes well-watered and in the valleys full-bodied streams swirl off to the ocean whence they came. They're broad hills, attractive hills, but they lack the majesty of those more rugged landscapes found a little farther east in the High Pyrenees.

But after Pic d'Anie all this changes. The Cirque de Lescun presents a fresh perspective. Now there are limestone peaks rearing above green pastures. There are screes and boulder fields and conifer woods in the valleys, and save for a lack of glacier or permanent snowfield, the cirque is distinctively alpine in character.

Wander up-valley across the green pastures and through the conifer woods, and you come into another cirque; this one almost Dolomitic in the staggering architecture of its lofty aiguilles. The Cirque d'Ansabère.

On a bright September afternoon, at the end of what had been an energetic climbing trip, I emerged onto the summit of the modest Pic d'Ansabère (7,799 ft/2,377 m), and gazed at the panorama spread about me. All the country to the west was Basque; all that to the east was the High Pyrenees. I had one foot in France, the other in Spain. Around my boots Alpine asters were blooming. Choughs circled the grey crags that formed the walls of the cirque, their mournful croaking being thrown back in echoes of nostalgia. Far, far below, beyond the fan of screes that formed an uncomfortable ramp to the twin aiguilles that were my immediate neighbours, a shepherd was calling to his sheep. The light clanking of their bells came to me in the breeze. But what really caught my attention was the great welter of peaks and ridges and hinted valleys that formed the eastern horizon.

I looked now at familiar peaks I had known, not just from this trip, but from many previous climbing and walking holidays spent in the Pyrenees. I recognised at once Pic du Midi d'Ossau and Balaitous, and knew the valleys that separated them. There were ridges and buttresses seen in a new light. On them I had spent some of my happiest hours. Yet there were other peaks, too, that I did not know. Other peaks I could not put a name to. Valleys — no more than hinted at from this vantage point — that were a mystery, and I found myself yearning to know them.

It doesn't matter how many times one visits a

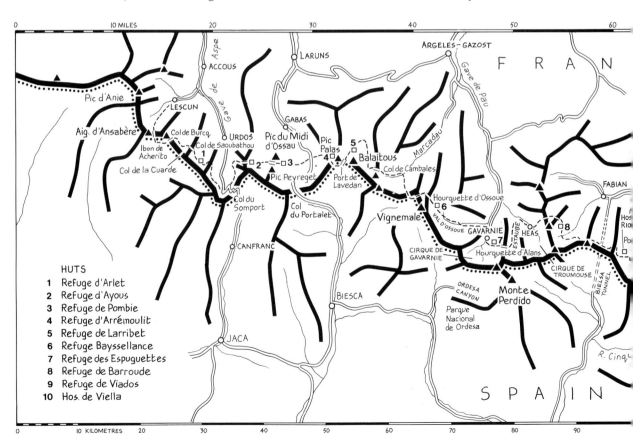

HUTS

1 Refuge d'Arlet
2 Refuge d'Ayous
3 Refuge de Pombie
4 Refuge d'Arrémoulit
5 Refuge de Larribet
6 Refuge Bayssellance
7 Refuge des Espuguettes
8 Refuge de Barroude
9 Refuge de Viados
10 Hos. de Viella

range of mountains to climb its summits, nor how often one wanders through its valleys, there will always be the unknown, the fresh angle from which to view a particular peak, the thrill of discovery of a new valley system. It seemed to me then, on the summit of Pic d'Ansabère, that it was time to adopt another approach in order to unravel some of the secrets that remained. How better than to attempt a high route through the High Pyrenees?

The Pyrenean High Route (Haute Randonnée Pyrénéenne) is undoubtedly one of the world's great walks. It links the 250 miles (400 kms) or so of mountains that stretch between the Atlantic and the Mediterranean by a series of high level trails – some clearly visible, others no more than a vague route along which a few remote cairns or paint flashes may be found. As the name suggests, the High Route attempts to remain as high as possible, often following the very crests of the mountains before dropping into the head of a secluded valley, or crossing a lofty pass. It is a challenging walk; a rewarding walk; a visually spectacular walk.

The first recorded full traverse of the Pyrenean range was completed in 1817 by Dr Frédéric Parrot who made his epic journey in 53 days. Along the way he was also able to find time to make the first ascent of one or two important mountains, including Pico de la Maladeta (10,853 ft/3,308 m), in the heart of the range that rises above the delectable Esera Valley. The High Route as worked out by members of the CAF (French Alpine Club), however, is rather more parochial than Dr Parrot's journey, for it remains as far as practicable on the northern side of the watershed, thus ignoring the splendours of certain Spanish massifs and valleys, other than during a few alternative stages. But having fallen under the spell of some of these areas in the past, I decided that my High Route through the High Pyrenees would stray from one side of the international frontier to the other, taking the best of each. As was the dream, so was reality.

We set out on a day of mist and drizzle, the cobbled stones of Lescun's narrow alleys black and shining with water. There were no mountains to be seen, nothing to suggest that above the sloping pastures were fine limestone peaks rising out of the forests, nor that ahead, peeking above converging ridges, were the slender aiguilles of Ansabère. Through the mist and damp came the rushing of streams, the dull clatter of cowbells. The smell of cowdung and freshly mown hay told us more about the country through which we were walking than anything we could actually see. I, at least, had

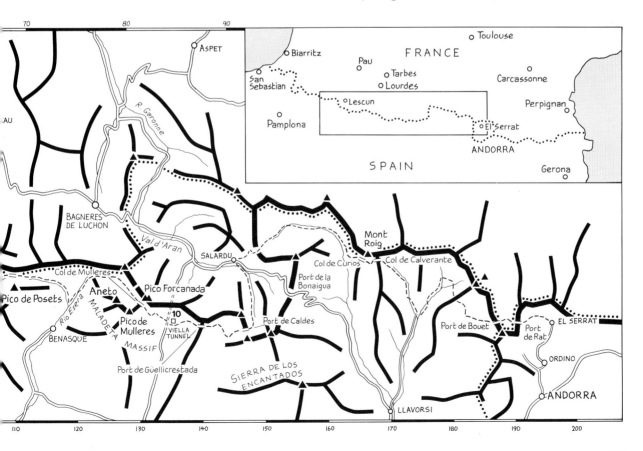

181

experienced the visual pleasures of this place before. Not so Pete, whose first visit this was, and I teased him with graphic descriptions of the peaks and pastures gathering all around us, only to be soundly cursed in return. But I promised him, too, that we would rise above it in due course, and merely hoped that it would be sooner rather than later.

Above the forest it was still raining. Still no mountains, just a damp, clinging mist. Then down into a grassy bowl of meadowland, across a stream or two and up the slopes opposite, into more woods that dripped on us while low-hanging branches threatened to drag the rucksacks from our shoulders. Out of the trees a boulderscape rose into the gloom. To our left a stream dashed down through a mass of giant dock leaves, and there, beside it, we planted our tent. At the end of our first day, we'd seen no mountains at all!

But when morning came there was a revelation. Soaring above the tent was the Petite Aiguille d'Ansabère, the bright stain of sunrise draining down its sheer limestone wall. In the valley, all the country through which we had walked the day before was hidden beneath a great cloud-sea. Lescun, just waking to the new day, would no doubt find it raining again. We, on the other hand, had the sun and clear skies.

A little above our overnight camping spot there is a shepherd's cabana, and as we wandered past, the shepherd was seated upon a three-legged stool milking one of his cows. Scattered about the grassy slopes were hundreds of sheep, and out of the slopes rose those fantastic rocky spires that had Pete reaching time and again for his camera. At last he began to believe my descriptions. They were no longer the wild exaggerations of a Pyrenean fanatic!

A trail took us to a tarn trapped on the

Right – First of the 10,000 ft (3,000 m) peaks along the route is that of the Balaïtous, seen above Col de Palas. Having crossed the exposed ledge of the Passage d'Orteig, the way then descends to Refuge d'Arrémoulit.

Below – On the west bank of the Aspe Valley, the stone-walled village of Lescun gazes over tranquil pastureland to the limestone peaks that mark the first of the so-called High Pyrenees.

hillside, then above that to our first pass of the day, the first pass of our high route; an unnamed, unmarked grassy saddle on the frontier ridge east of the Aiguilles d'Ansabère. From it we looked out into a Spain of huge vistas, where soft, autumn-tinged hills rolled far off towards the south, losing themselves among a welter of haze-blue sierras. Nothing in our field of vision was made by man, and there came to us the distant hum of indefinable sounds that we mistakenly call silence.

Down then into Spain over steep grass slopes damp with morning dew, towards a rocky spine leading from the ridge. Beyond that we found an intimate little cirque with another tarn nestling in its embrace. On its southern shore, we threw off our rucksacks and lazed in the sun among autumn crocuses and huge, stemless thistles whose centres were as large as dinner plates.

A stream pours from the lake's outflow, and one should make a point of filling water bottles from it. This is all limestone country, and limestone has a nasty habit of swallowing watercourses. The mountain trekker should always be aware of this simple fact and make certain that his bottle is filled at every available opportunity, for it may be a long time before another decent supply is located.

A clear path leads round the mountainside without shade, steadily losing height but never interest, its superb views of the big, empty country all around. Then up through a gully of grass and rock towards great, moorland-type hills with rocky crests above them. It's all wild, empty country suddenly and there is no real path to be seen, only one of a brace of passes to find which will lead back onto French soil again.

We headed through the more southerly of the two passes, Col de Burcq (6,768 ft/2,063 m), and there discovered all of France still slumbering beneath the same cloud-sea of dawn. Across this ocean of vapour we looked out at the lovely profile of Pic du Midi d'Ossau, the symbol of the Pyrenees. In two days' time we would be wandering in its shadow.

Bohi is one of the rare thriving villages on the Spanish side of the frontier.

The path that meanders along the high mountainside between Col de Burcq and Refuge d'Arlet is a pure gem. At first skirting a little below the actual crest, it leaves the ridge at Col de la Cuarde and traverses towards a subsidiary ridge, which it crosses at the saddle of Col de Saoubathou. Here there are a couple of tiny pools, and not far off, a spring of clear water – the first opportunity to refill water bottles since leaving Ibon de Acherito some hours earlier.

Refuge d'Arlet stands on a grassy knoll above its own tarn in a bowl of mountain and turf. Built by the National Park authorities, it provides a welcome and very useful overnight lodging for mountain trekkers. (All the countryside through which the High Route leads on the French side of the frontier, between the Cirque d'Ansabère and Cirque de Barroude east of Gavarnie, is included in the Parc National des Pyrénées – PNP.)

Two days later we came to another PNP hut, this one above the Lac d'Ayous. Above it we had topped Col d'Ayous (7,169 ft/2,185 m), to gain a sudden dramatic view of Pic du Midi rising in the east as mists came streaming, the air charged with electricity. Over on Pic du Midi there was a *son et lumière* being played out for our benefit as lightning sizzled and thunder roared. Knowing it would not be long in coming our way, we scurried down to the shelter of Refuge d'Ayous as the first squall of rain hit us.

I know of no mountain hut in all the Pyrenees with a finer view than that of Refuge d'Ayous. I know of no finer position anywhere from which to experience the glory of sunrise; and the morning after our storm-bound arrival we were treated to one of the most magical mountain day-breaks of my life. Rising early I peered from the window to see the first stain of sunrise breaking night's monopoly. Already Pic du Midi was standing on his head in the lake outside, but as the sun lifted itself from that obscure nest far off in the east, so colours sprayed across the sky, over the mountains walling the valley, and into the lake itself. In moments it was all over, but we took it with us, its impact lasting throughout our journey across the Pyrenees. It weighed nothing at all.

An easy day takes you from Ayous to Pombie, beside more tarns and over boulder fields and meadowlands where sheep and ponies graze, then up the rough, rock-strewn slopes below Pic du Midi's towering southern walls and buttresses, to Col de Peyreget (7,550 ft/2,300 m). The Col is a splendid dip in the southern ridge that links Pic du Midi with Pic Peyreget, and from it one gains an exciting glimpse of big new country ahead where tomorrow's route will lead. To the left burst savage rock walls. Tumbling from them are huge scree tips falling away out of sight. Steeply below the col, slopes plunge to brief levellings where tarns sparkle in the brilliant southern light. Below them shadows hide the mysteries of Pombie, lake and refuge.

Refuge de Pombie is probably the busiest of all Pyrenean huts, for climbers gather there to tackle the huge walls rising beyond the lake; trekkers use it as a staging post along the High Route; and those who are wandering along the classic tour of Pic du Midi are often drawn to its shelter, if not for the night, at least as a refreshment stop before climbing to the next pass. Below it to the east lies the deep valley of the Gave de Brousset, and this forms a clear demarcation between the green pasturelands of Pic du Midi and the high granite wilderness of the Balaitous massif. In the valley stands a rough hut which serves as a café, and as we scurried down from Pombie's perch I promised Pete that we'd have time for a drink and could stock up with chocolate and maybe some fruit for the onward journey. On arrival our expectations were dashed when we found the windows shuttered and the door padlocked. There would be several more days of hard trekking before we'd have another opportunity to restock.

Up then towards Balaitous. Through forest, across a stream, and up a narrow, climbing valley into the granitelands that I love for their savagery and their uncompromising nature. From the first col the entry is dramatic, for one is suddenly faced with a narrow ledge carved out of the face of Pic du Lac d'Arrious, with a great drop of more than 1,000 ft (300 m) to Lac d'Artouste for the unwary. In truth, this Passage d'Orteig presents no real difficulty, as long as the trekker crossing it has his rucksack well balanced, and has a head for heights, and it leads to the great white boulder whales that bask in the sun below Pic Palas.

There's a pleasant refuge here, with a pass above it that takes the trekker briefly into Spain before traversing round the lip of a bowl of scree. Then comes a scramble over craggy Port de Lavedan and across a desperate plunge of slab and buttress and loose gully, and finally you have access to the wilds of Batcrabere to the west of Balaitous. Refuge de Larribet stands overlooking a rough splay of turf where, more than a century ago, that great Pyrenean pioneer, Charles Packe, spent the night prior to his first attempt on Balaitous, '... *on an elevated basin affording a scanty pasture, at the foot of the northern glacier.*' The High Route makes a detour round the northern expanse of Balaitous, then crosses the Col de Cambales and slopes down into a wonderland of grass and tarn and swirling streams; the Marcadau, one of my all-time favourite valleys. If ever a region deserved to be treated to a slow exploration, it was this, but on our High Route journey, Pete and I were anxious to continue eastward. The Marcadau's indisputable pleasures had to wait for another year.

On leaving the grasslands of the Marcadau comes a classic stage, when a brace of high passes leads to the glacial plain at the foot of the North Face of the Vignemale, one of the most dramatic mountain walls to be found anywhere in the Pyrenees. There's a good hut here too, but many trekkers choose to continue beyond it, slanting up the east wall of the valley to cross Hourquette d'Ossoue on the shoulder of the Petit Vignemale, and drop down to Refuge Bayssellance, a beehive of a hut from which climbers set out to climb the Vignemale's glacier

route. From this hut the trekker is gifted towards evening with lovely views down the length of the Ossoue Valley towards Gavarnie and its cirque; tomorrow's destination.

When Pete and I wound down through the Ossoue Valley winter was in the air, and Gavarnie gave us a day and a night of snow. At least it kept the crowds at bay!

Right – *Between the raw granite and ice of the Balaïtous to the west, and the savage rock pile of the Vignemale to the east, the High Route passes through a soft-turf pastureland sprinkled with tarns and sparkling streams – the Marcadau Valley.*

Below – *Any trek across the Pyrenees will present opportunities to watch eagles, vultures, isard and marmots in their natural habitats. There will also be cattle in some of the valleys and sheep on the hillsides. These goats were grazing on a rocky buff in the Barroude Cirque, apparently without anyone in charge.*

There were three of us on the next stage to the heart of the range, and we went up to the PNP hut above Gavarnie Village in swirling mist to be treated to a fabulous display of mist magic spiralling out of the valley, teasing among the huge tiers of rock and snow layered across the Cirque de Gavarnie in the south. Then over Hourquette d'Alans and down into the rough pasturelands of the Estaubé, whose amphitheatre headwall gave a tantalising glimpse of Monte Perdido – the 'lost mountain'. Through the Estaubé Valley we ambled, once more in full sunlight, down to the little hamlet of Héas, last habitation, other than 'alp' huts and refuges, for at least eight days. We treated ourselves to drinks and sandwiches to celebrate, then hastened back into the wilderness.

We had savoured the Cirque de Gavarnie in snow and mist. We had seen the Cirque d'Estaubé in mist and sunshine and Cirque de Troumouse dazzlingly clear with streams tumbling through its green gateway. From Héas our route took us over the mountains to the back of Troumouse where another cirque, this one of Barroude, curved in a great wall of sandwiched rock above a pair of tarns. That night the moon danced in the waters, turning the cirque walls on their heads and spilling stars about us.

One of the hardest of all High Route days follows a night at Barroude, for a long ridge walk, balanced between France and Spain, leads for nine or ten hours to Rioumajou. There is only one opportunity to escape from the ridge in the event of bad weather, so trekkers should check the forecast before setting out, and then make an early start. It's a great day's walking in the sky, with magnificent views spread in every direction, and Pico de Posets – second highest massif in the range at 11,072 ft (3,375 m) – luring you onward. The day after leaving Rioumajou brings you into its shadow.

Rioumajou is a deep valley of green, but there is an interminable slope of scree that leads out of it to the saddle of Port de Caouerere (8,287 ft/2,526 m) and into Spain once more. From this pass one gazes at the West Face of Posets, and the descent from the pass to the headwaters of the Cinqueta de la Pez, through acres of alpenroses and the fragrance of pine with cicadas leaping from beneath our boots, is one of the abiding memories of the Pyrenean High Route. A Sunday of sun and splendour. The grazing hamlet of Viados, with its simple refugio, comes as the ideal finalé to a glorious day of

The Refuge d'Arlet stands at over 6,000 feet beside a lonely tarn.

high mountain walking, and makes a good base from which to explore this delectable region.

Two days of pleasant walking lead from Viados to the upper reaches of the Esera Valley below the Maladeta massif and Aneto, the highest Pyrenean peak, which rises from the napkin of its glacier. Here Pete had to leave us, and it was left to Alan and me to complete the traverse to Andorra.

The Esera is a valley alive with memories of so many climbing trips of the past that I can never walk among its flowers without raising my eyes with nostalgia to the granite crests, the snow domes and icy aprons of the peaks that wall it. But when Alan and I crawled from our tent to see clouds tumbling from the heights, we had more concern than enthusiasm for the day ahead, for at the head of the valley and hidden by a grey scum of vapour I knew lay our highest pass – Col de Mulleres (9,606 ft/2,928 m). This was not a crossing to take lightly, and we deliberated for a couple of hours or so before the weather showed sign of improvement and we decided to chance it.

Up then through the undulating Valleta de la Escaleta where cascades boomed and streams ran into deep hollows to disappear. Then trading grass for rock we moved up the glacial pavement of ice-smoothed boulders in full view of the double-pronged Forcanada, and used compasses to guide us into the mist-wreathed wilderness that leads to the Mulleres ridge. Verglas frosted the rocks here, attractive but unwelcome as we clambered down the gully on the eastern side of the pass. Below lay a true wilderness tip of scree and boulderlands, with cold-looking tarns far off and only the faintest hint of grass on which to camp at the end of the day. An isard – the Pyrenean chamois – eyed our large rucksacks with disdain, and leapt away unencumbered. We were left with a bowl of grey, streaked with snow and a line of cairns to follow.

But next day was another of those magical times of which the very richest of memories are made. We had crossed the snout of the Viella road tunnel and headed up into a high region of granite peaks and lost tarns, far from humanity, far from trees and shrubs, where we threw off the rucksacks and treated ourselves to a half-day's holiday. There, basking in the sun on a mattress of soft turf, with white granite mountains hovering on each horizon, and the nearest thing to silence that this world knows clamping the afternoon, I came to recognize the very perfection of nature in maturity, and gave myself to the hills. They responded with more days of magic as we crossed other passes and explored the western edge of the Sierra de los

Encantados – the Enchanted Mountains. Enchanted by name and enchanted by nature; rolling, empty country littered with brilliant tarns and with savage peaks forming every boundary. As we moved slowly through this landscape of delight, so I recognised summit after summit from previous climbing trips and promised myself a return before long. This, after all, is country one could never grow tired of. Wilderness country with dozens of compelling peaks that will never make the glossy mountain magazines, it is none the less just the country I love.

There are few paths through this wilderness, but occasional cairns mark routes that lead over first Port de Güellicrestada, then Port de Caldes, which gives access to a new series of valley systems dominated by the Vall d'Aran. A long walk through the valley of the Riu d'Aiguamotx brings the weary trekker to Salardu and shops, hotels, restaurants and a refuge; the first real taste of civilisation since leaving the hamlet of Héas long days ago. From wilderness peace to the grinding of traffic heading up the Bonaigua pass is something of a culture shock, but its impact is made more bearable by the prospect of fresh food and the opportunity to restock for the final four or five days' stretch to Andorra.

Those days are worthy days that lead through little-known country, unsung and empty of anything but the glory of wild mountain landscapes. From lofty ridges one looks into a Spain that has no place on the tourist brochures, for it is a deserted country of lost villages being slowly strangled by unchecked briars; a Spain of knotted sierras, of remote tarns and rough cirques of trackless forests and deep gorges and a wonderland of flowers. A trekker's Spain. A country no less idyllic for its being 24 hours or so from London.

A long and tiring day took us from the valley of the Noguera Pallaresa to a hidden farm set beside a stream on the eastern side of Mont Roig. Ten hours of scrabbling over three high passes, among great ridges thrown out by frontier peaks towards the tangle that is upland Spain, among tarns and cascades, scree slopes and forest. A challenging day that rewarded with its immense variety.

There were pastures on the way to Col de Curios, and old barns of red stone with wild raspberries clambering up their walls in the lower reaches, but as we gained height, so we traded grass and streams for scree and boulders jettisoned over countless centuries from the cliffs above. Up there among those cliffs lay the nick of Col de Curios, a lovely pass and worthy of its name. To our left rose the crags of Mont Roig, to our right fading hills that moulded into haze, while directly below lay two small lakes linked by a stream. Swifts swooped low over the water catching insects as they flew. Down we went to the swift-bombed tarns, then across to the scooped ridge of the Sierra de Mitjana and up steeply to find another tarn caught below the upper Col de Calverante. A million tadpoles blackened the water's edge, but we continued up to the col and there were weary enough to sprawl in the midday sun and glory in the world that was laid out especially for our contemplation. We shared it with no one but a lone buzzard riding updraughts of air overhead.

The descent from this high col is a long and taxing one, but at all times is it enjoyable for the breadth of vision it allows, for the constant variety and the leaf-bound conclusion at the end of the day. A clear stream, wild raspberries, birches and shrubs and a collection of ageless farm dwellings totally devoid of modern amenities, and with a levelling of turf beside a pool, we knew we had discovered somewhere rather special as twilight drew across the limited sky. The tent was pitched in a haven of luxury that neither of us would have exchanged for the most extravagant of civilization's inventions. There are times when perfection is simply to stop walking and to lie on an unspoilt bed of turf.

A couple of days later we came down into the Vall Ferrera, happy once more to be in familiar country. But as we wandered down the path out of the forest, we disturbed an isard resting on our track. Catching our scent it scrambled to its feet, but there was clearly something wrong, for

it stumbled in panic-crazed circles down towards the river. We dumped our rucksacks and took up the chase, intending to head him off, but the creature fell into the water and, although I managed to hold him long enough to see the cataracts filming his eyes, he twisted so much that I lost my grasp, and we watched, helpless and hopeless, as the doomed animal was swept away and drowned.

In a misery of if-onlys we continued into the valley lost in pity and sorrow.

A new day, a last day, takes the Pyrenean trekker out of the Vall Ferrera and out of Spain by way of the Port de Bouet (8,668 ft/2,520 m). Ahead lies a brief enclave of France, but the mountains opposite and at the head of the valley are Andorran. All that remains is to descend among the alpenroses to the valley floor, then climb steeply on the far side towards the classic and much-loved Port de Rat. Behind lies a complex of wild mountain country, undisturbed, indisputably rich in its timeless nature, mature yet uncompromising, challenging and rewarding. A backpacker's dream world. A trekker's delight.

Ahead lies Andorra where commercial avarice has branded the mountain kingdom with a multi-faced pollution, and taken from it the essential peace. To the wilderness lover it simply spells Hell.

A hard day's ridge-walking leads from Cirque de Barroude to the green luxury of the Rioumajou; a day of full commitment with barely one bad-weather escape route. The steep descent to the valley offers little respite, for endless slopes of grass, bogs and shrubbery threaten weary legs and ankles and can be hazardous when damp.

Astride the Frontier – Pyrenean High Route   **Fact Sheet**

Difficulty/dangers

Where the route passes along French territory, the trails are almost invariably well-used and, where faint on the ground, are aided by cairns or paint flashes on rocks. On the Spanish side of the frontier, however, there are a number of passages that are a little obscure and in these cases careful study of the map is necessary. In poor visibility, good compass work is essential. It is a strenuous route with several stiff days' activity. Particular care should be taken for the crossing of the Passage d'Orteig between Refuge de Pombie and Refuge d'Arrémoulit; for the crossing of the Port de Lavedan; on the long ridge-walk stretch between Barroude and Rioumajou; the crossing of the highest pass, Col de Mulleres, and the energetic three-pass day that leads from the valley of the Noguera Pallaresa to Cuanca, near Tabescan.
Highest point: 9,606 ft/2,928 m – Col de Mulleres. Snow can lie on the eastern side of the pass late into the summer, but even July can see a snowfall at this altitude and precautions should be taken for the crossing of this pass should there be any suspicion of snow still lying.

Distances/times

As the crow flies the basic distance from Lescun to Andorra is some 145 miles (200 kms), but the actual route will be well in excess of this. There are 35 passes to cross which, naturally, entails a great deal of height gain and loss. In terms of days' walking allow about 24, then add extras for rest days, bad weather days etc.

The High Route through the High Pyrenees may conveniently be divided into three sections dictated by the availability of rail links with Paris and bus links to and from the final road heads. These are as follows:
Lescun to Gavarnie: 10/11 days.
Outward rail link: Paris–Pau–Bedous
Return rail link: Lourdes–Paris
Gavarnie to Maladeta: 6/7 days.
Outward: Paris–Lourdes
Return: Luchon–Toulouse–Paris
Maladeta to Andorra: 8/9 days.
Outward: Paris–Toulouse–Luchon
Return: Ax-les-Thermes–Toulouse–Paris

Season/weather

Summer is the only safe time to contemplate this route, between July and September.

Late August and early September are best, for snow should be clear from all major crossings, although one should always be prepared for the worst. From personal experience September is finest of all for lengthy Pyrenean treks, with fairly settled weather conditions and sparkling views. The light is as exhilarating as champagne, although night frosts are by no means uncommon then. Anything earlier than July is to risk the danger of avalanche, although for wild flowers in these mountains June will not be bettered.

On the fringe of the Enchanted Mountains, the route enters a wonderland of tarns and granite peaklets with an overwhelming sense of solitude.

Equipment

Standard mountain walking gear will suffice. Dress for summer, but be prepared for the occasional taste of winter. In other words, warm clothing should be taken, although duvets will normally be surplus to requirements. Warm pullovers, windproof anorak, gloves and hat are recommended, as are breeches and shorts, plus waterproof cagoule and overtrousers. Comfortable, well-fitting mountain boots are essential.

A 'three season' sleeping bag will be your best bet for hut-less nights. Be prepared either to camp or bivouac on those occasions when there is no refuge nearby. There will be several such nights. Cooking equipment will need to be taken, plus some food carried.

An ice axe should be carried – and an ability to use it safely will be a requirement of all the party.

Language

French or Spanish will be spoken by hut guardians and shepherds. English is not generally understood by the local people, but then on a trek such as this, there will be few opportunities to mingle with village folk.

Other considerations

It should be stressed that this trek is a serious undertaking, and that an ability to read a map and compass is essential. Since there are several stages with no possibility of overnight accommodation, tents should be carried – or be prepared to bivouac beneath the stars. Rucksacks are therefore likely to be heavy, especially as food for several days must be carried, and there are few opportunities en route to restock with supplies.

On certain stages there are no escape routes should weather conditions turn threatening, and there are some sections when it is quite likely that you'll see no one else for a couple of days or more. Accidents, then, could prove very serious unless the party is able to provide self-help. Do not be lulled into a sense of false security by virtue of the Pyrenees being so close to major centres of commerce and habitation. To the trekker they offer a very real wilderness area, and should not be taken lightly.

Reading
Maps:

These are readily available at major UK stockists. Those for the French side of the mountains are published by *IGN* and are mostly very accurate, but for the Spanish mountains and valleys the *Editorial Alpina* sheets, although improving with each new edition, still leave something to be desired. They are, however, probably the best available at present.

Guide books:

Walks and Climbs in the Pyrenees – Kev Reynolds (Cicerone Press)
Pyrenees High Level Route – Georges Véron (Gastons/West Col)

Literature:

Mountains of the Pyrenees – Kev Reynolds (Cicerone Press)
Backpacking in the Alps and Pyrenees – Showell Styles (Gollancz)

Kev Reynolds is a full-time writer and lecturer specializing in mountain and countryside topics. He has published seven books to date and has several more in progress. Born in 1943, he began climbing and hill-walking at the age of sixteen with a typically wet trip to Snowdonia, and has been 'hooked' ever since. For nearly 30 years he has been active throughout the Alps, the High Atlas Mountains of Morocco and Corsica as well as in the British hills. But perhaps he is best known for his activities in the Pyrenees, a range of mountains he has visited on a score or more occasions, climbing all the major peaks and numerous lesser-known mountains, as well as exploring many remote and rarely-visited corners.

He lives with his wife and two daughters in a small village among the greensand hills of Kent.

THROUGH THE SOUTHERN ALPS – NEW ZEALAND'S ROUTEBURN TRACK

by Colin Monteath

'... and like a carpet at your feet, in endless gradations of light and shade, the New Zealand bush spreads out in green waves downwards to the edge of the ocean.'
Andreas Reischek, 1884

A brisk southerly pranced in from the Tasman Sea last night, leaving a dusting of powder snow on the razorbacked ridges of Fiordland's granite peaks. Even the mottled green mosaic of the beech tree canopy that winds down the Hollyford Valley to Martin's Bay is outlined in white as shafts of morning sun climb over the Southern Alps.

The wind that roared through the tops only a few hours before has dropped, creating a feeling of inner peace as we sit on top of Conical Hill in tussock grass beside a frozen tarn. Perched above Harris Saddle, this is the highest point on the Routeburn Track. Only the raucous screech of the Kea mountain parrot disturbs the silence, as a pair arc overhead, flashing the deep red of their underwing feathers.

Streamers of mist rise lazily from the Hollyford, lighting up the northern flank of Mt Tutoko, perched above the valley floor. At 9,061 ft (2,762 m), Tutoko is the highest peak in the massive Fiordland National Park – one of the most inspiring wilderness regions left on Earth. Fiordland and the adjoining Mt Aspiring National Park form part of the newly designated World Heritage region of south-western New Zealand. Although a few roads cut through the deep U-shaped valleys to creep down to the sea in places like Milford Sound, and some walking tracks struggle through the tangled forest, the vast majority of the park remains wild and untamed, commanding respect even from experienced local trampers and climbers.

The Routeburn Track is perhaps the easiest walk in the whole region. At 24 miles (39 kms) it is certainly not a long traverse, although after a pleasant meander through beech forest and grassy river flats it climbs steadily to cross Harris Saddle (4,214 ft/1,284 m), an impressive gateway between the Mt Aspiring and Fiordland Parks. Justifiably, the Routeburn has become popular in recent years, for to spend three or four days winding along the well-made trail, stopping each night in a cabin maintained by park staff, is one of the best possible introductions to the New Zealand high country.

The great benefit of doing the Routeburn is that it is not only a superb experience in itself but it opens up a whole network of tracks that can be undertaken from either the Glenorchy (Mt Aspiring) or the Milford Road end. The Rees/Dart, the Greenstone/Caples, the Hollyford, the Kepler and of course the famous Milford Track are all memorable walks, each with its own special character.

Everyone is talking about New Zealand. While newspaper headlines focus on New Zealand's nuclear-free policy or another All-Black triumph on the rugby field, avid walkers dreaming of spectacular mountains and deep, forested valleys are quietly saving for a holiday in the far-flung South Pacific. Visitors keen on a month's solid walking plan their trip to link together at least two or three of the tracks mentioned, thereby sampling a whole range of environments from coastal to alpine. It is possible to reprovision between each walk and keep pack weight down.

The Southern Alps were once sufficiently remote that even the ardent British explorers Shipton and Tilman never managed to venture there. Although affordable air travel has now brought New Zealand within range of many mountain folk and New Zealanders themselves are enthusiastic mountain travellers, it is extremely rare to find the crowds that plague the European Alps or even the popular trails of Nepal.

Many of course combine walks in the Fiordland area with trips in other New Zealand scenic spots. The high peaks of the Mt Cook National Park have their own special attraction for skiers, climbers and walkers. Many choose to traverse the Copland Pass on the Main Divide near the Mt Cook Village (a route that requires ice axe and crampons) and drop down to the hot springs at Welcome Flat not far from the wild west coast beaches. There is nothing quite like soaking tired muscles in a steaming pool while gazing at icy summits rising 10,000 ft (3,000 m) over the tree ferns.

Coastal walks in the northern part of the South Island, such as the Heaphy Track or along the golden beaches in Abel Tasman National Park, are also becoming increasingly popular, particularly with family groups. For a complete contrast, the network of walks in the volcanic centre of the North Island is a must. Active volcanoes Ruapehu and Ngauruhoe dominate the Tongariro National Park, blending alpine grandeur with sub-tropical bush, thermal springs and Maori culture. Tongariro is the oldest National Park in New Zealand, celebrating its centenary in 1987.

The friendly, unhurried 'kiwi' lifestyle is a major attraction for visitors. Those with a rucksack are particularly likely to be given a good feed and a bed for the night, or driven out of the way to the start of a walking track. Unlike Australia there are no dangerous animals, so it

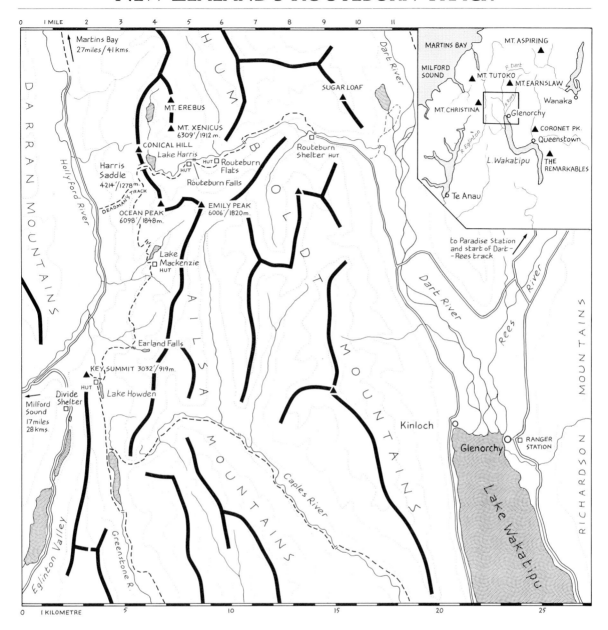

doesn't take long to feel relaxed in the bush. The water is so clean that foreign companies vie with each other to export it to the northern hemisphere in supertankers.

It is a pleasant six hour drive from Christchurch on the east coast down to the resort town of Queenstown in the heart of the Southern Lakes. Strolling through the shopping arcades in Queenstown, it doesn't take us long to buy fresh fruit, vegetables and wholemeal bread for our planned five day trek on the Routeburn, returning over the Greenstone–Caples track – a neat round trip that would bring us back to our car on the Mt Aspiring Park side of the Humboldt Mountains.

It was mid May so Queenstown was showing off its autumn leaves. Farmers were reaping hay for their stock on cardboard cut-out lowland hills; mustard-coloured tussock grass glistened in the low afternoon sun; a tinge of snow graced the peaks surrounding the town hinting that winter was just around the corner. Flocks of skiers would soon be coming to play on the nearby Coronet and Remarkable ski fields, thronging in to the modern restaurants and nightclubs as the moon and southern stars glint across the mirrored surface of Lake Wakatipu.

The vintage steamship *Earnslaw* glided into the wharf in the centre of Queenstown, scattering the ducks and massive trout that were being fed crumbs by a horde of little boys. The

Left – *Perched above Harris Saddle, Conical Hill is the highest point on the Routeburn Track at 4,300 ft (1,310 m), and provides a superb vista of the Darran Mountains – the loftiest range within the Fjordland National Park.*

Inset – *The beautiful Earland Falls plunge 300 ft (90 m) into rainbowed pools to drench in spray passing trekkers on the Routeburn Track as they near Lake Howden.*

lake water was so clear we could see every pebble.

The *Earnslaw*, built in Dunedin in 1912, is now used for pleasure cruises, taking passengers up the lake to a sheep farm for tea and scones while burly shearers in sweaty black singlets demonstrate blade-shearing. When I first did the Routeburn Track in 1968 the *Earnslaw* was the only transport up to Kinloch and Glenorchy at the head of the lake. Mail bags and fresh provisions were delivered to homestead wharfs on the way.

Wakatipu is the longest lake in New Zealand (48 miles/77 kms), so it took well over an hour to wind our way up the narrow, fern-lined road to the little township of Glenorchy. Edging through a bleating mob of sheep being pushed along by a dusty horseman slowed us to the pace of the land. We had left the bustle of city life behind.

Calling in to the newly-built Ranger Station at Glenorchy gave us the opportunity to register our walking intentions, buy a map and look at the latest weather forecast. With a rum and raisin ice-cream in hand we drove on for half an hour to the Routeburn Shelter and road terminus. Noisy Paradise ducks scattered across the braided flats of the Rees and Dart Rivers that merge just past Glenorchy. Paradise ducks can be found throughout the Southern Alps though this is their true home. Paradise Station is only five miles up the road near the start of the Dart–Rees Track, one of the best walks in the region and one that has become popular recently for its impressive views of the Forbes Mountains.

It was good to leave the car behind at Routeburn Shelter after a night in the tent under a glade of beech trees. The tall grass sparkled and the river boulders were slightly glazed with frost as we entered the forest and began the three hour walk up to Routeburn Flats. We climbed steadily up to a little gorge on a well-made track that threads its way over the twisted roots of Red Beech. Vivid green

The comfortable hut at Mackenzie Lake.

parakeets chattered in the canopy high above our heads, fantails and riflemen tittered about us, darting for sandflies or hovering a few feet from our outstretched hands. The bellbirds and tuis filled the forest with song in the early morning.

The Routeburn region has long been important to the South Island Maori as a source of Pounamu or Greenstone (nephritic jade), a prized material for both weapons and ornaments. This was Moa country too, before the giant bird was driven to extinction. There are traces of Maori villages near the mouth of the Routeburn River and the route itself was used as a link by the native inhabitants of coastal South Westland and both Southland and Otago. The Routeburn was known to the Maori as *Te Komama* ('running through a small opening').

The Otago gold rushes began in 1861 and it did not take prospectors long to try their luck in the hills at the head of Lake Wakatipu. With access to the Queenstown region from the city of Dunedin on the east coast still uncertain or at best slow, rumours of an easy route to the west coast created considerable interest. If a pass was found, a port could be established at Martin's Bay that would allow trading links with Australia. Following the discoveries of Harris Saddle and access to the Hollyford Valley in 1863 by pioneers Caples and Hector, the Dunedin business community pushed for the completion of roads to the east rather than through the Routeburn, determined that Otago gold should remain in New Zealand rather than ending up in Victoria or New South Wales banks.

Although accidents and starvation in the roughest bush country imaginable took its toll on the prospectors, many continued to use the Routeburn until gold fever further up the west coast drew them northward.

In 1870, the fledgling farming community at Martin's Bay warranted the cutting of a bridle track through the Routeburn. After four year's effort however, work ground to a halt somewhere near the Harris Saddle. Nevertheless mail was carried this way for two years until the settlement was abandoned, with the Hollyford and Routeburn tracks rapidly becoming overgrown.

Enterprising Glenorchy and Kinloch families developed the Routeburn side of the track and by the 1880s were guiding parties up to Harris Saddle for the view of Fiordland, going as far as Routeburn Flats on horseback. In this role, it predated the Milford Track by 15 years.

It was not until 1912 that the track was pushed through to Lake Howden from Harris Saddle. Before World War II, walking the Routeburn meant a return journey over the track or down the Greenstone Valley, to catch the *Earnslaw* steamer. During the Great Depression of the '30s, relief workers built the road from Te Anau up the Eglinton Valley towards Milford and work began on the Homer Tunnel to gain access to Milford Sound. In 1938, the final section of the Routeburn was cut from Lake Howden to Key Summit and out to the new Milford Road.

Warm sunshine greeted us as we emerged from the forested hillsides of the gorge onto the open Routeburn Flats to get the first view of the climb to Routeburn Falls, our destination for the night. As we strode through dewy tussocks up to our knees, a pair of Paradise ducks skittered across a jade-green pool where we stopped for a drink and welcome rest.

Regeneration in the beech forest on either side of Routeburn Flats is now visible following the rigorous culling of introduced mammals such as red deer during the 1950s and '60s. Deer are now farmed for their prized velvet, venison and hide throughout the South Island.

After an easy half-hour walk across the flats we stopped for a quick cup of tea brewed-up outside the National Park hut. Opposite, a good view opened up of the rarely climbed Mt Somnus (7527 ft/2,294 m), a fine snowy peak at the head of the Routeburn's North Branch.

The sun was strong now so we stripped to T-shirts for the hour long climb to Routeburn Falls. The forest floor was littered with fungi, mosses and ferns giving the air a fresh clean smell. Coprosma, native fuchsia and ribbonwood add colour and texture to the forest. The blocky summit pyramids of Mt Earnslaw (9,302 ft/2,835 m), the highest peak in the Forbes Mountains, stood proudly above the Dart–Rees Valleys as we approached the Falls hut at the edge of the tree line.

There was plenty of room for us in the 20-bunk hut, for only three American and four New Zealand trampers had spread their gear out on the double bunk mattresses. The hut warden read quietly in a sunny nook on the verandah, disturbed occasionally by the resident hut Kea clattering down the tin roof to pester her for a snack. We had to look after our gear carefully for the strong-beaked Kea took delight in tearing holes in boots or pack.

The sun leaves the steep-sided valley early. Lengthening shadows sent us scurrying down from our perch on the bluff above the hut where we had spent a delightful afternoon exploring a high alpine basin dotted with tarns. The view down across Routeburn Flats in the evening light is stunning. The coal-fired, pot-belly stove

The rocky knoll of Key Summit, reached easily in half
an hour from the Lake Howden Hut, is a superb viewpoint.
Northward rise the imposing peaks of the Darrans – on the
left is Mount Christina (8,256 ft/2,516 m).

The comfortable little Mackenzie Hut stands at the edge of the tangled beech woods close to the shore of Lake Mackenzie, a scene somehow reminiscent of the fantasy world of J. R. Tolkien.

warmed the cabin as frosty night air clamped around the hut. Dinner simmered on the hut's gas stove as the moon rose, its tentacles behind Mt Earnslaw casting eerie shadows across the forest 1,500 ft (500 m) below.

It was an exciting two hour walk next morning to Harris Saddle. We had now entered the high alpine world of tussock, squat, berried plants, swirling mist and rocky crags. The track is still easy, though boggy in spots as it winds across the moor towards Lake Harris. The saddle itself is quite narrow, suddenly appearing around a corner in the track as you climb between the buttresses of Ocean Peak (6,098 ft/1,859 m) and the lake itself, crouched below Mt Xenicus (6,309 ft/1,923 m).

We were lucky with the weather and had already changed from walking in long underwear to shorts. Harris Saddle can be a nasty place to

be caught in driving wet mist, or worse, one of the many vicious storms that come pounding in from the Tasman Sea, a mere 20 miles (30 kms) away down the Hollyford Valley. We dumped our packs at the Saddle outside the foam-lined tin bivi erected for those stranded by injury or storm. With no load and a pocket full of nuts and sultanas we scampered up the frozen track towards Conical Hill.

Ice on the track requires care. As we climbed for half an hour towards the summit the rocks became increasingly coated in snow, and long, curling fingers of frost heaved skyward from the rich black earth. Clusters of grey and yellow Edelweiss surprised us as we grasped for handholds on the scramble up the final rocks.

Conical Hill's reward is an unfettered panorama of Fiordland's Darran Mountains from the giant wedge of Mt Christina

The Maori used the native flax for many purposes: a clump is seen growing beside the Routeburn Track as morning mists boil from the Hollyford Valley.

(8,256 ft/2,516 m) in the south to the graceful Tutoko, wind-worn master of the Hollyford. For the serious climber the Darrans contain vast walls of steep granite in summer and in winter long, committing ice routes for the very bold. Tutoko received its first winter ascent as recently as 1976 after a saga of attempts spanning three years. These peaks may not be high in altitude but they can still throw a few punches.

By now we had left the Mt Aspiring National Park behind. Lake Mackenzie and its comfortable hut beckoned so we dropped down to our packs on the Saddle and began the long traverse across the Hollyford Face above the tree line. It is a steady three hour walk to the Mackenzie hut but the beauty of the vegetation is not conducive to speed and several tumbling brooks demand to be sampled. This section of the Routeburn is the most exposed, lashing many a tramper with angry, wind-driven mist and rain. That day the mist was calm, lazing around the tops of the Silver Beech and making the mountain flax bushes look like bronzed, spread-eagled statues.

A steep track dropped away below us, disappearing into the forest above the Hollyford. Deadman's Track is a shortcut (five hours) to the Hollyford Road but is only for those with strong knees.

I've always loved the view down onto Lake Mackenzie. The emerald green lake sparkled in the afternoon sun as we began the 1,000 ft (300 m) descent on the steep zigzag track. Fifteen keas charged overhead like drunken warlords, batting each other with their wings as they flitted from crag to crag. Tendrils of 'Old Man's Beard' lichen brushed our faces as we entered the tangled, twisted forest near the lake. Lush, moss-covered boulders guard the access to the lake shore. It was as if we had entered a scene from Tolkien's *Lord of the Rings*.

The Mackenzie hut warden, Sue, welcomed us with a cup of coffee and invited us to share some home-baked biscuits in her little cabin attached to the main 40-bunk hut. It was too nice an afternoon to spend long indoors, so Sue recommended we explore around the edge of the lake for views and reflections of Emily Peak. It would be so easy to spend a whole day clambering over boulders or lounging on the little sandy beach that looks up towards Emily Peak. This has to be the most tranquil spot in the whole Southern Alps. Even the twittery fantails seem at peace, perhaps because there are so few sandflies here.

It is only a three hour walk to Lake Howden so we spent the following morning sitting in the sun at Lake Mackenzie, reading and watching the myriad of birds feeding around the lake shore.

Bellbirds tinkled in the trees behind the hut and a giant New Zealand bush pigeon glided overhead in search of another succulent patch of berries. It is not easy to leave Mackenzie behind.

Sidling for two hours through the forest and under mossy bluffs, the track passes right underneath the 300 ft (100 m) Earland Falls. Ferns and flowering koromikos are drenched in spray, and dripped onto us as we lingered, peering up through a vivid rainbow that spanned the pools at the foot of the falls. It was almost impossible to keep our cameras dry in the deluge but our antics produced lots of giggles as we tip-toed around the water's edge.

Suddenly, the beech-fringed Lake Howden appeared before us. The occasional trout leapt for a fly, sending ripples across the glassy surface. Nothing else moved. Even the column of smoke from the pot-belly stove in the hut appeared to be asleep in the dusky amber light of early evening.

Lake Howden is an important junction as the Greenstone track takes off here in a southerly direction. More importantly, it is only an hour's walk out to the Milford Road although most, like us, prefer to spend the night here in the cosy upstairs bunkroom. We yarned long into the night in front of the stove with other 'kiwi' trampers who had joined the Routeburn from an impressive circuit of other tracks in the area.

Our sojourn on the Routeburn was all but over, for we had to return to Lake Wakatipu on a two day trip via the upper Greenstone track and the Caples Valley, emerging onto the lake at Elfin Bay. While the details of this journey remain for you to discover for yourself no description of the Routeburn could be complete without a visit to Key Summit.

Key Summit (3,032 ft/924 m) was first climbed in 1861. Today, although there is an easy, 30-minute trail winding up from Lake Howden hut, the little rocky knoll retains its original charm as a vantage point and botanist's delight. I jogged up the track in time to watch the sun rise over Harris Saddle, able to see the whole of the Routeburn from the Saddle until it dropped towards Lake Mackenzie. Reflections in tarns on the summit mirrored the big peaks of the Darrans – Christina, Crosscut and Lyttle – and I was able to look right down the overlapping, blue-green ridges of the Hollyford to Martin's Bay.

As I turned to leave the Routeburn, I was reminded of surveyor Wilmot's lines written in 1882:

The peaks in every direction are crowded and crushed together, till looking over the scene one appears to be viewing a petrified ocean.

Mists drift round treetops of native beech and the forested crags that fall steeply from the Darrens into the Hollyford Valley near the western end of the Routeburn Track.

Through the Southern Alps – New Zealand's Routeburn Track

Difficulty/hazards
Well-used, well-marked, properly graded track all the way. Strong bridges mean river crossing is not the problem it can be on many other New Zealand walking or trans-alpine trips. The track, bridges and huts are well maintained by both Mt Aspiring and Fiordland National Park staff. Hut Wardens are in residence during summer months (Nov–May) and are trained to deal with any mishap.

The climb to Routeburn Falls hut and descent to Lake Mackenzie hut are the only steep sections of the trail. Highest point at Harris Saddle is 4300 ft (1,300 m) above sea level. The main danger is being caught in severe southerly or north-westerly storms coming in from the Tasman Sea. Warm undergarments and good waterproof outer clothing are essential. Snow and wind storms can occur in any season. Symptoms of hypothermia need to be monitored carefully in young or weak members of a group. Although the trail is technically easy it should not be underestimated. People have got into serious difficulties through misjudging the severity of the weather.

Some side trips such as the half hour climb to Conical Hill can be extremely icy, even in summer.

Avalanche danger may exist in winter months in the Lake Harris basin or on the traverse across the Hollyford Face above Lake Mackenzie.

Distances/times
The basic trail is 24 miles (39 kms) long and can be walked from either end. The average travelling time on the trail totals 13 hours but most parties take three days, split into days of 4–5 hours walking. Extra days spent at Routeburn Falls, Lake Mackenzie and Lake Howden allow for a great variety of side trips to investigate the flora or sample the views from vantage points such as Conical Hill and Key Summit. (Times taken if trail walked from Mt Aspiring National Park end)

Routeburn Shelter to Routeburn Flats: 5 miles (8 kms) – 2–3 hours.
Routeburn Flats – Routeburn Falls hut: 2 miles (3 kms) – 1–2 hours.
Routeburn Falls to Harris Saddle: 3 miles (5 kms) – 2 hours.

Harris Saddle – Lake Mackenzie hut: 6 miles (10 kms) – 3–4 hours.
Lake Mackenzie – Lake Howden hut: 6 miles (10 kms) – 3 hours.
Lake Howden – Divide Shelter (on Te Anau – Milford Sound Road): 2 miles (3 kms) – 1 hour.

Season/weather
Most parties walk the Routeburn during the summer months (mid-November to March) though the clear days of autumn through to mid-May are excellent and the track is less crowded at this time. It is very important to check first with the rangers as heavy snowfalls can occur in May. Wardens are not in residence during winter months though the huts are open and experienced parties do go winter mountaineering or skiing in the area.

Mid-summer is often a period of high rainfall in the Fiordland region so February–March is the best time for the walk with respect to clear views. Mountain flowers at their best Nov–Jan.

New Zealand has a cool temperate climate, modified by its proximity to the Tasman Sea on the western coast. Low pressure systems spin north from Antarctica and Tasmania bringing moist, westerly air streams onto the Southern Alps. These are then replaced by cold southerlies which often bring snow to the alpine zone even in summer.

Average summer maximum temperature: 72°F/22°C.
Average summer minimum temperature: 50°F/11°C.
Average winter maximum temperature: 46°F/8°C.
Average winter minimum temperature: 34°F/1°C.

Equipment
Normal summer conditions mean it is comfortable to walk during the day in shorts and T-shirt with lightweight boots or training shoes. A woollen jersey or fibrepile jacket is all that is required for evening wear in the huts or during breaks. Waterproof parkas, trousers and gaiters are essential. Woollen hat and mitts can be needed at Harris Saddle at any time. Lightweight polypropylene underwear makes ideal walking clothing in the early morning or when windy.

A single-weight down or synthetic sleeping bag is adequate for use in the huts. Food can be obtained in Queenstown or Te Anau. All huts in summer months have bottled gas on tap for cooking though personal pots and utensils need to be carried. Huts have coal-fired pot-belly stoves for warmth or drying clothing.

Auckland, Wellington, Christchurch, Dunedin and Queenstown have excellent shops for the purchase of outdoor equipment.

Access/National Park etiquette
International flights come into Auckland and Christchurch. Internal flights and daily buses service Queenstown or Te Anau. Local buses (the Magic Bus Co. – office in Queenstown) will transport walkers to either end of the Routeburn. Many parties stay in Glenorchy (31 miles/50 kms from Queenstown) at the Holiday Park. This company runs a vital taxi service to the start of the Routeburn (19 miles/30 kms) and other tracks in the area.

It is mandatory that walkers fill in their intentions at either the Mt Aspiring National Park Station at Glenorchy or the Fiordland National Park Headquarters at Te Anau. Rangers will advise on likely weather and local conditions. Maps and guidebooks can be purchased in the major centres, Queenstown, Te Anau or Glenorchy.

Rangers can suggest other walks to link up with the Routeburn, eg the Rees–Dart Valley System, or the Greenstone–Caples or Hollyford Tracks, depending on which way the Routeburn is walked. It is now common for walkers to start with the Rees–Dart, cross the Routeburn and walk the famous Milford or Hollyford Tracks (or perhaps the new Kepler Track) then return to the Mt Aspiring National Park by redoing the first part of the Routeburn as far as Lake Howden before returning to Glenorchy and Queenstown via the Greenstone or Caples Tracks – an excellent two to three week holiday.

Hut wardens will collect hut fees – under review at the time of writing but around $10 per person for hikers – and ensure that everyone does their share to keep the hut and its immediate environs clean. A strict rule is that all garbage must be carried out by the persons bringing it in.

Fact Sheet

Native flora and fauna are totally protected. Horses and trail bikes are prohibited. Permits are required for firearms.

Brown and Rainbow trout inhabit the lower Route Burn and brown trout can also be found in Lake Howden. Fishing requires a licence and visitors can obtain a one month permit from NZ Government Tourist offices. Native trout found throughout the Routeburn region are totally protected.

It is important to keep to formed tracks, particularly in the Lake Harris area, as the alpine vegetation is extremely vulnerable to abuse. For this reason camping is not allowed within 500 yards of the track by either national park. Very limited tent sites are available near the main huts.

Routeburn Walk Ltd (PO Box 271, Queenstown) offer a guided service across the Routeburn. They have their own huts adjacent to the National Park ones.

Medical considerations

Like other walks described in this book it pays to be reasonably fit before coming to New Zealand. Boots need to be broken-in before embarking on major walks to minimise sore feet or blisters.

Some personal first aid gear, suncream, and sandfly ointment should be carried. Huts do have good medical kits, stretchers and radios and wardens are trained in their use.

New Zealand takes pride in the cleanliness of its water. This should be respected when dealing with human waste and washing water. Toilets are located beside each hut – wait till you try the solar-powered 'Sunny Dunny' at Routeburn Falls! River pools may be used for swimming but to avoid water contamination use of soap is discouraged – and is totally prohibited in Lakes Howden and Mackenzie.

Reading
Maps:
Routeburn Track NZMS 316 Scale 1:75,000.
Mt Aspiring National Park NZMS 273 1:150,000.
Fiordland National Park NZMS 273/3 1:250,000.
Guide books:
The Shell Guide to the Routeburn Track – Philip Temple (Whitcoulls,

Christchurch, London. 4th edn. 1986)
The Greenstone/Caples – a track guide – Barry Brailsford and Derek Mitchell (Footprint Press, Christchurch (1986)
Insight Guide to New Zealand – Apa Productions, 1985.
General reading:
Ways to the Wilderness – Great New Zealand Walking Tracks – Philip Temple (Whitcoulls, 1977)
Wild New Zealand – Reader's Digest, Sydney, 1982.
Fiordland National Park Handbook – Cobb Horwood, 1987.

Mt. Aspiring National Park Handbook.

Further information
District Conservator, Lakes District: Dept of Conservation, PO Box 811, Queenstown. Phone 27933.
Senior Conservation Officer, Mt Aspiring National Park: PO Box 93, Wanaka. Phone 7660
Conservation Officer, Glenorchy Ranger Station: Phone Queenstown 299–09 or 299–37
District Conservator, Takitimu District, Fiordland National Park: PO Box 29, Te Anau. Phone 7591

Colin Monteath was born in Scotland but emigrated with his parents to Australia while still a child, graduated from the University of Sydney and moved to New Zealand in 1972 where he now lives in Christchurch with his Canadian wife and two small daughters.

He made 21 trips to the Antarctic and sub-Antarctic islands as a member of the New Zealand Antarctic Research Programme and has since returned to the continent several times as a photographer and tour leader. At one time a Guide on Mount Cook, Colin has travelled, climbed, skied and photographed extensively in the Himalaya, in Tibet, in Russia and in North and South America besides 'Down Under', and was a member of the small but highly successful Australian 1984 Mount Everest North Face Expedition during which he traversed the North Col.

Colin is now a widely published freelance photographer, photojournalist and author. Among his business interests are the Hedgehog House wilderness and polar picture library and the beautiful annual New Zealand Alpine and Antarctic calendars.

ACKNOWLEDGEMENTS

My sincere thanks are due to all those who made this book possible – to the contributing authors, to our cartographer, Don Sargeant, and to Michelle Ross who did the drawings: I hope they enjoy what we have done with their work.

I must thank also the many friends, acquaintances and friends of friends who have helped fill the gaps, check the details and clothe the author's reminiscences with hard facts. In this context I am especially grateful to: Geoff Darling in Cleveland, Robin Marston in Kathmandu, Nazir Sabir in Islamabad and Clive Ward and Ian Howell in Nairobi as well as Mountain Travel Nepal, Explorasia, London, and the Secretariat of the Indian Mountaineering Foundation in Delhi.

It has been a pleasure also to work with Melissa Shales, our editor, Nick Hand our designer and with Connie Austen Smith, Clare Ford and Barbara Fuller at Unwin Hyman. This book is very much a team effort.

TITLE AND CHAPTER TITLE PHOTOGRAPHS

Karakorum
This is the *jula* bridge at Askole – an apparently rickety construction of plaited twigs spanning the tumultuous Braldu River. Such bridges were once common throughout the Karakorum and Himalaya, and were traditionally never repaired until they broke!

Ultimate in Mountains – The Annapurna Circuit
A line of ancient *chortens* looks down on Muktinath while Dhaulagiri and Tukuche Peak rise in the distance beyond the Kali Gandaki. *Chortens*, which should be passed on the left, are stylized figures of the seated Buddha, built to pacify local demons or the spirits of the dead, and are greatly revered.

To the Source of the Ganges
A stormy evening at Gaumukh, close to the source of the Ganges. This inscription on a wayside boulder near the head of the pilgrim trail is marked with the trident of Shiva, the deity who lends his name to Shivling, the mountain that dominates this holy place.

To the Heart of the Karakorum
Perhaps the great peaks of the Karakorum appear even more impressive by moonlight? This is a midnight view, a lengthy time-exposure, of Chogolisa – the 'Bride Peak' – and her satellites seen from the north-east at the junction of the upper Baltoro and Abruzzi Glaciers.

Four Mohammeds and their Mules – Across the High Atlas
Although they lie just a short distance to the north of the Sahara Desert, the High Atlas Mountains are often snowbound above 10,000 ft (3,000 m) during winter. High valleys like this one close to the village of Amrezi are irrigated by ingenious irrigation systems.

Mountains of the Moon – A Ruwenzori Journey
Trekkers descend from the Scott Elliot Pass, through the giant groundsel, towards the upper of the two little Kitandara Lakes – said to be the most beautiful spot in the entire Ruwenzori. Beyond rises Mount Luigi di Savoia, on which McConnell's Prong is clearly seen.

The Towers of Paine – Stormswept Patagonia
The Rio Paine surrounds the Paine Massif on three sides. In this picture the river is seen from near Laguna Amarga flowing tranquilly southwards towards Lago Nordenskjold, beneath the snow-covered Paine Chico. The savage Paine Towers, at centre, provide a strong contrast to the abundant wild flowers and gentle riverside pampas. *Photo: Colin Monteath.*

ACKNOWLEDGMENTS

Royal Road of the Incas
Ollantaytambo's amazing structure contains terraced walls of monolithic blocks, some weighing up to a hundred tons; yet, without the benefit of wheel or mortar, each fits together so perfectly that even a razor blade cannot be inserted between them. Even today they are almost immovable, having defied earthquakes and sieges throughout the ages. *Photo: John Cleare.*

Tree by Tree – Walking the Darien Gap
In the tropical rainforest some of the larger trees develop buttress roots to give them stability in the shallow soil. Indians sometimes use the buttresses as convenient corrals for animals caught on hunting trips. *Photo: Roger Sampson.*

Peaks or Pipedreams? The Wind River Mountains
One of the most delightful features of the Wind River Range is the abundance of small and charming lakes, surrounded by granite boulders and cradled by rugged, pine-scattered hillsides. Double Lake is not only beautiful but refreshing, not as cold as I had expected when I stopped for a swim.

Pacific Shipwreck Trail – Around Vancouver Island
While most of the West Coast Trail is tucked away in heavy coniferous forest, you can pick and choose long sections of beach to walk beside the fecund tidal pools and playful ocean waves. the sights and smells of beachwalking make this trek one of the richest in variety in North America.

Rocky Spine of Greece – The Pindos Traverse
Climatic conditions make transhumance a way of life for shepherds in the south Balkans. Here a flock of Vlach sheep is moving into an abandoned sheepfold to make camp on the first night of the two week autumn journey to the plains.

Astride the Frontier – A Pyrenean High Route
Daybreak on the Pic du Midi d'Ossau, an isolated mountain of purple-brown granite that has been called the 'Symbol of the Pyrenees'. This is the view eastward from the Refuge d'Ayous, probably the most spectacularly sited of all the Pyrenean mountain huts.

Through the Southern Alps – New Zealand's Routeburn Track
Lake Howden, fringed with gnarled beech trees and silent in the still of early morning, is almost at the end of the Routeburn Track. Several trails join at the lake and the cosy hut near the lake shore is a favourite among Kiwi trampers.

Photographs are by the author of each chapter unless credited otherwise.

USEFUL ADDRESSES

Due to shortage of space, this list is necessarily brief. A much more detailed listing, worldwide, can be found in The Traveller's Handbook, edited by Melissa Shales and published by WEXAS Ltd. US edition published by The Globe Pequot Press. Also look in the Fact Sheets at the end of each chapter.

Map and Book Suppliers:
Audrey Salkeld, 7 Linden Close, Clevedon, Avon BS21 7SL. Tel: (0272) 875 631.

Edward Stanford Ltd, 12-14 Long Acre, Covent Garden, London WC2E 9LP. Tel: 01-836 1321.

Gregory's Publishing Co, 64 Talavera Road, North Ryde, Sydney, NSW, Australia. Tel: 02-888 1877.

Hammond Map and Travel Centre, 57 West 43rd St, New York, NY 10036, USA.

ITN Bookshop (mail order maps), 2120 28th St, Sacramento, CA 95818, USA. Tel: (916) 451 1592.

The London Map Centre, 22-24 Caxton St, London SW1. Tel: 01-222 2466.

The Map Center, 2440 Bancroft Way, Berkeley, CA 94704, USA. Tel: (415) 841 MAPS.

Map Centre, Inc, 2611 University Ave, San Diego, CA 92104-2894, USA. Tel: (619) 291 3830.

The Map Shop, 15 High Street, Upton-upon-Severn, Worcestershire WR8 0HJ. Tel: (06846) 3146.

McCarta Ltd, 122 Kings Cross Road, London WC1X 9DS. Tel: 01-278 8278.

Pacific Travellers Supply, 529 State Street, Santa Barbara, CA 93101, USA. Tel: (805) 963 4438.

The Travel Bookshop Ltd, 13 Blenheim Crescent, London W11. Tel: 01-229 5260.

The Wilderness Bookstore, PO Box 300, Lincoln Centre, ME 04458, USA. Tel: (207) 794 6062.

Map and Book Publishers and Distributors:
Bradt Enterprises, 41 Nortoft Rd, Chalfont St Peter, Bucks SL9 0LA. Tel: (02407) 3478.
and
95 Harvey St, Cambridge, MA 02140, USA.

Cicerone Press, 2 Police Square, Milnthorpe, Cumbria LA7 7PY. Tel: (04482) 2069.

Cordee Books, 3a De Montfort Street, Leicester LE1 7HD. Tel: (0533) 543 579.

Roger Lascelles, 47 York Road, Brentford, Middlesex TW8 0QP. Tel: 01-847 0935.

Rand McNally & Co, PO Box 3600, Chicago, IL 60680, USA.

Springfield Books Ltd, Norman Road, Denby Dale, Huddersfield, W. Yorks HD8 8TH. Tel: (0484) 864955.

Useful Organizations:
The Alpine Club, 74 South Audley St, London W1Y 5FF. Tel: 01-499 1542. (Excellent library open to the public, phone first).

Alpine Club of Canada, PO Box 1026, Banff, Alberta.

American Adventurer's Association, Suite 301, 444 NE Ravenna Blvd, Seattle, WA 98115, USA. Tel: (206) 527 1621.

American Alpine Club, 113 East 90th St, New York, NY 10028, USA.

British Mountaineering Council, Crawford House, Precinct Centre, Booth Street East, Manchester M13 9RZ. Tel: 061-146 0492.

The Explorers Club, 46 East 70th St, New York, NY 10021, USA. Tel: (212) 628 8383.

Himalayan Club, PO Box 1905, Bombay 400 001, India.

Himalayan Rescue Association, c/o Mountain Travel (Nepal) Pvt Ltd, PO Box 170, Kathmandu, Nepal.

Indian Mountaineering Foundation, Headquarters Complex, Benito Juarez Road, Anand Niketan, New Delhi 110021, India. Tel: 671 211.

Mountain Club of Kenya, PO Box 45741, Nairobi, Kenya. Tel: 27747.

USEFUL ADDRESSES

National Geographical Society, 17th and M Sts, Washington DC 20036, USA.

Nepal Mountaineering Association, Sports Council Building, Kathmandu, Nepal.

New Zealand Alpine Club, PO Box 41-038, Eastbourne, Wellington, New Zealand. (Many sections in NZ and Australia.)

The Ramblers Association, 1-5 Wandsworth Road, London SW8 2XX.

Royal Geographical Society, 1 Kensington Gore, London SW7 2AR. Tel: 01-589 5466. (Publishes maps and expedition books. Excellent Map Room open to the public. Also runs the Expedition Advisory Centre. Tel: 01-581 2057. Phone first for an appointment.)

Sierra Club, 530 Bush Street, San Francisco, CA 94108, USA.

South American Explorers Club, Casilla 3714, Lima 100, Peru. Tel: 314 480.
and
1510 York Street 214, Denver, Colorado, 80206, USA. Tel: (303) 320 0388.

Helpful Commercial Firms:

Ausventure, PO Box 54, Mosman, NSW 2088, Australia. Tel: 960 1677.

Explorandes, Av Bolognesi No 159, Miraflores, Lima 18, Peru. Tel: 46-9889.

Explorasia, 13 Chapter St, London SW1P 4NY. Tel: 01-630 7102.

Mountain Travel (India) Pvt Ltd, 1/1 Rani Jhansi Road, New Delhi 110005, India. Tel: 523 057.

Mountain Travel International SA, Redgasse 21A, 4058 Basle, Switzerland. Tel: 061-323 279.

Mountain Travel (Nepal) Pvt Ltd, PO Box 170, Kathmandu, Nepal. Tel: 128–08.

Mountain Travel (USA) Inc, 1398 Solano Ave, Albany, CA 94706, USA. Tel: (415) 527 8100.

Nazir Sabir Expeditions, PO Box 1442, Islamabad, Pakistan. Tel: (92-51) 853 672.

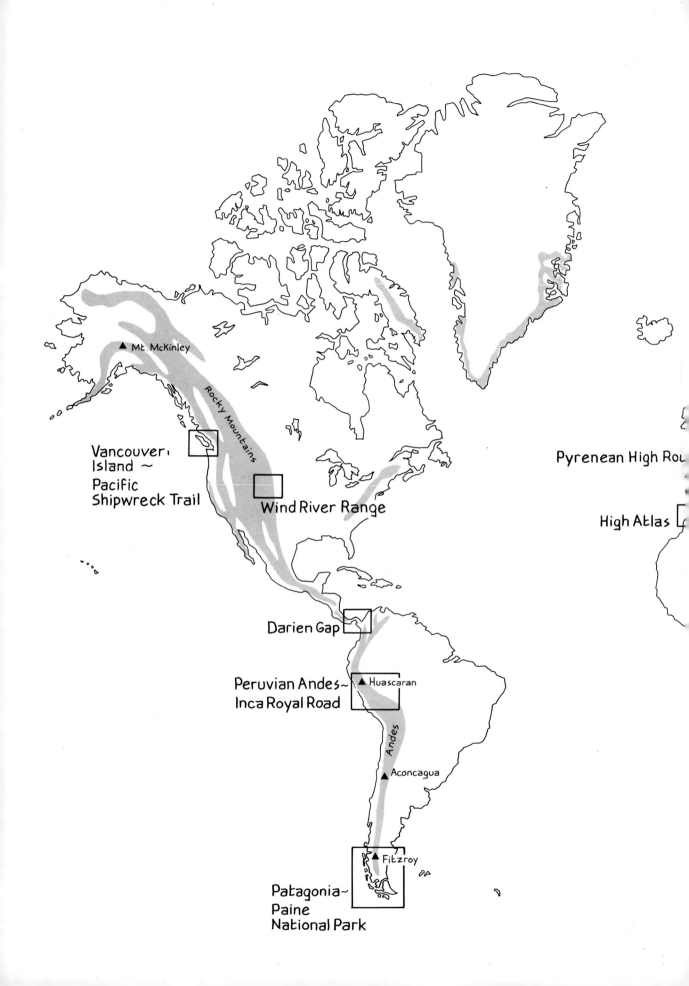

▲ Mt. McKinley

Rocky Mountains

Vancouver
Island ~
Pacific
Shipwreck Trail

Wind River Range

Pyrenean High Rou

High Atlas

Darien Gap

Peruvian Andes~
Inca Royal Road

▲ Huascaran

Andes

▲ Aconcagua

▲ Fitzroy

Patagonia~
Paine
National Park